From Science to Star

Anil Sethi

From Science to Startup

The Inside Track of Technology Entrepreneurship

Copernicus Books is a brand of Springer

Anil Sethi
Swiss Extension GmbH
Russikon, Switzerland

ISBN 978-3-319-30422-9   ISBN 978-3-319-30424-3   (eBook)
DOI 10.1007/978-3-319-30424-3

Library of Congress Control Number: 2016937750

Book illustrations by Rohan Pore. Illustration copyrights with the author.

Printed on acid-free paper

This Copernicus imprint is published by Springer Nature
The registered company is Springer International Publishing AG Switzerland

Acknowledgements

This book began as a note to my children, Aakash and Aanya, to tell them about my trials and tribulations in starting my company. This was, perhaps, to tell them why I wasn't able to spend more time with them. It was supposed to be only a few pages long and my way of documenting the challenges I faced each step of the way. The idea was to create a reference for me, as well as a note for my children should they decide to be entrepreneurs. Along the way, both Aakash and Aanya proved to be a delightfully distractive influence. Many an evening did I spend telling them bedtime stories that always began with "Once upon a time, in a land far, far away", when I should have been working on my book. Without this constructive distraction, this book would have been finished in half the time. Every minute of the delay has been well worth it. To that extent, more than anything, it is a labour of love.

As I commenced working on this book, I recalled the words of my late father Dr. Dev Pal Sethi, who often told me that if you *do*, you can make a difference, but if you're able to communicate effectively, you inspire others to find their own spark, where each is able to make a difference. My mother also deserves an honourable mention, simply for believing in me during my darkest hours.

Mrs. Sadana, my English tutor who stood by me during my childhood when I was struggling with the language and patiently persevered to help me appreciate the nuances and how you can have fun with it. She helped me realise that much more can be said between the lines than words will ever capture.

Poonam and Harsh Dhanwatey have inspired me in so many ways with their perseverance in the cause they believe in, which is conservation of the tiger and mitigation of the man–animal conflict in India. My sister Poonam, as a matter of fact, is likely the only woman since the dawn of civilisation to have been bitten by a tiger as well as tasered. That, however, is clearly part of her own personal story.

My friends and well-wishers have been an indispensable part of my story. They have, knowingly or otherwise, helped me along my journey and been the basis of many an inspiration. They include Krishna Nagashwaran, Felix Schachter, Rajiv Chhabra, Ajay Saluja, Santanu Das, Ashutosh Tyagi, Adrian Kalt, Beat Weber and Sanjeev Sharma. They have, at various times, lent me an ear and helped uplift my spirits as well as boulders for my aspirational Zen garden at home. I also learnt much from Prof. A N Tiwari.

Many entrepreneurs have shared their stories and the challenges they faced from idea to commercial realisation. They include Felix Mayer, Patrick Galliker, Wulf Glatz, Stefan Tuchschmid and Manuel Aschwanden. The book is richer because of their stories.

I would also like to acknowledge and recognise the time and efforts of my friend Silvio Bonaccio, who patiently went through the entire manuscript and made some very valuable suggestions from a business as well as scientific perspective.

Prashanth Mahagaonkar of Springer has been instrumental in giving form to the manuscript that comes to you readers in the form of "From Science to Startup". Rohan Pore has skilfully added colour and life by way of his illustrations.

Lastly, and perhaps most importantly, I would like to place on record my appreciation for the patience of my wife Aradhna. She dealt with my idiosyncrasies as I struggled to balance the challenges in my startup and penning down my failures and learnings each step of the way. Aradhna also read the manuscript approximately n times without so much as a murmur. She has documented her own story in her book *The Entrepreneur's Wife*, for which I am largely to blame.

Anil Sethi
anil.sethi@swissextension.com
http://www.swissextension.com

Contents

1

Prologue

It was the conclusion of my MBA. I was still pretty clueless about what I wanted to do professionally. The one thing I was certain of was that I wanted to do my own thing.

Some of us just hold on to our dreams for longer than others. In fact, as soon as I started working with a big corporate after my MBA, I began saving, knowing fully well that I would be doing my own thing and that it was probably not going to pay - for a while at least. This implied that I would have to live off my savings for a number of years...

Finally, after six long years post-MBA and stints with startups and established corporate giants, I did start my own company, Flisom. Entrepreneurship came with strings attached. Be careful what you wish for, for it does come true if you hold on to it and keep working towards it. The road to being an entrepreneur included, among other things, working for two cups of coffee per day for much much longer than expected.

This book is about the things I wish I had known when I began my journey. This book is really a guide for what not to do and what to be careful about, because they *will* come and bite you (no, the most important thing is *not* the business plan or financial projections). It provides you with insights into the real world of entrepreneurship, which will be of interest to you if you're finishing your MBA and want to be an entrepreneur, but have no idea what to do. This book is also relevant for technology people and scientists who want to commercialise their innovations, because it helps them recognise their box and how to think outside it.

So why is all this relevant for you? How about over 200 failures? Team challenges related to managing a group of people who were predominantly

© Springer International Publishing Switzerland 2016

A. Sethi, *From Science to Startup*, DOI 10.1007/978-3-319-30424-3_1

scientists or PhDs at a minimum and consequently live in an alternate universe, where the laws of profitability or go-to-market do not apply. Also, a bunch of awards, both on the European and global level. And living to tell the tale.

What a journey it has been. As Winston Churchill once said, "If you're going through hell, keep going". On few other journeys would I have expected to bump into the heads of state of Israel and Palestine along the way, get approached by the minister of defence of Iraq, or not be able to respond to Michael Dell's interest, because I was occupied elsewhere.

This is my story. The book will help you create yours.

2

Are You Meant to Be an Entrepreneur?

This was in the autumn of 2004. I was with a big company in Switzerland. Post-MBA, I had slightly lost track of exactly where my existence was making an impact in the big scheme of things within the company, other than to adding a touch of cultural diversity in a European environment. Responsibility for autonomous areas and pseudo-entrepreneurship within the corporate environment had whetted my appetite for the real thing. The work was pretty okay as work goes, but it seemed like work. Plus, "the spark" had been ignited!

Clearly, I wanted to do something of my own. Towards this end, a process of evaluating startup ideas with the clear view of scalability and global impact began. I seemed to always be involved in this process—consciously and otherwise. So, once while dining with a friend, a professor who had been doing research on very efficient flexible solar cells for almost three decades at the Federal Institute of Technology of Zurich, or ETH, another thought process appeared. Incidentally, ETH happens to be the university that got Einstein as a professor just over 120 years ago, making me conclude that the well of knowledge runs pretty deep here.

This professor friend mentioned that he was considering commercialising his technology. He also happened to elaborate upon his rather brief meeting with an investor, who had thrown his documents in the dustbin before thanking him for his time. Now the Prof. was a respectable scientist and not given to frivolous behaviour. In fact, he had held the world record for the highest efficiency for several years. Efficiency, in this regard, means the percentage of light that is converted into electricity. On inquiring what exactly it was that he had given to the investor, he said he had taken the PhD thesis of one of his students.

© Springer International Publishing Switzerland 2016
A. Sethi, *From Science to Startup*, DOI 10.1007/978-3-319-30424-3_2

Realisation dawned immediately! This authority in the field of technical education was far, far away from reality! Instead of making a business plan and a slick presentation to the investor in the language the investor understood, he had buried the investor under a PhD thesis. Instead of telling the investor where the technology could make money, the professor had told the investor what areas could be interesting for PhD research.

Here was one professor who was in desperate need of some help, I thought. And instead of pointing him to a good doctor, yours truly decided to help him to develop the business plan. As I began to study the market, the excitement of being able to bring an amazing technology to the market began to mount rather quickly. However, the task ahead seemed challenging, with no terms of certainty; so I continued to try and find really good reasons why I should get involved with this. At this time, there was apparently one reason—the spark that wanted to flame up into something different, something big!

But that wasn't reason enough to let go of a good thing—a job with a neat monthly salary at the end of each month. Still, never say no to opportunity—and going by that, I delved a little further. There was no team as the professor wanted to continue working in the laboratory. Risking his salary for something with world-impacting potential was a distant and far-removed concept he was unwilling to bet on. Eventually, after many sessions of speaking to him, cajoling him, he was convinced enough to get his students to consider joining the team. He had been made to realise that investors were not likely to give money to a business driver who was doing this on weekends and a professor who planned to continue working full time in the university.

This was in late 2004. There seemed to be no business rationale for me to get involved with this technology. The day after Christmas, I heard news about a wave that had lashed out and, in its wake, had resulted in 200 people losing their lives. Within one hour the estimate had been increased to over 2000. The next day it seemed that over 50,000 people had lost their lives. This was now being reported as the tsunami in Banda Ache in Indonesia.

In the coming days, the news only got worse. Over 250,000 people had perished. Many of these people were children and elderly people. Most of them perished not because of the wave itself, but because of lack of access to clean water and medicine in the first 3 days after the tsunami. International organisations like the UN tried to get medicine and potable water to those in need. The problem however was that all communication had been wiped out.

If only the professor's flexible solar solution had been available, a roll weighing 2.5 kg would have generated enough electricity to purify water for 1000 people per day. It could perhaps have saved many lives. This really was the point when I decided that I was going to drive the commercialisation of the flexible solar cell technology. For someone who had spent his career in consulting for clients to look for reasonable solutions, this was the most illogical of reasons for a life-changing decision. But it was no different from most entrepreneurs who start off simply because they believe. The would-be entrepreneurs who wait till all the risks are mitigated often become insurance agents. As Yoda said to Luke Skywalker, "Do. Or do not. There is no try."

And thus we founded Flisom in 2005.

The next 3½ years were spent talking to investors and trying to get the funding. With a small amount of initial funding from an angel investor, in all my wisdom, I somehow ended up hiring engineers and building a prototype machine rather than paying myself any salary. It was at about this time that the appreciation of the value of coffee crept in, since for the next few years, I worked for two cups per day.

In early 2009, a much larger amount of funding was on its way. With this, the semiautomated pilot facility took shape. This would then commercialise the record-breaking solar modules. A semiautomated pilot means that the machines don't really work unless there's a PhD trying to figure it out. In that way, these machines were like a Harley Davidson bike, which are only for people who like to spend a major part of their weekends lying on the floor with a dirty oily cloth trying to make the thing work properly. By now, the technology team had improved on their own world record consistently for the highest efficiency for over 10 years. In the meantime, our competitors had raised between $500 million to over a billion dollars per company. To put it in perspective, we had raised, at this point, less than 2 % of the funding of our biggest competitors, in an area of technology where we were recognised for holding the world record for the highest efficiency.

By 2012, the possibility of manufacturing these flexible solar modules had been demonstrated, but had not quite actually been done. This potential itself enabled us to raise a significantly larger round of several tens of millions of dollars to create an automated pilot, which would also demonstrate that making the large-scale flexible solar cells was going to be possible without actually doing it. For that, a lot more money was needed. This is where the value of what's possible or as I call it, "the art of the possible" began to develop. More about this later.

Back to the spark. It didn't arise suddenly out of nowhere. Right from the time of completing my undergraduation, I always wanted to do something on my own. There were hints of this along the way. I started my work life with a consulting company. One day, still within the stated probation period, I requested for a meeting with the managing partner, who was roughly the equivalent of God. On inquiring about how my work was coming along and the areas of interest that were developing, I told him that I was mostly driven by new client acquisition. Once the managing partner realised the seriousness of this statement, he patiently explained that this was his prerogative. My role was to do the grunt work of tax compliance and financial advisory. Subsequently, I heard that my suggestion was the subject of much hilarity among the partners.

Like many of us, I simply didn't know how to get started. There was also the fear of not having any expertise and not knowing what it really took to be successful as an entrepreneur.

2.1   The MBA

Other than the experience of walking in a straight line after more drinks than could strictly be considered necessary at any point of time, the value of the MBA was not immediately obvious.

Interactions with global business leaders including Bill Gates, Laxmi Mittal and Michael Dell led me to believe that they were regular people, extraordinary and driven, but nevertheless, human. That's when I realised that *what you need is a vision; expertise can be hired.*

In retrospect, my greatest learning from my MBA was that I lost the fear of dreaming big. You do yourself a disservice if you do less than what you're capable of—both to yourself and for those who come after you. Remember, today's all you've got, and right now is the cumulation of all your yesterdays and the springboard into all your tomorrows. And finally, the only sustainable difference you make is the one that can live beyond your lifetime. I realised that the MBA taught entrepreneurship but couldn't make an entrepreneur out of you, unless you had the spark. Most of my classmates simply wanted to have a successful career with fixed holidays and a steady path to executive management.

I recall a time close to the conclusion of my MBA where we got together for drinks. We each tried to answer the question of what we expected to achieve in 10 years. All the answers included lots of money, very senior positions in banking, consulting or industry, large houses and fancy cars. Mine was simply to be doing my own thing. Or as the Chinese saying goes, "May you live in interesting times". It's meant as a curse, but for me, it became a motto to look up to - and follow at some point in time! (Fig. 2.1).

The world is full of managers who know far more than you about any given administrative task. All they require is the comfort of having boundaries within which they can do their jobs. Managing these managers is also an important challenge to entrepreneurs.

Fig. 2.1 Different perspectives, different futures

If you're reading this book, you are most likely to slip into the assumption that everyone you meet will be driven towards the vision of the company and willing to do whatever it takes to make it happen. This is rather the exception than the rule. Apple always had a counterculture and one of the key attributes they looked for was passion. There are not many companies that can sustain this excitement, although every once in a while, a Google might come along.

Ivy league MBA programmes attract a lot of bright people. This results in a phenomenal level of exposure due to the cross-cultural pollination of ideas. The other thing that the MBA provides is the polish, where you develop the capability of being taken seriously simply by virtue of the jargon that you can spew per square minute. This seems to be by far the greatest benefit of MBA, other than the stamp and the alumni network, since no one I know actually did his MBA for the education.

There is a problem with the MBA that was pinpointed by one of our professors. He said that after the intense exposure through the MBA, real life was going to be boring. He said, look around. The people around you are all on the highest rung of risk takers. Who else in their sane mind would consider leaving a relatively stable job in their home country and travel to another unfamiliar geography to pursue management education? And that, too, with no clear prospects of a job and yet feel comfortable about changing not only careers but also lines of work from industry to consulting to banking to startup to geography by the time they complete the MBA.

My professor couldn't have been more right. In experience terms, the simulated challenges provided by 2 years of an MBA is equal to 15–20 years of the challenges in real life. This is due to the sheer IQ, drive and geographical diversity of the MBA peer group.

Corporate life after MBA is frequently a shock in its slow and staid pace. Corporate life as a fresh graduate tends to be several corridors from the seat of power. Contrary to expectations, you are not immediately welcomed into the top echelons of Goldman and McKinsey to aid them in their global strategy. The normal corporate does not have alpha males with a high-risk approach to life. On the contrary, many companies discourage entrepreneurship since strategy is done at the top and the rest of the organisation is supposed to deliver solutions absolutely in line with that strategy.

2.2   Life After MBA

My own example post-MBA illustrates this. My large company had its head office in the USA. Being based in Europe, I was part of the delivery mechanism. Trying to forge business development and strategy within conservative Europe virtually ensured that I rubbed a lot of local managers the wrong way by trying to find synergies between their fiefdoms. It was only my headstrong manager who covered me, in part, due to his other leadership role, which I found out about accidently when the phone call to him got re-routed. It turned out that he was a senior person in the US military reserve and had been asked to go on a stint to Afghanistan. This was in 2002.

As MBA students, we were already off the charts so far as risk was concerned, since—as mentioned before—we had all left our stable jobs and frequently our countries for the MBA, with no clue about where we would end up afterwards. Again, as previously stated—the 2 years of exposure through graduate school crams business experience equal to about 20 years in senior management. This was not so much through the classrooms during school hours as it was during the breaks during cocktails hosted by all manner of banks, consulting companies and corporate houses. Whether we were sober enough to absorb much of it is, of course, a topic ripe for academic research.

Since you're expected to intellectually challenge each other at the MBA school and arrive at breakthrough solutions, two things happen when you get back to the workforce:

1. There simply aren't enough challenges going around.
2. Your peers don't like you that much if you look at their stable work critically and challenge the status quo. You could ease in and slow down to align with others. Or not.

That's when you might ask the critical question: if not now, then when? There could be several reasons for not starting your own company immediately. The more prosaic one is money. Since you may have stretched your funding to the limit and, in fact, have taken loans to do that MBA, you probably do not have funds to sustain yourself for a long period of time. One of the downsides with starting your company is that you can't start paying yourself unless you have the money. You can compensate for this funding challenge in two ways. One is to have a partner or spouse who is in a stable job. The second is to do the startup on the side while you bide time with a corporate job. Since a concerted search for an opportunity can take a period of months to a couple of years, having a full-time job to pay the bills is not a bad option.

Frequently, when people have a spark, they do not quite recognise it for what it is and try to join a new company or a new function. This can be a mistake, since you have to learn about the new role leaving you with less time to work on your original idea. Keeping status quo at your old role would of course limit your growth, but then, you already know the ropes, so you can consider working on your idea in parallel.

A frequently heard piece of advice is that working in a big company is good experience before starting your own. Now if you get to a senior position in a big company, you probably will get enough experience in dealing with your subordinates and dealing with uncertainty. However, this can be overrated, simply because you can't sit on a spark for years at a stretch in the hope of getting to a senior position in your corporate where you might get the relevant experience. And the value of working in a corporate can simply be overrated, since you could end up managing within an organisational setup, whereas in a startup, you have to make all the rules and create your set-up framework as you go along.

That you have to work diligently in order to have a successful idea is another often-heard notion. Frank[1] proved this wrong! Sometimes you simply had to observe. He was doing his graduation at St. Gallen University in Switzerland and

---

[1] Name changed to protect identity of individual (s)/entity

naturally had a messy room. Being too lazy to clean it himself, he and a friend organised to get cleaning ladies to tidy up and sort out their rooms. They paid them on a per hour basis. With a pub just down the road from the campus, they realised that they could probably do something more useful with their money than giving it to the cleaning women. They decided to organise to get the rooms of the other students cleaned as well, albeit at a slight premium. In the bargain, their own rooms got cleaned for free. Once they realised that they could also make a bit of money by doing this, they continued to expand this service. Once, when Frank spilled some powder on his laptop, he realised that most of it simply went into the keyboard. After cleaning the keyboard, he tested it for germs and was alarmed to find that the bacteria on the keyboard are as numerous as the number of bacteria in a WC. This was because Frank, like many of us, used to snack while working on his laptop and often had crumbs from his food dropping on his keyboard, creating conditions ripe for life to evolve.

He tested the keyboards of a few friends' laptops. On getting a similar result on the virulence of the bacteria, he went about developing a simple testing system for checking bacteria as well as a simple way to clean them from keyboards. When he had this, he went to the local bank and showed them how dirty their keyboards were. Tapping on the bank's concern that an unhealthy working environment might open it to liability if employees fell ill, he was quickly able to generate business of cleaning keyboards on a weekly basis, which he obviously outsourced. By the time he graduated from St. Gallen 2 years later, this was a nicely thriving business. He sold it to his partner and pocketed a tidy sum in the process.

Many people feel that their resume would show a nasty gap if they did not get a job immediately after they finished their education or if there is too much time between two jobs. This is when the silver strings of security become a chain that restraints you from achieving your vision. In reality, very seldom would employers look askance at entrepreneurial experience.

Takeaway *Never ignore your own problems to which a simple solution does not exist. If you would pay for a solution, so would other people.*

2.3   Time for Ideas

There is a time when ideas flow. This is as much the case for new business ideas as it is for poetry. Anyone who has ever written poetry will agree that there is a time in life like first love, perhaps in school, when writing poems seems a snap. I remember a time when I once wrote three poems on a particularly eventful day. Now, I can't seem to pen an ode to save my life.

We always take creativity for granted when we have it. We only begin to appreciate this creativity when it stops flowing. This is also called writers' block.

This creativity in young people is not only seen in wordsmiths but also in science. Albert Einstein was 26 when he wrote three papers that upended the world of science (including $E = MC^2$) and formed the basis for his future work.

There will be naysayers along the way. Strangely, these are more often than not your well-wishers, simply because they want to protect you from your own naivety. After all, if no one has ever come up with your idea or no one has approached the market the way you expect to, what makes you assume that you'll succeed.

For one, you are not too cautious when you are younger. Another reason is that you don't know enough or care too much about the status quo. A simple example illustrates this.

Show a new flat-screen TV to young children and tell them you're considering buying this because this is the latest technology. As an adult, your reasoning may be that this will give you better quality images than what you may currently have. A child, on the other hand, may ask any of these questions: What does latest technology mean? Will you get different information than what you're now getting? How long will the latest TV be latest? If a better TV comes up, will you throw this and get the new latest TV?

When you think of the difference between the responses, the child's response reflects a more long-term impact, whereas an *adult* mind seems more biased.

Takeaway *Never let anyone tell you that you're too young to come up with great idea. The best response when someone doubts you is "Watch me".*

2.4 The Clock Is Ticking

However good your business plan, it does take a certain amount of time to reach maturity. In many cases, clients look for stability in a business. They will not give you business till they are sure that you'll be around after a few months. With few exceptions, going from a back-of-the-envelope plan to initial revenue will take a period of over 2 years. This is a good reason for getting into a startup early since you won't have to give up a senior executive role to take a leap of faith.

People frequently say that an idea that you may have is not likely to work. This can be for a variety of reasons, ranging from "you don't have enough experience" to "if it was so good, someone else would have already done it before". Instead of merely looking at their arguments, it would also be useful to look at what *they* are doing. You may find that they have not done anything remotely entrepreneurial in their lives.

A distinction has to be made between the entrepreneurs and others who engage in subsistence ventures due to the lack of job opportunities. More than anything, the difference is vision and persistence. Entrepreneurs frequently seek to grow more and scale up and have an overarching vision that they work towards.

The reality is that you never know if it's going to work unless you try it. Consider the half-life of companies on the Fortune 500 list. A half century ago, this was 75 years. This has slowly reduced to 15 years today and shows no sign of abating. This implies that if the company itself has such a short survival rate, the likelihood of lifetime employment has effectively ceased to exist.

Even within the same company, job roles and responsibilities change every 2–3 years, meaning that you are looking for a new job inside or outside the company. This implies that any job has a half-life of about 2 years. From the risk point of view, the downside of a job is that you risk losing it every 3 years. The upside of a job is that you get a perceived sense of stability; and if you do really well, you get a bonus of a percentage of your salary. And then you start all over again in the same box. Sorry to disappoint you, but for the majority, these are the facts.

Compare it with doing your own thing. The downside is that it will fail. But it gives you a view that no job ever can. There's a good reason most companies have a requirement for an entrepreneurial mindset on senior level roles. The upside is of course that it may succeed. In case money drives you, it will interest you to know that the majority of billionaires are entrepreneurs. The only remaining ones are African dictators and Warren Buffet.

The adage "if it itches, itch it" has never been more apt.

Takeaway *If you only connect the dots with the number on them, you'll never build a new picture.*

2.5   Get Started!

Caterpillars, like startups, require a certain amount of time in the cocoon before they can emerge as butterflies. Experience shows that the average start-ups required between 2 and 3 years before they are able to commercialise their solutions. This is a time fraught with uncertainty and lack of systems. I recall each morning in the office, deciding and prioritising between following up with investors, partners, potential customers and suppliers. In addition, time had to be allocated to manage the operational functioning of the startup, which mostly entailed listening to the team members to ensure that there was no ego getting in the way of the teamwork required to make it all happen. Since the research was very early stage, it was not the right time to already start thinking in terms of the supply chain and logistics and strict timelines. This was a time when the precise ideas of how the machines and processes would look were mostly in the minds of the technical team. That's how early it was.

This can also be a time of intense frustration for you as the business driver since the technology teams will very seldom understand what you really do, let alone why. Additionally, feedback from investors is in long weeks. You cannot follow up on a daily basis. This can result in your being in the work mode 24 by 7—with nothing to really show to the technical side of the team (Fig. 2.2).

Fig. 2.2   A day in the life of an entrepreneur

There were times when there was little to do through the week—just a couple of questions from investors on Friday which would put paid to my entire weekend. Fortunately, I had two very small children at the time and was able to spend fantastic quality time with them. This also brought a certain amount of balance in life.

When one looks at founding a startup, there is tendency to see it through rose-tinted glasses and to refer to examples of startups that cracked it within 6 months to 1 year. It's good to keep in mind that these are the exceptions rather than the norm. It's also important to understand how you would function in an environment of uncertainty. This is particularly important since one of your key tasks would be to motivate people and give them a vision towards which they work and they would look up to you for this guidance.

2.6   Present: And Feel Good Doing It

A practical attribute of being a business driver in a startup is the selling and presenting that is required. I recall, on starting the company, most of my time was spent either preparing for presentations or presenting to investors, partners or—when the opportunity presented itself—at investor conferences. This is no different from business drivers of other startups. Your main focus is to get the message out, since this is the only thing that generates excitement about the startup and generates traction.

Investors also like to see that the individual presenting is able to sell the concept and vision convincingly, since if he can't sell it to them, there's not much chance that he'll be able to sell it to potential customers.

Fortunately, this is an art that one doesn't have to be born with. It is, as I learnt to my subsequent relief, something that can be honed with practice.

The technical co-founders are not people that you can necessarily trust to present to business investors. This is because they love to speak about technology, to the exclusion of how interesting the market is or how the technology can make a difference to the market and finally how the company can make a lot of money by doing so. These are matters alien to the technical mindset.

Being a business driver in a startup is not for the reticent or for those who expect to hide behind technology. For that, you have the technology team, anyway. One of the most important responsibilities of a business driver in a startup is being the face of the company.

Takeaway *Your challenge as a leader is to get others to want to do what needs to be done, to go where you want to go.*

2.7 Setting the Stage

The following chapters will take you through your own evolution as you move from defining the idea from the perspective of the technology as well as the difference that the technology can make. Your value is not in the technology itself. This will be the domain of the technology team that does magic with it. Your value would rather come from being able to see the changes that this technology can enable. This vision is why your ilk are called visionaries.

Intellectual property or IP will need to be looked at to determine if it can become your competitive advantage as the process of commercialisation commences. Advisors can augment the team in more ways than one. This then finally takes you to the investors and transitioning the idea into a living thing. Something that's bigger than yourself.

Takeaway *Perception is reality. Make it good.*

Takeaway *The impossibility of the vision is the mark of the man. And that's the only vision worth achieving.*

Takeaway Summary

1. *Never ignore your own problems to which a simple solution does not exist. If you would pay for a solution, so would other people.*
2. *Never let anyone tell you that you're too young to come up with great idea. The best response when someone doubts you is "Watch me".*
3. *If you only connect the dots with the number on them, you'll never build a new picture.*
4. *Your challenge as a leader is to get others to want to do what needs to be done, to go where you want to go.*
5. *Perception is reality. Make it good.*
6. *The impossibility of the vision is the mark of the man. And that's the only vision worth achieving.*

3

Ideas to Shoot and Root for

I was evaluating several ideas with the underlying certainty that I was going to quit my job and do something more meaningful with my life.

The idea of a crèche seemed viable due to the fact that there were not enough of them in Switzerland. However, the big challenge was that it would require a lifestyle change for many women, who were now mothers and homemakers, to go back to the job market. An online meeting point for retired persons linked to common activities was another business option that seemed to have huge potential. But, the market did not seem scalable fast enough.

It was at about this time that I came across a technical guy who was working on a certain technology for over two decades. Apparently, this technology was the best in the world at what it did. Now the challenge with technical persons is that they can very seldom relate to the rest of us. Have you ever tried asking a PhD, let alone a scientist, what he does and walked away with a clear answer at the end of his long monologue? This seems to be the main reason why many great technologies never see the light of day. Scientists are fantastic at developing and understanding their work, but they simply can't communicate how their work will make our lives better and how it could be put into practical use in ways that us normal folks can understand.

But back to the professor I met. He believed that his work was ripe for commercialisation, but he couldn't get funding. I asked him what exactly the funding was for. He spent a weekend trying to explain, by way of graphs and charts and technology papers, what exactly he was doing and how the nuances of his technological competence made it more future proof. A number of scientific articles also got thrown into the mix, ostensibly to make the differentiation more clear. It took a few more days for me to read, understand, research and distil what his work really stood for: a highly efficient solar cell,

© Springer International Publishing Switzerland 2016
A. Sethi, *From Science to Startup*, DOI 10.1007/978-3-319-30424-3_3

thin and flexible like a sheet of paper that would… that could potentially provide electricity as cheaply as from nuclear or fossil fuel!

Takeaway *Get back to the drawing board if you can't describe the idea in 10 seconds!*

If, like me, you were born into the world with no specific industry expertise, but only carried the tools of management imparted during the MBA like finance and strategy, you do face a dilemma. Where do you start?

But even before we start, it's good to know what kind of startups there are. After my experiences and much toying around with startup ideas, I've split them into three kinds.

3.1   Route-to-Market Startups

The first ones are startups that primarily focus on providing a new business model to as large a group of users as possible. These startups do not have a specific technological advantage. Their main focus is therefore the speed of scaling up.

These startups are defined by certain peculiarities.

The value of the ecosystem increases with an increase in the user base. This is similar to the customer base for a fax machine. One fax machine is effectively useless. However, each incremental fax machine becomes a potential additional node for all existing fax machines. In the same way, the route-to-market solution becomes an ecosystem, which tries to get a majority of the reachable user base into its platform. At the same time, each ecosystem strives to lock other similar ecosystems out while enabling their users to transition easily into itself. The purpose is to get users into the ecosystem and keep them there. Each incremental user increases the perceived value of the entire ecosystem.

The sector has one dominant player that controls a large segment of the reachable market. This player may control a majority of the market and attracts ever more users due to the already existing user base. Other players often exist in narrow niches defined by language, culture or geography. But in our increasingly flat world, not often do we see this.

Geography is another factor that makes a difference since a larger population of early adapters help in initial scale-up and demonstration of the value proposition. Facebook would probably not have succeeded if it did not have the early adapter user base that it did at Harvard. Having a location in Silicon Valley helps, since the population is comfortable with new technology and investors are comfortable in investing large amounts in startups that seem like winners.

It is very difficult to have a winner, since when only one company wins, all the countless others lose. Behind each winner like Facebook, Twitter, Youtube, LinkedIn and Groupon, are countless entities with similar route-to-market value propositions that did not work. There are also certain route-to-market segments in the real world where there are a number of competitors offering similar products. Coffee is a shining example of this, where companies like Starbucks, Costa Coffee and McDonalds coexist and thrive. These do so because they operate in different geographies or specific segments. They can also coexist because they translate their value propositions into brands. But frequently, their three key advantages, as McDonalds puts it, are location, location and location.

This book will *not* help you to start a company that focusses on route-to-market as the defining characteristic of the company. To have that kind of company, you only need a business model that can turn on a dime, speed and a prayer.

3.2   Starting from Pain Startups

These startups spring up organically from trying to address a pain point or problem. When you realise that you are not the only one to have this problem, you identify the opportunity to provide the solution to others.

These are the most common and historically the easiest to do. Most entrepreneurs begin this way. It just so happens that more often than not, they stay on the same level. The reason is twofold: First, these businesses do not often have a path to scalability. Second, when the startup relates to a business area that relies on the skill of the entrepreneur, this itself becomes the limiting factor.

One example is that of a teacher. The time of the teacher becomes the limiting factor. The opportunity to scale up occurs when the teacher steps back and, instead of teaching students, hires other teachers to teach, effectively managing the resources. Even this can become a limiting factor. There are opportunities to scale up and become a truly global business, though it's not easy. The example below illustrates an exception rather than the rule.

It was 2008. Jose Ferreira had been looking at the GMAT preparation as thousands of students around the world do. He knew that the way to prepare for the GMAT was to get a book and cram in order to crack the problems. It was standard. Having worked for Kaplan, the world's largest go-to for books for GMAT preparation, he knew how the standardised guides worked. He also knew that the test preparation was not customised for each student. In the pre-Internet days, customising would simply not have been possible. However, with smart software and testing on the Internet platform, it had become not only possible but easy to test the specific strengths of students and focus only on their weak points. This enabled time optimisation by students by improving areas that really needed improvement. This effectively moved customised teacher-student interaction to the Internet and, in the process, scaled up the one-teacher model. This idea became Knewton (Knewtoncom 2015), which has, at the time of writing, raised over $100 million and is well on its way to becoming a shaker in the online personalised educational content market.

Other examples relate to specific pain points that the individuals experience. As they look for a solution, they realise that none exists.

Sara's ambition was to become a lawyer. However, she couldn't crack the admission tests. She then went on to become a salesperson for fax machines. Being forced to wear pantyhose while selling these machines in Florida, which was perpetually hot and humid, she hated the webbed toes. But she liked the fact that these pantyhose made the panty lines disappear and made her lower body appear firmer. An easy solution was to cut the feet off her pantyhose and wear it under her slacks. She realised that other women also perceived the same problem and there was no solution in the market. She got a meeting with the buyers at Nieman Marcus Group. She changed into her hose solution that she had trademarked Spanx (Wikipediaorg 2015a). Based on her meeting, she got Spanx into seven of their stores. The rest, as Sara Blakely would say, is history. Who would have known that getting rid of the panty line was the road to becoming a billionaire.

This book is also *not* about the startup that starts with the pain.

3.3   Technology-Driven Startups (or Back-to-School Startups)

The company that this book will help you to start focusses on technology and assumes that you don't have a technology of your own. And if you're a tech founder, it'll help you think outside your box and align your thinking to the investors and the market, rather than limiting yourself to the technology.

This brings you—the non-techie—to a fork in the road. The first option is to clearly know what area you want to work in and find research groups in universities who are already working in that area. The risk here is that since you are predisposed to certain verticals, you may look favourably at the technologies or teams working in these, to your subsequent detriment. This is because the route to commercialisation is very brutal and will test even the strongest of business cases. You can be sure that any area of weakness that you brush over will come back to haunt you during the due diligence or worse during the subsequent commercialisation. We'll discuss these issues in more detail later.

Having stated this, I would also say that actually having a particular area of focus enables you to develop deeper insight into the market scenario and trends. Thus, you are better positioned to evaluate how close the technology is to commercialisation, so long as you reserve the capability to evaluate reasonably and—more importantly—walk away if the idea does not fit.

The second option is to begin by identifying and talking to spin-off departments of technology universities within the research domain that are in turn trying to support IP or speaking to teams involved in research who are trying to commercialise their work. In this way, you are in a better position to do the most important thing in your startup, which is to meet technology teams and understand their vision. However, remember that without the research team, the technology is worth little more than the substantial reams of paper covering it unless it is covered by patent.

In general, when you are looking for technologies, you have a far higher chance of finding one if you know the industry and the niche—and you also know that this is where you want to play. This is a prerequisite that will provide a clear sense of the market potential and the players within that vertical. This will in turn give confidence to the technology team, and they are then likely to take you much more seriously. This confidence is important since everything else you talk about like fundraising, go-to-market and strategy will be alien to the technology team and likely to be largely discounted. This confidence is also important since you will also be asking them to dilute their focus on their research and form a company led by you. Needless to say, getting them to focus 100 % of their efforts on the company will seem like an insurmountable challenge in itself.

It is fully likely that universities or research entities may not have a spin-off department, but I would perceive this as a positive rather than a negative factor. I've been known as an optimist; otherwise I would have committed suicide several times every quarter. Believe me, you'll need to be an optimist, too, to make it work.

The legwork involved with the second option is more since you will have to identify and talk to people working in different areas over more cups of coffee than is entirely good for you. What you may find is no secret—technology that is not clearly linked to commercialisation is normally more mature than technologies developed in regions where the commercialisation of research is common.

This is also the reason why technologies being commercialised in Silicon Valley startups have a much smaller chance of success than those developed in Europe. Since the startup culture is more developed in Silicon Valley, technologies are frequently taken towards commercialisation before they are fully mature, resulting in the high failure rates. In Europe, the rate of success is higher—but the startups are far fewer in number per capita of researcher.

Research (Ethzch 2015) done at ETH Zurich by the London Business School regarding the survival of technology-based startups in Switzerland found something shocking—about 90 % of all technology-based startups from the Federal Institute of Technology (ETH Zurich) in Switzerland were still around after 5 years during the 2000–2004 timeframe. This, compared to less than 50 % of all other companies, started in Switzerland during the same period.

What's even more interesting is that the survival of technology firms is better than the survival rate of a large-company employee in any given job. Thus, there seems to be little justification in *not* starting a technology company. For a business driver, the lack of focus on any given technology can almost be considered an advantage, since you are then not locked into that particular technology but are able to evaluate different ones from the point of view of viability.

Of course, once the technologies demonstrate their capability to be commercialised, Silicon Valley's culture ensures that a lot of money is available for a very rapid scale-up and towards global domination. The culture of operating around a comfort zone in Europe frequently results in a much slower scaling up to being a company with 5–10 people, operating in a niche area. This geographical is also discussed in more detail in the chapter "Teams".

Takeaway *Evaluate technologies dispassionately before you get involved. Avoid falling in love with the idea of falling in love.*

3.4   Geography Matters

When I considered ideas and opportunities, I knew that Switzerland was going to be my home for personal reasons. I thus looked at opportunities that would enable me to be based in Switzerland. This made it easier to look at market peculiarities and create a niche by transplanting solutions from other geographies where people either don't have a solution or pay too much since they don't know better.

There are other challenges and decision-making factors that come into play, too. After I started Flisom, the government of Germany was particularly insistent that we consider moving to Eastern Germany, where very significant financial support (up to €50 million) was being provided to next-generation clean energy companies. We decided not to move.

The reason was simple. In the early stage of commercialising, it is imperative to de-risk technology. Proximity to the research facility enables going back in case things don't work at the pilot. And take my word, more often than not—they don't.

The importance of geography, especially if this is your post-MBA home, is to be sensitive to the attitudes of end users. My first startup experience post my MBA brought me to Switzerland. It was with eBaraza, a photo-sharing startup and the year was 2000. This was a lifetime ago, when Google was a research project, Facebook's founder was 16 and twitter was the sound of a bird. In fact, this was in the time when digital cameras were only catching on and Kodak still had strong growth forecasts. This was also the time before phones had cameras. Yes, it was that long ago.

eBaraza had developed a good business model and our website was backed by excellent software. What we did not factor in was the conservative Swiss mentality. The second thing that we did not look into was the sheer diversity, multiple languages and attitudes of people in Europe. Hence, we could not go to market with a one-size-fits-all strategy. Our competitors in the USA with arguably less ease-of-use websites were able to scale up faster since the mindset in the USA is to try new things. Having one language made things that much easier.

We had undertaken the challenge of changing the behaviour patterns of users. But since the starting behaviour of the various communities in Europe was different, we were unable to access a large segment with a common marketing focus. The multiple languages and cultures also hindered our progress since the buzz in one market segment did not translate to other segments. Subsequently, these competing photo-sharing companies got sold to larger players. In essence, simply because there was a population of 300 million in Europe, we had assumed that we could capture 1 % of that market. Like so many other startups that make this assumption, we were wrong. And we folded.

Takeaway *When developing an idea, understand the behaviour of the focus customer segment. It's easy to assume wrong and just as easy to fail.*

3.5   From Idea to Market

One of the main challenges when looking at any idea is how to get from research to commercialisation. The main questions are:

3.5.1 Timeline to Pilot

Researchers do research for the sake of doing research. Their primary focus is seldom to rush something to market. Their greatest motivation is often to get their papers published in scientific journals and get peer reviews on arcane parts of their work. Your challenge here is to figure out how to go through the morass of technical jargon and get some questions answered: What steps are required to start working on the pilot? Do any of the steps need fundamental research or is it a matter of developing manufacturing capability? Does the machine design exist, or can it be easily customised for the process in question? How critical is replicability? Are any of the materials used toxic? Even if these questions cannot be answered in the beginning of your evaluation, your awareness of these potential issues at least minimises the risk of any unpleasant surprise that hinders or delays commercialisation.

Investors will invest if the path to starting the pilot is clear *and short*. More importantly, investors will invest only if the path and time to completing the pilot are clearly defined since scale-up is where the commercial opportunities arise together with an opportunity for the investor to exit.

3.5.2 Sustainable Competitive Advantage

Your first customers will be your prospective investors. In order to sell the idea to them, you have to convince them that your idea has a competitive advantage that will still hold true for a number of years. This will enable them to recover and multiply their investment before China replicates at a lower cost.

3.5.3 Establishing Beachheads

The first market that your product will address has to be clearly defined. Sounds easier than it is as you will find a number of attractive addressable markets. The most difficult decision may be whether to go for high-value or high-volume markets. Investors look for markets that have an annual size of over a billion dollars in order to provide enough growth potential. And it is this potential that will enable them to exit with a healthy multiple.

3.6   Positioning: High-Value or High-Volume

One of the questions that need to be asked early on is the positioning of the solution or product enabled by the technology. This will bring to the fore the decisions that need to be made by a startup compared to those in an established company. This will also provide a flavour of the decisions that are made by CEOs of large corporates and are the reason that they are paid as much as they are.

The impact of these decisions even in large companies can clearly not be overstated. When Lou Gerstner was brought into IBM, his strategic focus was clear. "The last thing IBM needs now is a vision". Years later, his successor, Sam Palmisano, decided to exit the PC business while it was still in vogue and decided to focus on the higher-value service business. Compare this with HP, which not only delayed getting out of the PC business as it was commoditising but spent $25 billion (Nytimescom 2015) to buy Compaq, even as its business model was evolving and the manufacturing sector was moving to China. The result: IBM continues to outperform, whereas HP is languishing and seems to have gone astray.

When Steve Jobs came back to Apple, it was on the cusp of bankruptcy. Jobs dramatically reduced the product line from a whole plethora to a mere handful and clearly moved to the higher perceived value desirable products. Job's view was simple: "get rid of the crappy stuff and focus on the good stuff" (Carmine gallo 2015). Largely as a result of this, Apple is today seen as an example of leadership in turbulent times by staying true to its DNA. Years later, this exact DNA of very high perceived value has enabled Apple to continue increasing market share, in the face of competitors who previously had lambasted Apple and who now saw their market shares eroding even as their products are perceived as being commoditised.

Positioning determines whether the product will be high value or high volume. There are some obvious ways to arrive at the answer.

3.6.1   High-Value Positioning

Many mid-sized companies in Switzerland, Germany and Austria thrive on extremely high-value solutions that use precision-machining capabilities. Since the market is so small on these rarefied levels, it is not worth the while of other companies like Chinese manufacturers to replicate and go after these markets.

A classic case is of a company based in a village on the outskirts of Zurich. Each week, a helicopter used to land in the company's premises for a few minutes. On inquiring, I found that this company was making the washer mechanism for windscreen wipers of high-end luxury cars. The size of the components was so small and the value is so high that it was worth the while for the company to get the products picked up by helicopter every week. Due to the small volume of production and the precision of the work required, the company did not have competition, especially as it was able to provide adequate production with 100 % guarantees on delivery time schedules. The super profits from this high-value manufacture further enabled the company to do ongoing research on new alloys in order to retain its global competitive advantage.

3.6.2 High-Volume Positioning

Instead of being high precision, the company may rely on a new method which is covered by patent. In such case, the best option would be to go in for high-volume production. In this way, the company will be able to capture more value by scaling up rapidly. American companies frequently focus on high-volume positioning, where they keep their brand strategy and R&D operations local and ship their volume manufacturing overseas.

I recall a time when I went to a very large sports shoe store in New York and inquired about a pair of US-made Nike sports shoes. The salesgirl was unable to help, so she requested the store manager to help. He candidly responded that Nike only had their marketing and executive functions in the USA. All manufacturing had been outsourced to lower-cost countries. This is a bit scary, particularly since if there is no local manufacturing, over a period of time, the skills are lost. The next generation of engineers and mechanical workers miss learning from the more seasoned workforce resulting in loss of capability over an entire sector of manufacture. With no manufacturing jobs, students choose other fields of study, resulting in not only the loss of skills, but also of the next generation of educated workers to help in evolving the manufacturing knowhow. Perhaps this rash of outsourcing may come back to haunt these countries and industries in the not-too-distant future.

But back to the present, for technologies relying on a new method, failure to rapidly move to volume production entails two risks:

Risk 1 The first risk is that of replication or expansion, particularly in geographies where patent law is difficult to enforce. This afflicts not only young startups but also established companies.

Rolls Royce, one of the most recognised names in the automotive world, recently found to its chagrin that Geely of China had apparently copied the Rolls (The telegraph 2015). This had not only the look and feel but also details like the signature grill and the Flying Lady mascot. To be fair, not everything was copied. The price point for the Geely car was much lower.

China used to be a very large purchaser of Russian military aircraft. But over the years, the focus has shifted to indigenising high-tech equipment. From orders of 200 Su 27 fighter planes, the focus moved to smaller and smaller numbers, till, finally, China asked Russia for one Su 33 prototype aircraft (Pravdaru 2015). Since it appeared that the only reason China would want only one aircraft would be to copy the technology, by way of replication and indigenising, Russia refused, and China promptly acquired one aircraft from Ukraine. Fast forward a decade, China is now rapidly becoming a much more significant player than Russia in fighter aircraft export globally.

Risk 2 The second risk is that entities that scale up faster have the opportunity to establish standards. Once these standards are established, any firm that comes in later has to pay royalty to the companies which own patents used in creating the standards.

The advantage of these standards is that solutions requiring these products are customised to ensure that only these products work. Nespresso is a good example of this.

Nespresso produces its own coffee capsules but does not focus on producing the machines into which these capsules fit. However, since they have become a standard in coffee capsules, any other company that wants to produce coffee capsules that are compatible with these Nespresso machines would be blocked by Nespresso's patents and would thus not have the freedom to operate. Nespresso's exclusivity based on its patents would enable it to get global brand recognition and become the de facto standard by the time the patents expire.

3.6.3 Bridge Positioning

There are companies that move from high value to high volume while retaining their perception of high value by capturing the essence of value of superior engineering to build their brand. Apple is an excellent example, moving to high volume while retaining its perception of high quality. Swiss watch companies have also been moving in this direction, since they started with high-precision engineering that enabled these complicated automated machines to keep ticking on your wrist. Even though more precise quartz watches have deluged the market in the last few decades at price points which are sometimes only 1 % of that of Swiss watches, the Swiss watch companies have been able to leverage on the "made in Switzerland" tag to drive brand perceptions even as they focus on generating volumes.

Google is another good example of a new generation company to do bridge positioning. Google began as a superior search technology. However, over a period of time, it has captured our consciousness to such an extent that although there are other search companies and technologies out there that may be as good, we only remember Google. In fact, it has entered common parlance when talking of any research—we simply say, "Google it!" It has thus moved from a technology-driven company to a route-to-market or high-volume positioned company.

3.7   Change Required from Status Quo

Changing the status quo or behaviour patterns for end users is far more difficult than it first appears. Try brushing your teeth with your left hand; you'll know what I mean. Not only does the technology have to pass the test of being easier or cheaper than what is currently available, it should also resolve a problem that end users may have. Even that may not be enough. It is because of this reason that given the option, it is easier to address the B2B market rather than going for the B2C.

Boo.com is a classic example of how behaviour matters. It's an expensive example as well since it cost well over $135 million to find out what doesn't work! (Wikipediaorg 2015b). This was a startup that came out of the UK. The idea was simple: you bought clothes online by providing your size once. This avoided the hassle of going to different stores and effectively saved you a lot of time.

The founders did not recognise two things: people enjoy going to malls. In fact, for 50 % of the population, window-shopping needs no further explanation. The second element is that people buy clothes, not just based on how the clothes feel but how the clothes *make them feel*. This experience is impossible to recreate (at least with current technology) on the Internet, compared to buying electronic equipment online, where you only care about the functionality. Since shopping is considered a leisure activity by users compared to being a hassle as understood by the founders of Boo, this resulted in a gap in perceptions. Of course, other challenges like difficulty in opening heavy data pages due to slow connectivity in the pre-2000 world only accelerated the demise.

3.8   Emotions Rule

There are two ways to start a company. The first way is to do a proper evaluation of the business case, look at the competition and do a competitive analysis, look at the strengths of the team and take tentative steps towards involvement. The second is to simply believe in the capability of the technology to deliver and, in spite of wiser counsel, go right ahead with the conviction that failure in your chosen path will be more fulfilling than relative success in your current labour.

Your advantage compared to that of the technology team is that you can afford to be objective about the viability of the technology to become a business idea. The technology team's work of their lifetime depends on their passion for the technology, so they can hardly be expected to be objective about it. This is however only in the initial stages of your involvement, since as you get deeper into the technology, your objectivity will wane.

3.9   Rocket Science

I was once trying to explain the concept of world-class innovations to my niece who's a physiotherapist.

What it is that really distinguishes scientists who do something really special? This was in relation to my startup, where the technology co-founders had once sent their solar cell sample into space with the space shuttle to understand the impact on exposure to space radiation.

I said you couldn't really do research that was more rocket science than this. But having seen these scientists up close, I realised that in addition to being bright, they were very very patient. So if things didn't work, they would get up next morning and try to tweak something minute and see the impact of this change—however, miniscule it might be.

In physiotherapy-speak (in a slightly exaggerated manner though), it was like trying to invent a new technique of physiotherapy. Each day, you tried something new and, oops, the patient suddenly died. After sending about 10,000 patients to a better place, one fine day, one patient suddenly got better. You say, "Whoa, how did that happen?" Then, you try to replicate what you did and try to get them to survive.

Takeaway *Up close, rocket science is about really small simple steps and a serious amount of patience.*

3.10 Seeing the Bigger Picture

An oft repeated but seldom recognised trait of truly successful entrepreneurs is that they see something different from others. They are driven by the power of conviction.

Many years ago, in one of his rare interviews, Laxmi Mittal was asked about the wisdom of his strategy of acquisition and consolidation in steel, which was at the time globally acknowledged to be a sector of terminal decline and bankruptcy. His response was "I can see what others cannot see" (Wwwftcom 2015). It would have been a pompous claim if it hadn't been true. And testament to his foresight was the fact that a few years later, his conviction that steel would be the bedrock of industrialisation was realised, incidentally making him one of the richest men in the world (Fig. 3.1).

My technology team was a prime example of working in a limited area compared to having conviction about the bigger picture. After I got involved in discussions with the technology group who would later be the co-founders and team members, I realised that they had a particularly risk-averse attitude to risk. Once, when I remarked that investors like to see the founders' skin in the game, their reaction was as though I had contracted a particularly virulent strain of the bubonic plague. I realised that they were not likely to leave their stable jobs at the university till the funding came through.

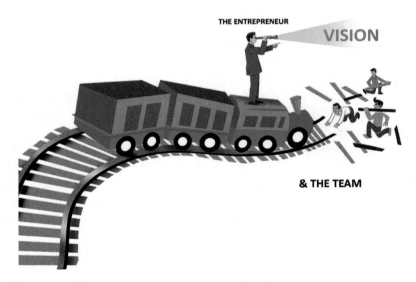

Fig. 3.1 Carving the future in line with his vision

When I had decided to take the leap and tender my resignation to my corporate employer, the first reaction from the technical team was to ask if I had taken leave of my senses. This was definitely not the excited or positive reaction that I had expected since I would now be fully committed to the idea. The difference between them and me was that they could see the research as their daily bread and saw the challenges that needed to be resolved to improve it further. I, on the other hand, could visualise the impact of the technology on the real world and the potential to bring change by way of providing low-cost electricity using flexible PV.

For me, the risk of failing in something that was clearly bigger than me was worth taking and worth more than succeeding as a mid-level executive of a larger company. This book is a validation of my decision.

3.11 The Right Idea = Patience and Perseverance

The value in any idea is not always what the team perceives but what the market is willing to pay for. Yahoo, considered a successful company (or at least a company that's still around, at the time of writing), changed its business model over ten times in the first 2 years of its existence. It began by having editors catalogue information available on the web and compile them into logical categories. In 2004, Yahoo's focus was so clearly driven towards having a catalogue that they outsourced the search component to Inktomi and then to Google. After all, there was no way search could enable Yahoo to make money, was there?

Google is one of the most spectacularly successful companies of our time. Yet, in the early stages of its existence, search was not a clearly defined idea. Different companies were experimenting with different business models. Yahoo's view was that artificial intelligence was not smart enough to understand what users really wanted. Even companies that were doing search like AltaVista were trying to create other revenue streams by incorporating news travel and shopping. Google had only focussed on search and resisted the temptation to do more things. Its focus was a limitation in the beginning and it struggled in the early years of its existence.

At one point, the Google founders were open to selling it to Excite, another search engine. The only reason the deal did not fructify was because the Google founders wanted $750,000 (Wikipediaorg 2015c) and Excite thought the price was too high. George Bell, the CEO of Excite, reportedly threw Vinod Khosla out of his office when Khosla brought the deal to the table. The focus on search did pay off when over a period of time, there were just too many websites to remember or even to catalogue. Users did not want to go to websites anymore; they wanted the information to come to them. Finally, Google's vision of the future was recognised by users and became a convenient reality. And the rest of Google's story, like they say, is history.

Again, Apple is another classic case of having the right idea. Its original idea was ease of use and great look and feel. After the founder Steve Jobs was unceremoniously shunted out of the company in the late 1980s, the company lost its focus by not realising why users brought its products in the first place. It was only when the company was on the cusp of bankruptcy that Jobs was brought back again. He realigned the vision of Apple to what it was. From there to becoming the most valuable company in the world was no mere chance but only an unrelenting focus on the two things that defined its true north—ease of use and fantastic look and feel.

Whereas Google's vision was to get information to the user's search on the computer, Apple's was to make the individual's life easier. This included being able to get information to the user even if he did not use a computer. Where the original requirement was to type queries in order to access information, Apple made even typing redundant. In Apple's view, not only should users not have to remember where a particular piece of information resides on the web but that they should not even have to go to a computer or have to type. Information should be ubiquitous to be relevant. One step in this direction was word-phrase suggestion before you get to type your entire query. The other was the introduction of Siri. Information without relevance, as they say, is just data.

Flexibility is an important attribute of successful companies. This is because, frequently, the value the market perceives and is willing to pay money for in an idea is different from what the team originally thought. However, technology founders do tend to be rigid about their ideas since they visualised them in their purest form much before they became a startup. If the founders consider any modification of the idea sacrilege, know that this rigidity can cost you (Fig. 3.2).

Takeaway *The value of the idea is only as good as the capability of the team to execute it.*

3.12 My "Aha" Moment

When I began to look at the thin-film technology, one of the first questions in my mind was how to get it to market. This question vexed me for a long time. I reiterate here, it was in 2004, to be precise—the day after Christmas when I

Fig. 3.2 The best product is the one that works

was evaluating why I should get involved in this and what the route-to-market should be. Then, I heard about a wave in Asia that wiped out a few villages and killed over 200 people.

We now know that the total number of deaths was over 250,000 (Wikipediaorg 2015d). I realised that many of the persons who perished in the days following the tsunami were children or the sick as they were unable to get water and medicine since all communication channels had been wiped out. Thus, although there was enough food and medicine being flown in from all parts of the world, no one clearly knew precisely which islands or the isolated parts of the mainland had what requirement. All power generation solutions connected to the grid had been wiped out till miles inland leaving no way to power communications or water purification and cold storage for medicine.

This was my "aha moment", the moment when I realised what I had to do. I had to drive the commercialisation of the flexible solar technology that had been in the lab for over 25 years. In case of another natural disaster, providing lightweight and mobile power with flexible solar modules could mitigate the loss of lives in the days immediately following the disaster. The long-term vision of providing flexible modules that provide electricity at costs competitive with electricity from the grid could come later, with significant scale-up and the requisite investment.

This is when I also realised that to try and fail in the commercialisation of this technology would be preferable to success in my regular job in a large company, where I could keep getting sporadic promotions, taking regular holidays and creating nothing dramatically new towards the evolution of mankind. I took my plunge. And though my dream of commercialisation is taking slightly longer than expected to be realised, I still continue to support it.

It just goes to show that when you feel strongly enough about the idea, it's like falling in love. Dangerous, since for both things, the right attitude would normally be to evaluate the current position, the risk profile, the background of the other partner in the mix, and the financial alignment. How many of these things do you recall doing when you last fell in love? For me to consider even a modicum of success in your reading, this book would imply that you consider some of these practical challenges and risks before jumping into your startup compared to falling in love. And may both your endeavours be equally fruitful.

3.13 Industry Standard

From the point of finding the right idea, the question is always whether to take small steps or gigantic leaps towards a quick scale-up. This largely depends on the mindset of the founders. Some founder teams are contented to remain small and specialised.

The advantage of this approach is that you have complete freedom to pursue your own qualitative projects. You also have no additional pressure imposed by investors whose main focus is as high a financial return as possible in as little time as possible.

The disadvantage of remaining small and specialised is that if you really have a solution whose cost reduces as you scale up, you could be crushed or marginalised by competitors who see a global scale-up. Without scale, you are unlikely to have a sustainable competitive advantage enabling you to win new businesses other than the ongoing relationships that you may have.

Assuming the team does not want to keep the solution small and specialised, the best option is to scale up fast, *if* conditions are right.

Here's what happens when they are not: The field of flexible solar was still early stage in the early 2000s.

The processes for enabling commercialisation of highly efficient solar cells were not fully mature. Nor was the machinery design for large-volume manufacture finalised. Yet, what was there was the buzz. Governments began to consider it as part of their competitive advantage to provide support to alternative energy. Part of the funding flowed to technologies that were not fully mature. One of these was Nanosolar.

Nanosolar was founded by Martin Roscheisen (Wikipediaorg 2015e). Martin had experience with startups, having successfully started and sold several companies prior to founding Nanosolar. The vision of Nanosolar was always bigger than its capability to deliver. But in early stage companies, it's all about how you're perceived. This is particularly true if the investors are unaware of the technology and the challenges that need to be resolved prior to commercialisation.

Since the window of opportunity to raise funding was limited, Nanosolar applied to the US government for funds in addition to the $500 million (Crunchbasecom 2015) that the company had raised from investors. The US government provided another $400 million to the company. This funding was for scale-up.

What was interesting was that although Nanosolar was all set to scale up and commercialise, the technology to be used in its flexible solar cells had not been finalised. The company started with one technology and when it did not deliver or where the manufacturing challenges were deemed too steep, it moved to another technology. Nanosolar switched technologies several times including quantum dots, then moving to the semiconductor copper indium gallium selenium or CIGS. This was going on even as the company was raising funds from investors for large-scale commercialisation.

Now in a mature technology environment where a number of alternative technologies are available and the solution is distinguished by the look and feel, not finalising the technology to be used till just before production is no big deal. But in an emerging industry where the technology is the key and probably the only driver of whether the company can provide solutions, to get funding for scale-up before the technology has demonstrated manufacturing viability is nothing short of incredible.

At the height of this mania, Nanosolar raised funds at a pre-money valuation of $2.1 billion. That was then. Since reality has a tendency to catch up, eventually the investors realised that the company was not going to deliver. This resulted in the next round of funding at a pre-money valuation of $50 million. Loss to investors: $2 billion.

Takeaway *Keep in mind that investors' money will not make you rich. Only delivering on your promises will.*

Frequently, conditions are right for a rapid scale-up. This is when the technology been demonstrated, the pilot has been done successfully to ensure scale up, and the machines and the necessary maturity of processes are in place to ensure rapid commercialisation. This is when the right strategy towards commercialisation becomes important.

It is said that the best solution does not always take market share. The solution that takes market share is the one that gets to the threshold market size first.

A key part of the commercialisation strategy is forging relationships with key players in the industry. This will ensure that the solution becomes an industry standard. Blu-ray and HD DVD are good examples of relationships.

Both Blu-ray and HD were debuted in early 2000s as the next generation of home movie players. They both delivered a much higher visual performance compared to DVD players.

HD, backed by Toshiba, focussed on providing a smaller size for movies and cheaper players. Blu-ray, backed by Sony, had larger storage capacity. The battle was won by Sony's Blu-ray format, not because of Blu-ray's superiority, which was not demonstrated, but because Warner Bros, a key movie studio, decided to drop the support for HD (Wikipediaorg 2015f).

It's not an ideal world, since otherwise we would have the same kind of plug points for electricity all over.

Takeaway *When you get that far, remember that being the standard matters more than technical excellence in capturing and monetising value. The tech co-founders will never understand and that's okay.*

3.14 No Certainty

Like love at first sight, people frequently believe they'll know when the right idea comes by. Unfortunately, this is very seldom the case.

When you start looking for your great idea, it's normal to come across a number of ideas and not be absolutely certain which one you want to be fully involved with. At this stage, entrepreneurship is not about taking unnecessary risks but understanding what risks are worth taking. When you have a number of ideas, a good option is to evaluate them. Take them for a test drive.

Surprisingly enough, involvement with more than one idea doesn't necessarily double the effort and time investment. This is because the strategies relating to markets for different ideas and commercialising different technologies tend to be similar.

You can start by getting involved from the outside, helping these technologies and the technology people to take the first steps before you fully commit. More than the sustainability of the idea, this will also enable you to understand how committed the technology team is.

A reasonable approach is to have equity in the idea and have a commitment that in case you get fully involved in commercialising on the idea, you have the right to get a larger equity stake. This then limits your downside and at the same time protects and safeguards your upside by having equity in the commercialising entity. If one idea begins to get more traction, you can move that on a full-time basis, thereby mitigating your own risk.

An unexpected benefit of supporting multiple ideas is that you will be able to cross-pollinate commercialisation ideas from one to the other. This is because there is a significant learning curve involved with each technology. You help in mitigating mistakes since you see the impact of a mistake on one technology's commercialisation and are in a position to avoid it the next time around.

Takeaway Summary

1. *Get back to the drawing board if you can't describe the idea in 10 s!*
2. *Evaluate technologies dispassionately before you get involved. Avoid falling in love with the idea of falling in love.*
3. *When developing an idea, understand the behaviour of the focus customer segment. It's easy to assume wrong and just as easy to fail.*
4. *Up close, rocket science is about really small simple steps and a serious amount of patience.*
5. *The value of the idea is only as good as the capability of the team to execute it.*
6. *Keep in mind that investors' money will not make you rich. Only delivering on your promises will.*
7. *When you get that far, remember that being the standard matters more than technical excellence in capturing and monetising value. The tech co-founders will never understand and that's okay.*

References

Carmine gallo. (2015). *Forbes*. Retrieved December 1, 2015, from http://www.forbes.com/sites/carminegallo/2011/05/16/steve-jobs-get-rid-of-the-crappy-stuff/

Crunchbasecom. (2015). *Crunchbasecom*. Retrieved December 1, 2015, from https://www.crunchbase.com/organization/nanosolar/funding-rounds

Ethzch. (2015). *Ethzch*. Retrieved December 1, 2015, from https://www.ethz.ch/content/dam/ethz/main/industry-and-society/transfer/dokumente/The performance of ETH spin-offs Jan 2015.pdf

Knewtoncom. (2015). *Knewtoncom*. Retrieved December 1, 2015, from https://www.knewton.com

Nytimescom. (2015). *Nytimescom*. Retrieved December 1, 2015, from http://www.nytimes.com/2001/09/04/business/hewlett-packard-in-deal-to-buy-compaq-for-25-billion-in-stock.html

Pravdaru. (2015). *PravdaReport*. Retrieved December 1, 2015, from http://english.pravda.ru/world/asia/04-06-2010/113664-china_pirate-0/

The telegraph. (2015). *Telegraphcouk*. Retrieved December 1, 2015, from http://www.telegraph.co.uk/motoring/5205369/Rolls-Royce-considers-legal-action-against-30000-Chinese-copycat.html

Wikipediaorg. (2015a). *Wikipediaorg*. Retrieved December 1, 2015, from https://en.wikipedia.org/wiki/Spanx

Wikipediaorg. (2015b). *Wikipediaorg*. Retrieved December 1, 2015, from https://en.wikipedia.org/wiki/Boo.com

Wikipediaorg. (2015c). *Wikipediaorg*. Retrieved December 1, 2015, from https://en.wikipedia.org/wiki/Excite

Wikipediaorg. (2015d). *Wikipediaorg*. Retrieved December 1, 2015, from https://en.wikipedia.org/wiki/2004_Indian_Ocean_earthquake_and_tsunami

Wikipediaorg. (2015e). *Wikipediaorg*. Retrieved December 1, 2015, from https://en.wikipedia.org/wiki/Nanosolar

Wikipediaorg. (2015f). *Wikipediaorg*. Retrieved December 1, 2015, from https://en.wikipedia.org/wiki/High_definition_optical_disc_format_war

Wwwftcom. (2015). *Wwwftcom*. Retrieved December 1, 2015, from http://www.ft.com/cms/s/0/df17a9f4-26b9-11d9-9157-00000e2511c8.html

4

Technology Evaluation: Is It Ripe for Commercialisation?

Larry Page and Sergey Brin are blessed in a way, for they came up with a technology that had a clear market focus - search! Most technology people come up with technologies that are wonderful - but have no real market focus and a pre-defined usability factor. And for the rest of us with a business background and a yearning towards having a startup, there is a myriad of options, primarily focussing on technology or route-to-market. A startup that relies on a route-to-market is a logical starting point since it can rely on existing technologies to provide a better service to a target market. So far, so good. But the biggest challenge is the barrier-to-entry.

Barrier-to-entry implies the difficulty for a potential competitor to replicate your idea or to provide a similar solution to your customer group. This can be very different for a route-to-market from a technology. The protection can also be different (more about this in the chapter on patents). The ecosystem is key for an idea that depends on route-to-market. Facebook would have been much more difficult in another part of the world.

Amazon is a classic example of a route-to-market solution. The solution is centred around buyers purchasing books online rather than from bookstores. In 1999, there were over 50 online booksellers similar to Amazon, since there was no technology involved which could be protected. Naturally, each of these assumed that all they had to get was a 1 % share in the online market place. The reality is that there is one entity that gets the majority of the share (45–65 %) of the online market and two to three that have between 10 and 15 % each. The remaining survivors share whatever remains. Barrier-to-entry in case of route-to-market typically comes by scaling up quickly enough to become the predominant solution in the market. The competitive advantage is based on being the one company that users think of when they want to buy

© Springer International Publishing Switzerland 2016   **39**
A. Sethi, *From Science to Startup*, DOI 10.1007/978-3-319-30424-3_4

books online. As an example, try to name one other online bookseller other than Amazon.

Interestingly, Amazon's main product is not only books, as is commonly assumed. It is you. Once they have you visiting their site, they can provide whatever it takes to keep you coming back. Their value is in touting the number of users, also called eyeballs, or, in the brick-and-mortar world, footfalls. A more current example is Facebook. At its initial public offering, it had a value exceeding $60 billion. This is only partly made of revenue. The majority of the value (and indeed the revenue) is due to the number of users. The perceived value of Facebook is based on a net profit of over $2 (Investorfbcom 2015) *per user* for about 1.5 billion users. Again, the main product of Facebook is you and your personal data.

A technology-based company, on the other hand, has a barrier-to-entry based on knowledge that may be covered by patents or trade secrets. This is far more difficult to replicate by other companies that are based on route-to-market. Unfortunately, this is also difficult to understand by B-school graduates. A technology is also not something you can come up with sitting in a strategy class.

Which brings us to the secret recipe for increasing chances of success in a startup.

Unless you happen to be in Silicon Valley and have the blessing of one of the top VC firms, there is a significant risk that your route-to-market idea may be replicated and scaled up far more quickly with *n*-times more funding by a startup in the Valley. There are obviously exceptions, such as startups with strong relationship with key customers.

A very powerful route-to-market may also be a combination of existing solution components or technologies which already exist. I call this product focus.

One of the most powerful marketers of our generation is Steve Jobs. Apple is driven by having a more user-friendly product. The obvious examples are the reactions of persons who have an Apple computer. Without exception, they all feel very strongly about their computers. I am yet to find this reaction in anyone with a Microsoft-based computer.

For the uninitiated, Macworld is the Mecca for Apple devotees. The main highlight at this annual event used to be Steve Jobs' keynote. It was here that the full impact of the reality distortion field of Apple was felt. The product focus that Apple has elevated to an art could be recognised by the presentation. Jobs' presentation slides sometimes displayed only one word or a number. Just one. But whatever that single representation is, it pointed to the essence of clarity on what you deliver to the customer. I mentioned earlier that a good solution can be defined in one line. A truly great solution can be defined in one word. The word for Starbucks would be *escape*.

4.1   Think Secret

A technology-based solution is far more difficult to replicate and thus has much more value, especially if it has a patent protection or a secret recipe or a combination of both. Both Google and Coca Cola have trade secrets.

Coca Cola began over 120 years ago, primarily as a cure for drug addiction. Other than the brand name, the most important element was the *formula* (Wikipediaorg 2015a) itself. Had this formula been patented, it would have been fully protected till 1906. The strategy was to have a trade secret, which does not have any time limitation. However, there is the risk of a disgruntled ex-employee walking away with the formula. Of course, over a period of time, the value of the trade secret becomes negligible, and the company's perceived value is derived by its brand recall and its profit by its lower cost compared to new entrants.

In today's world, there is a very small likelihood of a startup with an idea like Coca Cola succeeding. But it's possible, which brings us to another company with a formula.

4.2   It "Gives You Wings"

Dietrich Mateschitz was an Austrian marketing executive with a penchant for trying new stuff. His travels took him to Thailand where he chanced to try the local drink Krating Daeng (Thai for "water buffalo"), which was consumed locally to keep long-distance truckers awake. He realised that drinking this immediately cured his jet lag. With his hectic travel, he could be active longer and felt less sleepy. He soon began having this drink up to eight times a day.

At about this time, Dietrich came across an article that stated that the top taxpayer in Japan that year was a company that marketed these tonics. Clearly, these tonics had huge earning potential if marketed right. He came up with a simple idea; he would market Krating Daeng in the West as Red Bull (Wikipediaorg 2015b).

This was where his experience in consumer brands came to the fore. He imagined this being an efficiency drink. As he said in *BusinessWeek*, the focus was "improving endurance, concentration, reaction time, speed, vigilance and emotional status. Taste is of no importance whatsoever".

Dietrich carbonated the drink and gave it the look and feel that he felt would appeal to the target audience. And the tag line reflected his vision for the drink: "*Red Bull gives you wings*".

To fuel the suspense, he encouraged rather than squashed rumours that included allegations and suspicions that taurine—an amino acid and one of the ingredients—was derived from the bulls' testicles or even bulls' semen. The company even set up a website devoted to the rumours.

The most important element was where the drink was pitched. This was focussed on extreme sports. These sports include BASE jumping (building, antenna, span or bridge and Earth), ice climbing, kite surfing, inline and speed skating (mostly down mountain roads) and free climbing.

The company also provided the drink for free to DJs and staff at clubs and the all-night party circuit. It began to be seen as the drink with the edge, the drink you wouldn't mind be seen drinking in a bar if you had to drive home.

Testament to the success of Red Bull as a new category of drink are the imitators. At the time of writing, there are already over 150 companies or drinks trying to cash in on the *energy drink* market.

The one thing that's interesting about the Red Bull story is how rare this is. Route-to-market is not easy to find success in, and the number of companies that succeed in this completely belies the number of companies that tried and failed. Companies like Red Bull and Coca Cola are the exceptions that prove the rule: the percentage chance of success in startups that focus on route-to-market is far smaller than startups driven by technology.

Takeaway *Unless your strength of conviction in a route-to-market play is backed by global investors, a technology-backed company is a better bet to succeed.*

4.3   Cost and Price

Ajit Gulabchand is the chairman of HCC, one of India's largest construction companies. In spite of being a large company in a high-growth sector, the company still operates like an entrepreneur—taking risks and trying new solutions. One of the most fascinating projects HCC envisioned was to build an entire town called Lavasa (Wikipediaorg 2015c). This is the first full planned city to be built since India gained independence from the British over 65 years ago.

Ajit once said that far more companies would be successful in entering India if they could recognise the difference between price-based costing and cost-based pricing. For most products, companies do cost-based pricing where they calculate the total cost of making the product, add the profit margin and create the price. But to enter the market of a developing country like India successfully, you have to start by understanding how much your prospective customers are willing to pay, and that defines your price. You then have to see if the costs fit and if they don't, you have to innovate—think frugal innovation—and get the costs down in order to crack the market.

In other words, the decision between whether to have price-based costing or cost-based pricing is driven by whether your solution is value driven or cost-competitive.

Here lies a really important lesson that many entrepreneurs, particularly technology entrepreneurs, do not fully understand. There are some products that become brands and their price can be defined by perceived value. However, these are few and far in between. The majority of products need to be able to compete on price while providing an innovative solution.

Over-engineering runs the risk of making the product too expensive to compete with other solutions out there. However innovative your solution, it is new, and in the eyes of the customer, it runs the risk of not working as well as the established solutions. Keeping the price the customer may be willing to pay in mind can remove the crucial barrier.

As Adam Smith said in his treatise, *The Wealth of Nations* in 1776, "The value of any commodity, therefore, to the person who possesses it, and who means not to use or consume it himself, but to exchange it for other commodities, is equal to the quantity of labour which it enables him to purchase or command. Labour, therefore, is the real measure of the exchangeable value of all commodities. The real price of everything, what everything really costs to the man who wants to acquire it, is the toil and trouble of acquiring it".

The benefit of rethinking costs when looking at the technology is that since you're already at the drawing board, thinking about cost reduction potential can simply mean a greater focus on processes that are suitable for rapid manufacture or easy replication. Technology teams cannot relate to this since their primary focus is to do something innovative. However, a process that enables lower-cost potential can be worth a lot more than simply a world record. Our team learnt this the hard way.

The scientists I started Flisom with had set up the world record for the highest efficiency back in 1999. The efficiency however was achieved by a complex process that was possible to do only in the lab. After getting over the euphoria of having achieved something no one else had done, the team realised in their wisdom that the lift-off approach, whereby two layers are created on two different surfaces and then brought together to form a solar cell, could only be done in a lab setting. The agonisingly slow speed of getting the two layers together and the problems with replicability made this unsuitable for commercial production at a price that the customers would be willing to pay.

It took another 5 years to get to a sensible efficiency with a process of making these flexible solar cells that was commercially replicable and another 8 years till we were finally able to *begin* the automated pilot. No one told me it was going to be easy, but the most difficult lesson was the most obvious; innovation without a relevant price point was just that: an innovation.

Takeaway *Customers don't pay for the world record—they pay for a solution that either saves them money, makes them money or makes their lives better.*

4.4   Technology Weakness

Technologies have an inherent weakness when they are solely run by technology people and scientists.

With all due respect, scientists are the not the smartest people on earth based on average intelligence. The more they specialise, the narrower their field of expertise becomes. Scientists thus know more and more than anyone else about less and less. Not that one wants to take this inference to its logical conclusion. Yes, they are highly specialized to genius levels when it comes to their area of focus - but beyond their focus realm, they are more often than not, clueless and out of their depth about the demands and functioning of the real world.

Technology people are thus not aware of whatever is required to take their technology to market, and, more's the pity, they have no respect for this knowledge, i.e. the business element. Technology people do not speak the business language required to talk to investors, who frequently are your first customers, if we assume that the customer is the one who pays you.

Early on in the formative process within the team, it is important to define the responsibilities of the various team members. This helps in avoiding much heartache as the startup progresses.

4.5   Red Flags

As you proceed with discussions with a technology team, there is a risk that the proximity may take away some objectivity of looking at the technology. Since your most precious asset is your time and it may easily take 3–4 years from idea to initial commercialisation, it is worth looking at the red flags very carefully. There are certain things that should raise a red flag for you as the business driver (Fig. 4.1).

Fig. 4.1 Ignore at your own peril

4.5.1 Different vs. Superior

Coming up with different ways of doing the same thing or coming up with a different output is what scientists do for a living. However, *different* does not always equate to *better*. This is particularly important if you're looking at the differentiation of the technology. But for the end user, differentiation in the function is far more important than differentiation in the technology.

Apple, once again, provides an excellent example of differentiating on the end use. The touch screen technology used by Apple for their iPhones was not invented by them. Apple, however, was the entity that began by focussing on what would provide a differentiated experience for the end user. It was then that the technology was integrated on the iPhone at the cost of buttons. Steve Jobs was famous for saying that the most difficult decisions did not involve what to put in the device but what to keep out. So when other laptop manufacturers today are talking about more than more complicated hardware and software, Apple is distinguished due to its focus on the end-user experience.

4.5.2 Replicable

Penicillin was discovered by accident by Alexander Fleming because he kept his windows open, letting in bacteria in the otherwise sterile environment of his lab.

In the same way, there are always extraneous factors that are unknown to the scientists. There is sometimes a particular combination of variables, some known to the researcher and some unknown, which sometimes comes together to give a superior result. However, the result only has value if it can be replicated.

When our team was working on flexible solar cells, they sometimes were able to obtain very high efficiencies. However, replication of these results was not always possible on the same machine. This clearly implied that of all the steps and processes involved, some variables behaved in a manner that improved the efficiency. But since there were thousands of variables involved, it was impossible to know precisely what variables contributed to the spike in efficiency. Thus, a superior result that could not be replicated was considered an outlier and not considered when looking at performance.

To ensure that the result was truly replicable, the same processes and variables were considered on a different machine and the results compared. This mitigated the variables specific to the particular machine that the team were not aware of.

What made our solar cell so challenging was not the theory. The theory had been known for a few decades. It was the precise configuration of the exact percentage of the four materials in the beginning, the middle and the end of the process, so that the 1–2 μm layer was different at the bottom, middle and top. The challenge for the scientists was how to make the highest possible efficiency, i.e. make the new world record on a standard cell. The size of the standard cell in research was less than 1 cm.

The challenge for me as the business driver was to ensure a mindset in the company that would result in a manufacture of not 1 cm pieces but of rolls with a width of 0.5–1 m and length of 1 km with reasonable efficiency. In fact, to compete on the global scale, the volume produced would have to be thousands of such rolls every year.

4.5.3 Timeline

If the solution takes more than 3 years to get to the black, be aware that the potential investor base that can support this will become limited. Most financial investors require a return on their investment in that time period. Thus, only the very-long-term investors like strategic investors or family funds will continue to be comfortable with this kind of timeline.

4.5.4 Overlapping Patents

Frequently, different geographies have patents that overlap. Technology teams are normally aware of this and from their perspective, this is no big deal. Their nonchalance in this regard should be treated with caution, since this seemingly minor fly in the ointment has sunk many a startup having huge growth prospects.

4.5.5 Technology Published

Technology people like to publish their work in scientific journals. This is one of the things that drive them and provide them with credibility among their peers. However, once a technology is published, it becomes *prior art* or information that is then already available. Patents cannot be filed on anything that is already known.

4.5.6 Technology Across Multiple Segments

It is easy to consider multiple segments where a given technology may have slight relevance. It is also just as easy to confuse the sheer number of customer segments where it may have some relevance with the one particular customer segment where the given technology will have absolute leadership.

4.5.7 Proof of Concept

Much of research tends to be fundamental. It is what builds the careers of researchers to enable them to reach the higher echelons of Godhood or, in other words, make professor. The downstream research that veers towards development is frequently not considered challenging enough. Fortunately, the lure of untold wealth on commercialisation is gradually changing this view.

Researchers in Silicon Valley and indeed much of the USA have fully embraced the route to commercialisation. However, Continental Europe is still lagging behind. China, on the other hand, is trying to leapfrog the West by setting up very large research facilities for fundamental as well as applied research. However, the mindset among researchers there is still very top-down and it may well take a generation before true creative work begins to emerge from China.

The problem of fundamental research is that it takes a long time to get to a practical proof of concept to demonstrate the theoretical concept. From the commercialisation perspective, not only should the timeline for the technology be clear, it is preferable that this proof of concept should already have been demonstrated. There will be enough challenges along the way without having to deal with an uncertain timeline of the proof of concept.

4.5.8 Funding for Proof of Concept

There are normally thresholds beyond which it becomes more difficult to get funding. The situation becomes even more untenable if there is no clarity about the precise funding requirement to get to or to complete the proof of concept.

Another question that needs to be asked is who pays for the funding of the proof of concept. In case the university pays for it, the ownership of the patent arising from this will most likely belong to the university. You need to navigate through this minefield with a degree of caution. This is discussed in more detail later.

4.6 Competitive Advantage

Technology leadership is certainly important in a technology-driven startup. But here's what happens when the startup is run by technology people.

I was recently advising a technology startup focussing on multi-fluid dynamics. The team of two extremely bright technology co-founders had been running the company for over a decade, and were sustainable with over 10 employees, all driven with organic growth and without external investment. In a tough market, where the leaders were frequently billion-dollar companies, this was extremely creditable. They now realised that they wanted to get external funding in order to drive growth and capture market share.

As we were fine-tuning their investor documents, I chanced upon their slide stating their competitive advantage compared to their global competitors in one word. With this one word, they had demonstrated how far they had to go to get aligned with the language that investors relate to. The word: "Physics".

4.7 Time to Market

One of the first things to investigate in any technology is how long it would take to get to the market. Once the proof of concept has demonstrated the concept by way of a prototype, it proves that the technology works *in the lab*. The second is the timeline for the pilot, since it is the pilot that will demonstrate that the technology can be transferred from lab equipment into commercial equipment. And just because the prototype exists does not automatically imply that the pilot will be easy, fast or inexpensive. My own experience below demonstrates some of the challenges.

Our lab solution was a 5×5 cm^2 solar cell which was created using machines that could make one such cell every few hours. Since breakthrough technology was of the essence rather than faster turnaround time, this was not a problem. Further, the evaporation sources were point sources, which evaporated layers in a circular shape around the point source, a bit like an ice cream cone.

For commercial manufacture, the big breakthrough required was to develop line sources. The technology was a bit like rocket science, since the materials had to be evaporated in high vacuum which were heated to a temperature to between 700 and 1300 °C with a maximum allowed variation of 3 °C. To add further complication, the proportion of the various materials in the vapour changed from the beginning to the end of the process. In fact, it was so like rocket science that our team did send one cell into space in 2002 on the Endeavour space shuttle.

Making the pilot equipment, however, took several years and many rounds of failure. This was because not only was the process new but even the machines that were required were not commercially available. Our team was thus developing the process appropriate for the pilot while simultaneously working on designing the machine and the line evaporation sources. And this was only for one of the several process steps. Only on the successful completion of the pilot would we get to the large-scale commercialisation.

As if this was not enough, we were working on a new evolving industry. Prospective investors and customers also wanted to compare us with conventional industries like nuclear, coal and wind-based electricity generation. At least no one had told me this was going to be easy.

4.8 Pilot to Black

Simply being able to do the pilot only demonstrates that the concept can be transferred from lab equipment to commercial manufacture. Then comes the real test of commercialisation: is the technology capable of being scaled up to a commercial viable level and deliver a clear and quantifiable benefit in cost or perceived value to the target customers?

Software companies have an advantage of moving from pilot to scale-up. This is because there is very little if any customisation that needs to be done. Additionally, once one solution is done, there is no incremental technology or engineering development effort to replicate and make copies. With the web as today's de facto distribution channel, there is also no effort in setting up the logistics of the distribution channel.

Flisom was a manufacturing startup. At the conclusion of the pilot, the scale-up funding requirement was of over $150 million. Without this, the only thing that the pilot would have been able to do was to demonstrate the viability of the scale-up, without actually producing any meaningful quantities.

This funding requirement and timeline for revenue needs to be clear up-front. In particular, the time to get to the black needs to be as clear as possible. A manufacturing startup can easily take 5–6 years to get to revenue from the scale-up from completion of the lab prototype.

As the business driver, your risk as well as your learning will be much more than that of the technology team. So will your capability to transition your knowledge and experience gleaned from your first venture as an entrepreneur.

4.9   Research and Manufacturing

Scientists always perceive of research as the ultimate voyage of discovery. Due to this, they have a propensity to look down upon those who are not engaged in such lofty efforts. This category firmly includes engineers, who do the prosaic work setting up manufacturing plants. However, researchers often fail to realise that research without the capability or possibility to finally manufacture something useable and tangible is of no commercial relevance.

Sometimes, researchers resist getting manufacturing experts into the team too long. This hurts the ability of the company to understand what real challenges lie in taking the research to commercial manufacture.

We were a classic case of the company driven too long by the technology team. When we began, we were very strong on technology but with non-existent manufacturing capabilities. As we went from the lab to the pilot, our technology team began looking at the manufacturing equipment available in the market. Since this was an emerging field, fully turnkey equipment, where the machine comes with fully integrated process, was not available. The benefit of turnkey equipment is when you switch it on and it works, like a coffee machine. The slight disadvantage is your competitors can turn it on, too. Without the integrated process control, our machine was more like a pizza oven than one where next-generation solar cells can be created.

The more our team looked at machines available in the market, the more they were struck by how expensive these machines were—their view being that they would be able to make it with components for much less. Little did we realise at the time that we were making the classic mistake of technology-driven startups, assuming that the best way to commercialise was to do everything ourselves.

Building our own machines was fine during the pilot, but on scale-up, where we would require tens, if not hundreds of machines, we just did not have the mindset of managing the logistics of machine manufacture. On the other hand, working with machine manufacturers during the pilot itself would enable us to focus on our core competence, while enabling the machine manufacturers to focus on theirs.

Takeaway *Be aware of the long-term impact of short-term benefits; it's a long winding road to commercialisation.*

4.10 It's Okay to Not Know

It is commonly assumed that like love, you absolutely know when the right idea happens. I would like to argue that in both love and inspiration, it doesn't simply happen. It has to be nurtured. Unlike love, however, it's not a bad thing to look at more than one idea at the same time. Rather, it's the prudent thing to do. In this way, in case one idea does not stand scrutiny, you have the other ideas that you've been discussing with their respective technical teams.

When you begin looking at technology-driven ideas and the teams driving them, you realise that it's not often easy to know exactly which idea will really fly. In this case, a sound strategy to mitigate your own risk is to diversity. Instead of identifying the *one*, a reasonable option is to work on multiple technologies.

Initially, the work will be more, since you will have to prepare business plans including competitive analysis for different technologies. However, since the process of making the business plan is standard across different technologies, working on two technologies does not imply double the effort.

Working on more than one technology also has two more benefits. The first benefit is that you don't get infatuated by the feeling of working on a startup, where you may be the only one taking the risk, given that the technology team cannot be expected to leave their salaried jobs to jump in, in spite of owning the technology. In this way, you avoid jumping into something that is less likely to fly. The second benefit is that you can challenge key success factors including competitive advantage and commitment of the technical team if you're working on more than one idea together. This ultimately makes your own chances of making the startup succeed far greater.

The additional effort put in more than one idea also has a payback, since you concentrate the mistakes that you're likely to make. There is really no substitute for your own mistakes, so if some of those mistakes are made with the idea that you do not progress, you can use the learning in the idea that you do decide to run with and you're that much ahead in the game.

Takeaway *Diversify risk. The best chance of looking at options is before you get fully committed to one.*

4.11 Maturing vs. Mature

I once had the opportunity to meet Howard Berke, the founder of Konarka (Wikipediaorg 2015d). Now Konarka was a poster child of the arrival of flexible solar cell solutions into the mainstream. By 2012, the company had raised over 170 million dollars of funding. Howard had famously said back in 2003 that Konarka was 6 months from commercialisation.

Konarka had ticked all the boxes, including having a Nobel Laureate as an advisor and receiving state funds signed off by the US 2012 presidential contender Mitt Romney.

During our conversation, Howard mentioned that they had capacity of 1 GW per year. This surprised me, since this is more than the capacity of a nuclear power plant. I felt this company's reputation clearly was well deserved and not based on vapourware.

As our conversation continued, I realised that the output capability was based on an assumption of 10 % efficiency and 20-year lifetime. The long lifetime was important since it was not possible or cost-efficient to change the solar modules on buildings and rooftops every few months. It transpired that with its technology, Konarka was able to get efficiency, which, if slightly improved, would touch 3 %. More importantly, the technology used by Konarka to make solar modules was unique in one aspect. It was organic. As the joke went, organic thin-film solar technologies work fine so long as they are under vacuum and in the dark, since moisture and UV radiation kill the devices quickly. The then lifetime of the solar modules of Konarka was in weeks to months. While this was eminently suitable for applications like emergency response, where the module had a one-time use, it was not ideal for buildings, where replacement was difficult and expensive.

The assumption of Konarka of having a capacity of 1 GW was then wildly inflated, since the technology itself had not demonstrated its capability to last for 20 years, which was over 100 times its current life, and an optimal and desired efficiency of 10 %, which was almost four times the current efficiency. Howard really believed that these were the *only* two issues to be resolved to have the capacity of 1 GW *and* that they were manageable in the lifetime of Konarka.

In a field where a 1 % improvement was considered noteworthy by the global press, Konarka's assumption that the only thing hindering success and global domination was a fourfold improvement in performance was something meant to excite the more impressionable investors.

Unfortunately for Konarka, the investors lost patience in Konarka's vision and in June 2012, the company finally closed its doors.

Takeaway *There is a huge chasm between emerging technologies and mature ones. Not recognising this spells the difference between success and bust.*

Takeaway Summary

1. *Unless your strength of conviction in a route-to-market play is backed by global investors, a technology-backed company is a better bet to succeed.*
2. *Customers don't pay for the world record—they pay for a solution that either saves them money, makes them money or makes their lives better.*
3. *Be aware of the long-term impact of short-term benefits; it's a long winding road to commercialisation.*
4. *Diversify risk. The best chance of looking at options is before you get fully committed to one.*
5. *There is a huge chasm between emerging technologies and mature ones. Not recognising this spells the difference between success and bust.*

References

Investorfbcom. (2015). *Investorfbcom*. Retrieved December 1, 2015, from http://investor.fb.com/releasedetail.cfm?ReleaseID=893395

Wikipediaorg. (2015a). *Wikipediaorg*. Retrieved December 1, 2015, from https://en.wikipedia.org/wiki/Coca-Cola_formula

Wikipediaorg. (2015b). *Wikipediaorg*. Retrieved December 1, 2015, from https://en.wikipedia.org/wiki/Red_Bull

Wikipediaorg. (2015c). *Wikipediaorg*. Retrieved December 1, 2015, from https://en.wikipedia.org/wiki/Lavasa

Wikipediaorg. (2015d). *Wikipediaorg*. Retrieved December 1, 2015, from https://en.wikipedia.org/wiki/Konarka_Technologies

5

The Team: Recognising the Red Flags

The team is by far the most important component of any young business. Having the perfect team members is not a luxury we often have. It's healthy to have some level of dissent since it's by being challenged that the business idea becomes more robust. At the same time, a startup team is not a team that can operate from 8 to 5 like in a regular job. Work in a startup is a lot more than a job. And it takes a lot more from the team to make it happen.

The initial interaction with the technical team is very important since it provides a sense of the dedication to making it work. If the team truly wants to make the technology get to the real world, they have to be ready to make sacrifices. At the same time, it is also normal that the technical team be nervous as they will be stepping out of their zone of comfort, since the things required to make a company out of a technology are very different from the technology itself (Fig. 5.1).

This is a great time for you to tell the team that it'll be okay. They need to hear it. At the same time, this is also a good time to look out for red flags since you want to get a fit team, not a therapy group.

Even within conventionally business-savvy people, there are points when the team members become less than rational or simply opportunistic, as the story below illustrates.

One of my MBA classmates, fondly referred to as the Greek God by the girls, the guys never knew why, was clearly very intelligent. A reflection of his genius was getting hired by McKinsey and subsequently becoming global head of strategy for a major alcohol brand company, despite or perhaps due to consistent absence from all MBA classes, which he more than compensated

© Springer International Publishing Switzerland 2016
A. Sethi, *From Science to Startup*, DOI 10.1007/978-3-319-30424-3_5

Fig. 5.1 More than just 9–5

by doing much to strengthen his liver at the apéros by prospective employers organised through the MBA.

The Greek God finally saw an opportunity to set up an online car insurance company in Greece, which has very cost-conscious consumers. The timing seemed ideal, since the country was undergoing fiscal restructuring and growth had stalled, resulting in high unemployment. He got together with three other people from the industry and began talking to potential investors. At the same time, one of the other three persons assumed the title of CEO of the venture.

He asked me for ideas to commercialise. On my inquiring how much stake he held in the company, it transpired that the idea was still on paper and had not been formalised in the form of a legal entity. His view was that this had not been discussed between the four co-founders but that he assumed that he would get 25 %. My suggestion, based on challenges in any team arising from uncertainty and misalignment of expectations, was to incorporate, so that the shares could be distributed between the four founders in a mutually agreeable manner. This would then take any uncertainty off the table so that the founders could focus on the real challenges.

As soon as he spoke to the other co-founders about the incorporation and distribution of the shares, the person who had been the acting CEO said that since he was doing the maximum face time with external entities, he was going to own 100% of the company and the other three individuals would be eligible for stock options based on performance. Needless to say, this led to acrimonious arguments resulting in the dissolution of the team. As if that was not bad enough, the four people split into two teams of two, each competing for the same market.

It turned out that the most important advice he had received since he began to work on the idea was "incorporate".

Takeaway *Tick the "stupid" things first: incorporation, equity, defining roles and responsibilities and authority will enable you to focus on the core task of making it happen.*

5.1 The Spouse

This is by far the most important element of your team. As they say, travel is great if you have a really nice place to come home to.

The main risk of doing a startup is not being fully aligned with your spouse regarding the time and effort it will entail and the uncertainty of it all. Indeed, even in case of success, the seas tend to be stormy. The surprises can come not only from the wind but also the currents. In such case, the last thing you want is for the ship to spring a leak or your partner to stop rowing (Fig. 5.2).

Many founders take their spouses and *their* aspirations for granted. Similarly, some spouses tend to expect glory, money and fame relatively quickly from the founders' activities. Founders keep the reality away from the spouses for multiple reasons. One major reason can be—not wanting to share frustration of things not moving forward. This happens more than you imagine and can relate to investor discussions not progressing, lack of technical progress, co-founder issues, disproportionate risk being taken by one founder and money running out. Other reasons include not wanting to let the spouse down since you have left your job to go after your dream. You are probably dipping into your savings and putting extra burden, not only financial but also emotional, on your spouse.

I know of more than one case where the wife of the founder told him that she wanted to be able to look up to him and his startup was taking too long. She was now wearing the pants in the house by way of being the breadwinner. She mentioned that it was time he became the man of the house and really consider taking up his role seriously by getting into a stable job and be responsible

ROLE OF SPOUSE

STABILITY THAT CAN ENABLE FLIGHT

Fig. 5.2 The spouse will balance the boat—make sure you're in the same one

for financial stability. It was now getting embarrassing to go out together because his status was "trying", which was akin to being unemployed.

One simple advantage of having a spouse who understands and appreciates the challenges that startups entail is that you are 100 % sure that your spouse is on your side and has your best interest at heart. This cannot be said of any of the other co-founders, let alone the investors, as the examples in the following pages illustrate. And your spouse doesn't need to be a legal eagle to pinpoint areas that may end up being relevant. It's worth keeping in mind that lawyers are excellent at protecting your interest in areas that you pinpoint. What about areas that you forget to mention?

Being straight upfront with your spouse also helps to clear another thing. It may happen that your spouse is not comfortable with the risk or uncertainty of your getting into a startup. If push comes to shove, it's better to decide upfront whether, in such case, you want the spouse or the startup, rather than having to let one of them go after investing years of effort. Another founder I know is clear on this point. If the funding requires him to move to Silicon Valley and his partner if unwilling to come along, tough for her. Push may not come to shove, but in such case, he's at least clear what he'll do.

But without undue philosophising, it's nice to have a partner who'll stick with you since the journey can be tough, and very few outsiders will understand, let alone stick around through the equivalent of your sustained hormone imbalance and "flipping out" frustrating behaviour at times.

5.2 Conflicting Vision of Team

Very often, the core team is driven by different motivations. When there is a clash between the conflicting visions of different members of the team, the best-case scenario is a departure of some team members. In a worst-case situation, this can result in the dilution of the company.

Teams where some of the members are very senior sometimes fail because these older members like to have back-up scenarios. Younger people give it their all, since they have less legacy reputation and distractions at stake. This may seem obvious, but during the early stage of the company, all members of the team have to be driven by the same vision. Not only that, they also have to get hurt the same way if it does not work. If some of the members have a back-up just in case the base case does not succeed, they will be driven by completely different motivations. More than anything else, this will undermine all efforts of the other team members (Fig. 5.3).

A team of co-founders of a technology startup may have a senior researcher, probably a professor. It is unlikely that the professor will relinquish his tenured position to become part of the startup. On the contrary, he's more likely

Fig. 5.3 You'll never get there, unless you all agree where you want to go

to see other opportunities to commercialise his research into other startups. His motivation is therefore already different from that of the younger co-founders, who are fully committed to the startup.

In one particular case, a senior scientific lead continued to work in at the university, whereas the others joined the startup full time. The full-time employment with the university gave the senior lead the luxury of looking for something better, which became a huge drag on the timeline. Because of this, the executive team began looking for the perfect solution rather than moving forward with simple solutions and customising them to fit. This resulted in a loss of time that could otherwise have been used in commercialising faster. Since one of the senior scientific lead was doing the startup as a hobby and had the luxury of being able to exert authority over the technical component of the startup, he continued to keep the status quo rather than focussing on getting a manufacturing lead to transition towards manufacturability. The company ultimately missed the opportunity to commercialise successfully because the technology lead was driven by considerations different from that of the company's.

Commercialising a startup is mostly self-driven, where no one tells you how fast you should go. It is thus relatively easy to delay since it's not possible to imagine the future impact of delaying one particular action. However, the delays and dithering set the tone of the startup, dooming it in the face of the more hungry competitors.

5.3   Problems in Technology People in Europe vs Silicon Valley

The concept of having a back-up scenario is probably the greatest difference between technologists in Silicon Valley and Continental Europe. In Silicon Valley, technology people are usually the first ones to jump into an entrepreneurial role and see how their concepts may be applied to real life. Technology people in Continental Europe fail in startups not because their concepts are inferior in any way but because they don't have the guts to take a stand on any technology and work towards taking it to market.

Going to market is difficult since it entails taking hard decisions and full-time commitment to a unified vision. This is not something technology people are comfortable with, since research is all about working with several concepts at the same time. The reality however is that it is only the market that will determine what will be successful; no amount of procrastination will improve the odds.

We were once having a conversation with a UN entity responsible for providing solutions in the strife-torn area of Africa. The entity was very interested in our flexible solar solutions. Our view was that this interest was due to the lightweight nature of our solution that could have been installed on rooftops of houses in villages. On discussion, we realised that the perceived value of the flexible solar modules was so high that there was a significant risk of them being stolen. The main advantage was not the lightweight nature of our solution but the fact that these could be rolled when not in use.

Takeaway *The market will frequently put a higher perceived value on the solution than what the technology people imagine, but this will only be known once you get there.*

5.4   Companies Driven by Lifestyle of Team

It is common to find companies in Switzerland with 5–7 people who have been providing a specialised solution in a high-end market. Their reason not to grow despite huge latent demand is fear of loss of control and change in their comfortable lifestyle. These companies continue to thrive with the same number of people for years. Normally, they are zero-debt and continue to focus on the same thing as a sustainable business, without going upstream or downstream.

Technology people are most comfortable with running or being in such companies, since their comfort zone lies in technology rather than the strategy related to growth, with all the growing-up pains of managing more people and having a consistent vision. (There are probably important lessons to be learnt about how this may be replicated in order to avoid large companies crashing and burning due to total disconnect of the senior management from what the customers want or, indeed, who the end customers really are, as well as tackling the challenge of the next generation of leaders running these enterprises. However, that clearly is the subject of another delightful tome.)

5.5   Business Team vs Technical Team

The two teams come from different planets. Business people understand that you need a very solid technology with a competitive advantage around which a business may be built. Technical teams, however, frequently have a biased view towards commercialisation and, more often than not, do not even understand the challenges. It is this approach that can come back to haunt these technical persons and startups driven solely by them.

Take Flisom. The technical co-founders had a clear understanding of the results of their experiments, which was "yes" or "no". There was no middle way or uncertainty. A lifetime of working in technology had completely disabled their capability to see the value in non-technical areas like business projections and strategy to such an extent that they questioned the very need or relevance of such non-technical criteria. Their inability to comprehend a business universe where plans and projections were not black or white was probably the reason why they were the best in the world at what they single-mindedly did at their laboratory. But this did little to help the commercialisation.

This was not limited to the initial company formation stage but also after we obtained our first round of funding. One of the technology co-founders asked me if I would now be looking for another job, since my work of getting the funding was done and the focus was on scaling up the technology. His view was that areas other than technology on a larger scale were only administrative like paying salaries and ensuring the stationery was always adequately stocked. The company, in his view, would run itself.

Takeaway *Don't assume that the tech team has all the answers simply because they are the best in what they do. Your vision may be the only right one, simply because you have one.*

5.6   Ethics

Simple words can have hugely different implications when understood by people from different backgrounds.

The first time this struck me was during my MBA at the London Business School, where the class had people from over 50 nationalities. We were once discussing a case study on ethics. The Chinese group could not relate to this at all, the Japanese lot was agreeable to whatever their team lead suggested and the Indians were not in complete agreement with any particular view and had significant discord even within the team, but were still willing to be flexible to accommodate everyone. The sole Swiss student wanted to read the fine print to ensure that he understood the financial implications of his decision.

But it was Felix, my friend from Israel, whose reaction was the most memorable. As he told the ethics professor, "I don't believe this class is relevant, since all ethics are inculcated by the time a child is 5". On being asked to share more of his background based on which he came to this conclusion, having come from the Israel military, Felix only said, "I could tell you, but I'd have to kill you". Till date, no one knows if he was joking.

Another time was when Ajay, a friend of mine, joined the London office of a young software company that had recently IPO'ed in India, at the conclusion of his MBA. He did the due diligence and it seemed to check out, other than the share price, which seemed to have a significant variability.

After he joined the company, he realised the reason for the stock variation. The modus operandi was simple, elegant and illegal.

The owner and majority shareholder would get two letters from a company: one stating that the company had bagged a large deal, and the second letter stating that the contract had been cancelled. His job was to go to India and talk to some chartered accountants about the deal. These chartered accountants, who were on the take of the company, would inform selected analysts who were covering the company about the deal. These analysts would then inform their clients who would then buy the shares of the company, driving up the share price from Rs. 10 to 40. The owner would then sell a large number of his shares.

The owner would then get the second letter out, which stated that the contract had been cancelled. The share price would slowly get back to Rs. 10. At this time, the owner would buy shares back from the market and the cycle would begin again.

Takeaway *Simple, elegant and criminal—if everything checks out, remember that it'll only work for you if the ethics line up.*

5.7 Commitment

Commitment can also mean different things to different people. A scientist will only commit when he's absolutely sure that something is possible. In fact, in my own company, I once asked my technology team when they expected their new and heightened efficiency to be achievable. Their consistent response was, "let's only promise what we've already achieved to the investor". My attempts to share a view that investors may be looking for stretch objectives and a team desperate to make it happen were not considered to be relevant. When I stated that if we promised something, the investors were likely to *take one third off*, the technical team said this did not appear to be based on scientific fact.

As a business driver, however, I recognised that a commitment is a target that we expect we will reach at a particular time in the future, given a best guess on internal progress with a constantly shifting customer base in a market that will hopefully still be around by the time we got there. Business drivers also recognise that the uncertainty of the assumptions made for future performance and progress are some of the key factors why startup companies have a slightly lower valuation than IBM.

A business school once selected us for a startup case study. The professor committed to support us in any way possible. On my inquiry, he stated that his interest was to write a possible business case. I considered this to be good commitment from his side to support us in the best way possible ... till I remembered our own business cases done during my MBA. The evolution of a young company is just as valuable as a business case for a professor, irrespective of whether the company succeeds or fails.

One thing that technology teams share is a conservative attitude (read pessimism). They see the challenges of their research and progress and frequently only agree to promise what they can comfortably deliver. Business drivers, on the other hand, are more clearly able to see the possibilities with the technology. Due to this, "business realistic" implies stretch objectives, whereas "technology realistic" implies objectives done in the regular course of work.

This is particularly true for technology teams in Continental Europe, since there is a very conservative attitude towards risk combined with a lack of vision regarding the business possibilities that the technologies are capable of. Very seldom do these technology teams agree on stretch objectives, which make it easier for them to achieve these objectives. At the same time, not having stretch objectives enables these same technology teams to continue working 8 h days, 5 days a week, rather than 24/7 to make it happen. The ease of getting employment for educated people in Europe hinders their hunger to do great things that require significant sacrifices, like shortening their skiing vacation.

Takeaway *As a business driver, align the right expectation with your technology team. Keep in mind that they do **not** understand your business vision.*

5.8   Perception Is Reality

When you get started, there is the excitement of doing your own thing that has the potential to become the next Google. However, it's also slightly unreal, particularly when you look around at the disparate members of the team, who look eerily like regular people rather than ones likely to change the world.

Even the startup infrastructure, if any, seems woefully inadequate. It is easy to question why any investor might pay a lot of money for getting a slice of something so ephemeral.

For this reason, it's also difficult to perceive it beyond what it appears. Investors see the potential of the technology to gain leadership in an evolving industry, which is why they often agree to pay valuations that appear outlandish to technology entrepreneurs. There are times where perceptions are also far from reality. Like the life of an entreprenuer. From the outside, the life of an entrepreneur may appear extravagant and enviable. However, the inside track is different. Let me compare this with skiing. If you've been born in Switzerland, you don't think twice about wearing your skis on a crisp winter day and heading to the snow-covered mountains, where you take the ski lift straight to the black slope (the surest way to breaking your neck) and ski down a mountain at upwards of 80 km an hour and making it look effortless in the bargain. However, if like me, you only took up skiing when you were 35; your brain was wired to consider any speed above 20 km/h as something appropriate for a sprint, particularly when someone else was doing it. Anything faster than 30 required a seat belt and anything over 60 risked getting a speeding ticket.

I remember, the first time I went down a black slope was purely by accident, since I really wanted to try the red (only risking severe injury to various limbs). I had taken the wrong exit when I got off the ski lift. After the first few hundred metres, I realised the magnitude of that catastrophic error. Anyway, there was nothing to be done other than to ski down as slowly as I possibly could on angles averaging 45°. I kept thinking about what sadistic pleasure a person would possibly get, going down that slope. In case of an unfortunate fall, it's not as if the snow is soft and fluffy. The first inch is slightly soft, and below that is hard snow with no bounce whatsoever below which of course is the mountain.

After sitting and contemplating for a bit, I realised that this was not going to get me anywhere and most definitely not back to the base. In fact, the only thing that was going to get me down were my skis. So I began by trying to fight the mountain and go at a pace that I considered safe, but then, as Newton had realised with a fruit, gravity was not always on my side. Finally, after what seemed like an eternity of flying and falling, I finally did get to the base… and was hooked. And that's what happened with entrepreneurship.

Takeaway *Entrepreneurship shifts your perception… and perception is everything.*

5.9   Woods and Trees

Being modest about one's accomplishments is one thing, but scientists, particularly those in Continental Europe, tend to think very little about the commercial value of their efforts. This also percolates down to the serfs doing the grunt work that research entails.

Just how little vision the teams have for the difference that the technology may be able to make in the real world was brought forth to me during our investment finalisation discussions with investors. My technology cofounders raised a huge flag when they saw the $15 million penalty in case the team wilfully leaked out core company secrets about our technology. This penalty was for the timeframe during the process of investment finalisation between the time when investors committed to investing by signing the formal binding transaction documents and the formal company board meeting stating that shares could be issued to the investors.

Our team members raised this issue and stated that this was not acceptable. Our own lawyers explained more than once that this was standard practice, since after all the investors were only investing in our team and our promises. This discussion went back and forth and we lost 3 months in trying to resolve it. The final result was indeed what the investors had stated in the beginning: we would pay a penalty if we knowingly leaked company secrets after they were locked in and before shares were issued to them.

The team's assumption was that there would be a gap of weeks between the two steps: (1) the investors committing and (2) the shares being issued to them. In fact, the two meetings happened within a minute of each other, so that as soon as the investors committed, we began the board meeting and signed the standard letter stating that, of course, the investors were going to get shares.

Takeaway *Being an entrepreneur is about the art of the possible. Scientists only understand the science of reality. Don't ever assume the technical team members will understand.*

5.10   Respect

Often, the technology lead becomes dismissive of the efforts of the technology team and manufacturing-related team members. While this may be the norm at a research institution where the technology lead or professor is considered God, the company is a very different animal. In the company, this attitude may have detrimental implications on the morale of the team members. Larry Ellison of Oracle has always been a completely autocratic driver of Oracle. Due to this behaviour, senior executives of Oracle who simply couldn't stick Ellison's behaviour went ahead and started many successful companies in Silicon Valley.

And then again, companies can become global leaders simply due to the force of the vision and drive of the founder. Exemplifying this is Steve Jobs. Jobs was always considered autocratic and was known to be downright dismissive of employees who failed to deliver according to his expectation. But contrary to what one may expect, these same individuals who worked directly with Jobs and often bore the brunt all say that this element was the most exhilarating experience of their working lives, after which their subsequent careers have been defined by the pursuit of excellence.

The above examples are the exceptions rather than the rules.

Most startups are about teams working in alignment towards a common vision. If a technology lead runs roughshod over the other members during the early stages of a startup, the risks are on two accounts. Firstly, the company may tend towards becoming a technology-focussed entity, rather than one focussed on manufacturing and commercialising the innovation. This, after all, is the comfort zone of the technology lead. The second and greater risk is of the other members of the management team simply becoming subservient to the commands of the technology lead and blindly following his diktat.

We saw that in our company, where the technology lead was a professor and the other technology co-founders were his students. The co-founders never considered themselves to be on par with him during the process of early commercialisation. This often resulted in situations where the co-founders found themselves following technology steps simply because the technology lead had told them to do so. This was particularly scary since the process of technology innovation was being made subservient to the mind, creativity and limitation of one individual.

The final result was that the pilot phase went on for 7 years, before a real pilot was even attempted, which would eventually lead to commercialisation. With the *final* pilot taking another additional 2 years, this made close to 10 years. I don't know of any other company that was able to go on without making revenue, let alone still be on the pilot stage, for this long.

Takeaway *However bright your team, listen to your gut and never lose your nerve. Never forget, they are scientists and are clueless about what makes the world of commerce tick.*

5.11 Inside Out

The technology lead or the scientist frequently has the tendency to refrain from detailed involvement in the operations through the initial stages of the venture. This is just as well, since even within research, his work is often limited to simply sifting through ideas and oversight of research.

By remaining out and looking in, the scientist can easily begin critiquing the efforts of the team working on the venture, ostensibly to provide an outside view. This can easily make the team feel that the scientist is absolving himself of operational responsibility. Constant critiques can also sag the motivation of the team at the time when they should all be putting their souls into making it happen.

If this is not flagged out early, the scientist is likely to project the same critical attitude even after investors come in. On the face of it, the scientist's attitude may remove him from direct responsibility of the team's lower performance when investors sit around the table. However, this misses the point that the scientist and the rest of the team will always be on one side of the table and the investors on the other side.

Takeaway *If the technical lead gives "constructive" criticism, it may be to ensconce himself from investors when targets are not achieved. Remember you succeed or fail together.*

5.12 First Love

Business drivers tend to give their all once they get involved with technologies to enable them to become successful. This tends to be very different for technology team members. Technology founders don't start off with a view that they will be unethical or less than fair towards the company. They often can't help it.

A technology co-founder who continues to work with the research institution is wearing two hats at the same time, being a senior researcher at the institution and being the technology lead at the spin-off. There are many opportunities that can give rise to conflict.

The research being done at the institution often requires external project funding where some commercial entity needs to be involved. The most obvious option for the technology lead is to get the startup to be the commercial entity. However, with the funding, which comes to the research entity, some work needs to be done by the commercial entity. The spin-off ends up doing this work even if it distracts from the core mission.

The technology lead also has the propensity to spend more time with research and his research group. This is his area of competence and also because he's the master of this universe. Work at the startup, on the other hand, poses challenges to which the technology lead often does not have the competence to resolve. The conflict becomes more pronounced where the technology lead has to decide where to invest more of his time. Unfortunately, in most cases the startup suffers because the technology lead continues to consider the startup as a hobby and the research as the mainstay.

Investors recognise this very well, which is why they devise the golden handcuffs. This is where the technology lead gets a quasi-salary. The lure of money is meant to buy his loyalty but, more importantly, to keep him on the straight and narrow.

As the business driver, it then becomes your responsibility to ensure that the spin-off remains the first priority of the technology team. Without conscious effort on your part, anyone in the team wearing two hats is likely to put a lower priority on the startup due to the uncertainty. It also becomes your responsibility to share the vision and make it real for the tech team. Finally, your loyalty to the startup also implies that sometimes you have to flag these concerns to the investors. This doesn't make you a turncoat, since you're only doing what's in the best interest of your startup.

Takeaway *Be aware of priorities of co-founders who continue to work at the research institution. Know that their first love is research—the company is but a dalliance.*

5.13 Perfect vs Market Ready

Scientists like to strive constantly for ever-better results (read "research-focussed" results). Business drivers focus on getting the solution to the market. It is only by being in touch with the market that you realise not only what the market challenges are but also what the perceived value to the end customer is.

I recall having a conversation with NATO with regard to our flexible solar cells. After we explained the benefits of high efficiency, flexibility, lightweight, etc., their question was "*can this come in different colours?*". We were told that since the NATO troops frequently operated in conflict areas, a black solar module could stick out in certain surroundings making them easy targets.

In Flisom, our edge was PV cells with the highest efficiency in the world of converting light into electricity. The market, on the other hand, did not care about the precise efficiency but how much the electricity from these cells would cost, once they were installed on rooftops.

The scientific team's focus continued to be to improve efficiency, whereas the focus that was really required was to replicate so that we would be able to make millions of pieces of the same efficiency. The result was that we spent far too much time in the lab, where our lead scientist's focus was to continue to hold the world record rather than to take the leap of "productionising" the research on the basis of which the company was founded.

The greatest risk now was of technology obsolescence. This could be by way of cheaper Chinese replication. Alternatively, this could also imply slightly lower efficiency solutions that got to the market first and created the standard or integrated with key devices. The jury is still out on how real the risk was, but delay did not do us any favours.

5.14 What Else Is Possible vs First to Market

Scientists like to experiment. That's a good reason why they're called scientists. What makes them excellent researchers is their main drawback when it comes to going to market—tinkering. Scientists do research for the sake of research and this is what enables new discoveries. The more breakthrough the work of the scientist, the more likely it is that he sings to his own tune. This makes it very challenging to tune the focus of the scientist towards getting his innovation to market.

But then, once you have identified the technology that has a clear edge in the marketplace, the focus has to be to get it to the market as soon as possible. And since the technology is nothing without the technical team, it implies that the technical team has to be motivated to focus on getting the technology to market with the greatest possible speed. Otherwise, two things can happen—a better or cheaper technology or an inferior technology that works will get there first (as mentioned above) or the market will shift making your solution lose its relevance.

Takeaway *Even with a breakthrough technology, let no one convince you that it will be easy. The most challenging task is tuning the scientists' mindset to the company's future success.*

5.15 Does the Current Flow vs Evolving Business Models

Planning for business is an important part of transitioning from a research group into a commercial entity. Science is all about tinkering and seeing the result, which is either positive or negative. Here again, the scientists find it easier to think of *yes*- or *no*-type solutions.

Business, on the other hand, is more fluid and entails addressing new markets and planning targets, which have to be aligned, realigned and aligned yet again. Business models and routes-to-market have to be modified with changes in the marketplace.

Our business began with a view to commercialising the PV modules by taking them from the lab to pilot and then to large-scale production. Along the way, we realised that it was going to take longer than we anticipated to simply do the pilot. A lot longer.

In the meantime, our American competitors made promises and projections that seemed a bit optimistic to us. China began to look at clean energy and the PV business seriously.

Fast forward 3 years. Many of the American companies filed for Chapter 11, and all the companies focussing on PV lost their technology founders. Some US companies got loans and loan guarantees from the government averaging $300–500 million. They failed as a consequence, the USA risks losing its appetite for new-generation clean energy companies. In the meantime, China became a powerhouse in PV and each of the Chinese companies secured financial support in the form of soft loans averaging $4 to 9+ billion (that's right, billion) (Wikipedia and Reuters) (Fig. 5.4).

Our strategy had to evolve to address this change in the marketplace to ensure that we did not become irrelevant. One option was to move from manufacturing solar modules to machine manufacture, which would enable our customers to manufacture solar modules. The second was to consider licensing our technology and revert to becoming a technology provider.

Making decisions in the face of this kind of uncertainty is what technology persons find very difficult to deal with. This is also the uncertainty where a good business driver earns his keep.

Takeaway *Your business model will evolve. This doesn't mean the scientists' innovation is less relevant, it only indicates that the perceived value for customers is different.*

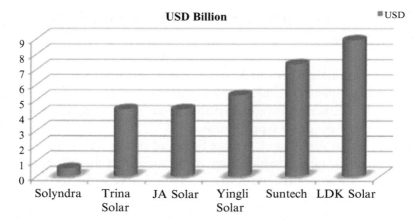

USD Billion   ■USD

Fig. 5.4   Government loans as source of financial competitive advantage

5.16 Research Overkill

It doesn't hurt to emphasise and reemphasise that researchers and scientists do research—that's what drives them, along with the peer reviews and the names of the journals where their research gets published. Even when the time to commercialise comes, they are best at doing research within their comfort zone. Not only do they very seldom (if at all) recognise the relevance of the business driver, they also do not see value in manufacturing expertise, since this is low tech and requires *simply* an engineering solution rather than a technological breakthrough.

This can lead to two risks, both with bad to disastrous consequences.

The first risk is that the delay in getting the manufacturing expert for the "*boring* work of replication" of the lab solution. This step is often continuously postponed because it's not considered urgent. The only redeeming industry where this can be condoned is software, since all you have to make is one copy that works. Replication of this software is seamless and does not entail additional effort or cost. In most manufacturing or technology-based industries, failure to replicate will doom you and pave the way to those who follow, since paving a new route-to-market is much tougher for the first entrant since he makes all the mistakes.

The second risk is that the research continues for simply too long resulting in a risk of the commercial obsolescence of the technology. It's like what makes truly great paintings—the artists know when to stop. In the same way, the really good technology teams know when to stop tinkering with the technology and focus on getting it out the door to the real world.

5.17 Too Much Rocket Science

For those of us who do not have a PhD but are in contact with reality, the world of scientists and research holds a certain aura and mystique. When you initiate discussions with a group of technical people for the purpose of commercialising their work and bringing it to market, one thing to be aware of is that scientists think differently from you and me. They are wired differently.

Scientists are involved in a lot of research and one is made to believe that they do something new every morning when they get to the lab. However, when you begin to go into commercialisation, your main focus is how soon you can get something to market. This is because the market defines how the solution will be used.

The iPhone is an excellent example. Before the iPhone was introduced, mobiles were largely used to make calls and send SMSs, with a small minority using other functions. Today, thanks to the iPhone and other smartphones that followed suit, your mobile is probably the first thing you see when you get up in the morning and the last thing you see before you go to sleep. The calling and SMS have been relegated to being two of the top 10–20 functions on your mobile. The market not only defined how the mobile would be used but also created the different uses. Witness the majority of the applications you use on your smartphone, which have been created by private entities and not by the mobile phone manufacturer. To understand how the market evolves, notice how often you use each application that you so enthusiastically downloaded when you first bought your smart device?

Frequently, solutions get over-engineered in the lab before you can get the scientists to take them to market. This—once again—runs two risks. The first risk is that the solution is far too expensive for the simple needs of the market. This is like developing a rocket engine for a bicycle. It's more than capable of doing the job. It will have the capability of running the cycle much faster than the cycle is ever likely to go, and it will run for a million miles before it breaks. It's over-engineered to death, making the cycle too expensive and completely out of reach of the target audience—and not really catering to the real requirement.

The second risk is more pervasive and similar to that defined above regarding research overkill. Yes, once again, this is the risk of commercial irrelevance or obsolescence. If the market is big enough and is developing fast enough,

Fig. 5.5   Technology excellence vs customer needs

it is more than likely that there are competitors out there. If they get there before you do, they may end up becoming the standard by forging alliances with the largest strategic players in the go-to-market.

It's for this reason that investors rightly motivate teams to start talking to customers. Otherwise you simply don't know what the market wants. And this is important since what the market wants is the only thing it will pay for (Fig. 5.5).

Takeaway *There is such a thing as too much rocket science. When you're being enamoured by what the technology is, ask what it can do and how soon it can do it for real people.*

5.18 Interesting Work vs Mere Manufacturing

Scientists often suffer from a common affliction. They dislike doing any work not related to scientific breakthroughs. The gap, however, between science in the lab and something of practical use to the real world is the engineering required to convert this science into a prototype.

Most scientists find this process of doing the engineering boring and not inspiring enough. For a business driver, it is particularly important to ensure that the scientists focus on the boring work of translating the research into practical and replicable solutions.

Takeaway *The greatest value in an innovation is not breakthrough science but translating this science into replicable solutions.*

5.19 Peer Review vs Go-to-Market

Before embarking on such a significant endeavour, it would be wise to know the motivations of the enablers and influencers.

Scientists are driven by one thing over all else—peer review. This external validation of their work gives them their sense of self-worth. It is only the foolhardy business driver who does not pay heed to this motivation.

The motivations of business drivers range from seeing a technology get to the real world to making a lot of money to making a difference. None of these are invalid. But the success of a happy marriage depends not on getting lost looking deep into each other's eyes, which often lasts till you blink, but to look at the horizon and share the same vision.

Takeaway *Assume that technical team members will not appreciate the business elements of what makes a company and likely question the existence or relevance of it and of your efforts.*

5.20 Money, Money, Money…

Money is frequently not the motivator for the scientists. This can be tough, simply because there is a fundamental gap between the end result desired by the scientists compared to the investors, who are looking for X times return on their investment. It is key to find the right buttons to ensure motivation, since motivation will ensure focus and reduce distractions.

My own technology team of co-founders is a good example of when money is not the motivator.

My technology co-founders were primarily driven by technology. Thus, when the time came to get funding and when the investors wanted to formalise the investment by way of legally binding conditions, the greater concern of the technology team members was the penalty clause in case they did not comply with the conditions stated. This was notwithstanding the fact that they did not even understand several conditions due to the complexity of the legal language involved. Our lawyers tried to explain that these were standard conditions to protect the investors since the investors were after all investing on the credibility and vision of the team. These technology co-founders were less driven by the millions of dollars that they stood to make in case of successful commercialisation and more concerned about the standard legal clauses that the investors wanted them to commit to.

This process of going from the term sheet (which is the nonbinding document) to the transaction documents (the legally binding agreement) took a period of *15 months*. Now the relevance of any technology is based on speed-to-market. From that point of view, not having cash as a driver leaves you with limited options of things to use as motivators.

At the same time, money can also be the sole motivator for the scientists. This can be even worse.

A cautionary tale concerns one of my technology leads. He could be considered to fall in the latter category of being driven by money. Since his motivation was clearly monetising on the knowledge that he had created as a scientist, his first idea was to identify *all* the technology innovations that he had achieved. He then proceeded to claim that he would like to keep these innovations in separate companies. He also dug up a name of a techie-turned-entrepreneur in the USA who had spun off several companies to commercialise his various innovations as a case in point.

This obviously had a detrimental impact on multiple counts. To start with, the other co-founders found it rather disconcerting that the technology lead could leave them in the lurch halfway through the technology commercialisation by diverting his attention to other projects that he considered more interesting or which gave him a greater financial return.

The greatest detrimental impact, however, was during discussions with potential investors. What investors look for is full commitment from the team, since this is what they invest in. As soon as potential investors realised that the technology lead was considering other potential spin-offs by keeping some technology innovations out of reach of the current company, their interest would cool off. More than one potential investor did not move beyond the initial stage of discussions due to a risk that the technology lead would start something else after they had invested in the primary venture.

Takeaway *Ensure that the technology team has the right motivation to commercialise. Bind them legally to ensure no other spin-offs result. Drive comes from focus.*

5.21 Techie's Hobby

One of the greatest risks to the business is the focus of the technical lead. This is particularly relevant in the initial stages of the startup.

In such case, the investors expect you to provide answers to all kinds of questions, many of which may appear inane to you. Imagine how puerile these questions appear to your technology lead. However, it is good to keep in mind that the investor is trying to understand the future size of the given market and your unassailable lead in this market to enable you to either take market share or superprofit, or both, for a period of time adequate for the investor to exit and make a lot of money in the process.

In my young company, we completed the business plan and began contacting investors. This became a very time-consuming process, especially since investors began to evince interest in the concept. It soon became apparent to me that Flisom was my highest priority, since I had left my salary-paying job due to my belief in what Flisom's technology could enable. However, the company was still an experiment or a hobby at best for my technical lead, since he was not aware of the timeline towards investment and also did not know how seriously to take this. His zone of comfort was still his research activities.

The impact of his lack of prioritisation was reflected in setting call or meeting dates with investors. After the first meetings with investors, we were sometimes unable to get the second meeting for weeks on end due to the research and conferences scheduled by the technology lead. Now, however important the research work is to the scientist, the commercial reality is that all the research is irrelevant unless there is a path to commercialisation. Investors pave this path. We lost not "just a few" investors due to this research mindset. It is also likely that this resulted in a delay in obtaining our funding. Tough lesson learnt, when I had falsely assumed that the technical lead's commitment would be the same as mine.

Takeaway *Don't assume that the technical team can see the same business vision as you or their commitment is more than 9–5. That's what makes you the visionary.*

5.22 More Equal than Others

Technology teams tend to be pretty special. This is the reason that they achieve something that no one has ever done or do it better than it has ever been done. Another attribute of technology teams that achieve spectacular results is that they try something no one's ever tried before. By achieving breakthrough results by following their own intuition, these teams sometimes begin to think of themselves as smarter than others even as the process of transitioning the technology into a company begins.

The danger of this thinking becomes apparent during investor discussions. Investors recognise their important role in enabling technologies to become real companies by providing cash to commercialise. In return, investors expect to get their questions relating to market size, technology uniqueness, path-to-profit and time-to-market answered. Investors also realise that without their support, technologies have very little scope for commercialising. The fact that investors can live without investing in a particular company but that the technology requires investors to proceed gives the investors an edge in the negotiation. After all, no investor ever gets fired for saying no to invest in a young company.

In Flisom, we began investor discussions with several investors since our technology provided the highest performance in the world in arguably one of the hottest sectors, clean energy. This gave my team the illusion that we had an edge over even the investors during the discussion. Even through the discussion, we used to clearly state what we thought we would want to do to commercialise the technology, giving the prospective investors very little flexibility in the discussions. This ego probably lost us several investors resulting in a delay in obtaining the funding.

Takeaway *Technology teams do not recognise that the scales are tipped in favour of the investors in the negotiation. Know that the investors are more equal than the founders.*

5.23 Rich vs King

If all is well with the technology, a very important factor for investors is to know the motivation of the founders. In many cases, the founders become fixated on continuing ownership and veto rights on the company. In this respect, it is important to know the motivation of the investors, particularly financial investors. Their motivation is to get a healthy multiple on their investment.

In order for the investors to make a lot of money from the investment, it is imperative that the founders work on achieving this. If a founder gets stuck on the title of the CEO or chairman of the company, the investors realise that this individual may become the bottleneck since the performance of the company in his area will be limited by his limited competence in his area. Similarly, if the founder's mindset is to continue having an ownership in the company, this may also limit the exit options of the investors, since some exit options may entail selling the entire company or technology.

For this reason, many founder-driven companies continue to be niche players with a size of 5–50 employees. But for you as the business driver, it is as important to know the motivations of the technical co-founders since if their vision is to continue with majority ownership, this will also reduce your exit options. Since you will be investing a minimum of 3–4 years of your life in the startup (and it becomes increasingly difficult to extricate yourself from the startup with time), it is wise to know what drives the technology team.

SD Consulting[1] was a 10-man company and was based in the UK, providing software to maximise the pricing of drugs that went off patent. The right pricing based on the different geographies could enable the company to make hundreds of millions of dollars and ensure effective competition with generics, due to brand recognition. SD Consulting facilitated the right price to ensure profit maximisation for by differential pricing for different markets, by use of statistical tools.

Due to the niche sector that SD Consulting operated in, there were two strategies for growth. The more aggressive approach was to scale-up by way of widening the scope of activities and eventually get acquired by the larger consulting companies that had not recognised the scope of the opportunity and had consequently no brand recognition for this particular vertical. The second approach was to continue to operate as a small niche player.

The two founders had a difference of opinion regarding how they perceived the growth of the company as well as their involvement or exit in the midterm. Simon, one of the founders, wanted to be king, by continuing to have full ownership and lead the company. The second founder Mark realised that the only option for survival was to scale-up quickly and get acquired by another larger player, since the market was growing and the larger competitors were making moves towards providing solutions in the area.

Disagreement over the vision resulted in paralysis in the decision-making. This escalated to such a high level of acrimony that eventually the company had to be dissolved. This was truly a pity since the company had revenues of over £2 million and was profitable. Now to have to close a company due to erosion of profits on account of competition was one thing, but to close the company when everything was going well and a profitable niche and brand name established was truly lamentable.

---

[1] Name changed to protect identity of individual(s)/entity

Takeaway *Establish the vision and drivers of the co-founders early on and align expectations; this can mitigate much pain later, especially if the company becomes successful.*

5.24 Align Expectations

During the early stages of our startup, we used to have formal board meetings every couple of months where the professors who were co-founders used to participate. Here, I used to often perceive that the professors who were not involved with the investor discussions were pointing their guns at me and taking pot shots every now and then. This was because they did not participate in investor discussions; their only question was when was the money coming in.

Fair question, but since they did not know how long and tough the procedure to getting investment is, their expectations were completely out of line with reality. They only knew that we were having discussions with investors and these discussions were going on and on… and on. Little did they realise how fortunate we were that investors were interested enough in us that they wanted to continue the discussions, despite the attitude of superiority of some of our own team members.

Thus, instead of feeling excited about these discussions and the ongoing due diligence procedure, these professors felt frustrated that the money was not yet in the bank. And the blame for not having $15 million in the bank fell squarely on the shoulders of the business driver, i.e. yours truly. The fault was mine because I was not aware how long these discussions could take. Additionally, I was not aware that the professors were clueless about investor discussions. I felt boxed in between these professors who were constantly questioning the lack of progress during the board meetings on the one side and the investors, whose questions seemed to go on and on.

An important learning was to make every technology co-founder aware of how long the discussions can take, what the steps towards investment are and what commitment they need to demonstrate to make it happen.

It's also very important to make the team aware of precisely what your role is as the business driver. During discussions with investors, one role is to make strategic choices between investors. This implies understanding the implications of certain kinds of investors on the startup and the founders in the years to come. The second role is to build consensus between the investor on one side and the technology team on the other. The final one is to focus on execution including prioritising it to make it happen as well as getting legal opinions if the technology team refuses to agree with any condition of an investor, to check for reasonableness.

Takeaway *Communication with the technology team is paramount; as with good presentations, tell them what you'll tell them, tell them and tell them what you told them.*

5.25 Growing Pains

Technology teams spend their lives working on technologies in the lab, surrounded by the comfort that their salaries will come at the end of the month and other individuals who also expect to spend their working lives in labs. However, transitioning the technology into a company brings new challenges every day, challenges these technology teams are ill equipped to cope with. The sudden change takes these individuals out of their comfort zones.

One of our senior scientists was such an individual. Although he was one of the earliest proponents within the technology team towards commercialising the technology, the change in focus from pure research to commercialisation brought forth a focus on things that were alien to him like business plans, financials, route-to-market and profitability. Another thing that changed the status quo was the new team members who, in spite of being younger than this senior scientist, brought these business skills that he did not have.

Now normally, any younger member of a research team is always subservient to the senior members since the senior members guide them. However, with the influx of individuals who conversed in this alien business language, the senior scientist began to regress into his lab as a comfort zone, while still wanting to know and understand the rationale behind every decision during board meetings. With time, he wanted to slow down the transition of the company back into a lab environment and became a stumbling block for the rest of the team. His three decades of work in the lab had ill prepared him for the rigours of commercialising. Eventually, it was only on the coming in of investors that the company made the painful transition from being a research entity to being a commercial-minded startup.

Takeaway *Reward senior technology leads with stock options, so that they get the upside without becoming stumbling blocks.*

5.26 Non-compete

Let me take you back to the fact that scientists frequently work on multiple areas of research. But when it is time to commercialise, investors want to see one technology being commercialised and making money before the scientist begins to work on commercialising other technologies or ideas.

A lead scientist considering a spin-off did not think this applied to him. Since he had worked on multiple technologies and had established world records on several, his view was that investors should only have access to the one that they were investing in, giving him the freedom to commercialise others as he pleased.

However, from the investors' perspective, the main thing they considered through the investment discussions was the technology team leader's commitment, since their investment was to the team and not the idea per se. Their view was that if the main person driving the technology considered the idea as a hobby, what stopped him from developing another side hobby with another one of his technologies, from which the current investors were excluded.

To preclude the risk of the lead scientist running off with another one of his ideas and leaving the current investors on the lurch, they decided to ensure that he was locked in with his idea that they were investing in and only got freedom to commercialise something else once the commercialisation milestones for the first one were achieved.

Locking the technology lead sounded far easier than it actually turned out to be. The technology lead tried team motivation tactics ("this will stop me and my team from pursuing research in this area, since we will no longer have motivation to do so"), financial tactics ("no one will give us funds to continue this research if we are not allowed to commercialise") and emotional tactics ("my research students will leave me and not remain with my group if they realise they are not allowed to commercialise"). It was in fact so challenging that it took over 1 year (that's right, over 1 year) to go from the term sheet to binding transaction documents. This process normally takes a maximum of 3 months, and normally much less, for a startup.

My investors had a similar cautionary tale. They invested in a mathematician who had an idea to building a low-cost supercomputer. They invested a lot of money in building the company around his idea. However, when the time came to sign the non-compete, the mathematician declined and walked away, stating that the terms were too onerous. The investors still assumed that the team that he had built up would be able to commercially replicate the idea. This however did not happen and the team just built a me-too computer. This again exemplified the risks of investing in one technology lead.

Takeaway Be aware investors will require the technology lead's non-compete. Misalignment of expectations with the technology team will come back to haunt you.

5.27 Hierarchy

Research teams are used to either working very independently or in very loosely defined teams. However, for any commercial enterprise to function, areas of responsibility have to be clearly defined. This also implies that some members report to others and areas of authority and responsibility do not overlap so as to avoid replication or gaps.

On paper, this is logical and easily defined. However, by their nature, scientists are a free species and best served in the lab. The problem is similar to that of commercialising spider silk; although much lighter and stronger than silk-worm silk, spider silk is difficult to make in commercial quantities due to the propensity of spiders to eat each other, particularly just after procreation, which isn't really conducive towards teamwork.

Ego also plays a major role in how scientists work. After all, the reason a scientist is able to achieve more than anyone else on earth is because he is driven by his own intuition and is egoistic enough to believe that he's right.

Now all of a sudden, if he's asked to report to someone else who does not necessarily realise the depth of what he's done or fails to appreciate his wisdom, or worse, is younger, this can really rock his cart. The equation is however best to clarify early on, since with time, system gives way to chaos.

Takeaway Realise that a hierarchy is needed, since everyone can't know everything and decisions can't be made collectively. This painful medicine will ensure the patient's survival.

5.28 People Past Their Prime

Augmenting your team with individuals who have retired can be a sterling option… if managed well.

We hired a person who had retired after working in an administrative role at one of the largest public sector enterprises in Switzerland. This individual brought a lifetime of experience in processes and managing systems. I dutifully heeded his input since my experience in institution building was limited. Till he suggested that for our requirement of accounting systems, we get an integrated system like SAP. At this point, we had four employees.

Now SAP is so complex that even enterprises like Novartis take periods of up to 10 years to fully integrate this into their systems and the cost runs into hundreds of millions of dollars. In fact, this is a dream system for the consulting companies who integrate it, and I know more than one person who has gone from junior consultant to the position of partner simply working on the implementation of one project.

The rigorous discipline that retired persons bring helps the team to grow with a structure, which is so critical in an organisation for it to function efficiently or, indeed, to function at all. The motivation of these retired persons is also different. They simply want to use their time and experience meaningfully and are less concerned about wanting to go up the hierarchy and have a particular title. They only want to be recognised for their efforts.

At the same time, these seasoned people do have a particular view of how things can or should be done. This is based on their decades of working in the middle management of a large corporate. This rigidity is good for inculcating discipline in the startup, but may stifle creative ideas of the team. Further, a rigid or too-organised organisation early on will not have the flexibility that is an absolute must in a young company since entire business models may have to change to cater to a dynamic customer base.

Takeaway *Hiring retired people is a high-value resource if they put systems in place, but if not managed well, this can cost much by hindering the agility of the organisation.*

5.29 Motivations

Commercialising an idea requires a very high degree of motivation, since each step is fraught with challenges and pitfalls. What's critical is an alignment of vision between the team members. If one team member wants to have a small company that is fully partner-owned, this will conflict with the vision of another member who perceives a global scale-up, where the latter will require many external stakeholders including short-term VC investors and long-term strategic partners.

Different technology team members have different motivations in being involved. In our case, three of the youngest technology members had just finished their PhD, and this was their first foray into the real world. They thus assumed that it was normal to start a company with a world-beating technology and get funding.

One of the original founders perceived the startup to be so passé that he decided to sell his shares to the other co-founders and exit because he felt that the travel distance of 1 h was too much. I did not understand his decision at that time and I don't believe I ever will, simply because life in Switzerland is so comfortable that people have very little appreciation for the privilege of starting your own company that may, as Steve Jobs once said, make a dent in the universe. My not understanding the founder's motivation to give it up notwithstanding, this was still fine since he was upfront.

Founders can have other motivations that drive their involvement in a startup. One is to get additional funding for their research projects from the government-funding agencies. However, the most detrimental motivation behind involvement in a startup is when the co-founder wants to have a slice of the pie without giving up his other commercial interests that may be too close to the startup. This is the risk when the founder wants that startup but not badly enough to give up his other interests or put them on ice.

Takeaway *Learn about the motivations early. It may define whether you indeed want to get involved with the particular technology team, the technology notwithstanding.*

5.30 Mindset of Harmless Lies

Technology teams sometimes completely overestimate the advancement of their technology and readiness to commercialise or the superiority of their technology to everything else that's in the market. This is less due to their wanting to consciously lie and more because of their delusion of grandeur that they perceive in their ivory tower.

More risky than their conscious lies about the superiority of their technology is their understating the challenges relating to commercialisation. The perceived superiority of the technology can be put to the test when you as the business driver evaluate the technology compared to other startups or mature technologies out there to define the advantages that this one may have. However, understating the challenges to commercialising or replicability is far more risky since these cannot be easily validated by anyone outside the technical team.

A reality check of the technology team is particularly helpful and indeed imperative since this will help in early identification of the risks towards commercialisation. Even if the risks are not fully identified, individual discussions with each member of the tech team separately will help understand the challenges towards commercialisation.

In our case, the manufacturing challenges were glossed over since they didn't fall into the domain of the tech team. The highlight was the high efficiency and the startup's chance to become the gorilla in this space. What was telling was that the technology lead at no point committed to moving fully to the startup. That was an early and important red flag.

One other member of the team, the naysayer, identified any number of problems which would preclude us from commercialising, from having no machine capability to vastly overestimating the capability to replicate the high efficiency achieved in the lab to the dysfunctional nature of the team, to me not fitting in by not having a clue about the technology. But as President Eisenhower of the USA once said, "Pessimism never won any battle". The naysayer member finally left the startup since he didn't fit into the unstructured culture. But his predictions about the challenges we would face did come to pass. These were our growing pains.

5.31 Perception of Risk

Close proximity often makes it difficult to perceive the risk associated with any activity. An excellent example is the tulip mania (Wikipediaorg 2015).

In the early 1630s in Holland, tulips were becoming exceedingly popular with the wealthy classes to showcase their wealth. The different colours and hues made them dramatically different from other flowers. The more rare the colour of the flower, the more prized the bulb. The irony was that the rare streaks of double colours were a result of virus infections in the bulbs.

In a short period of time, the price of the rarest of the bulbs went up to an extent where, at one point, they were more than 5 years of salary paid to a skilled worker. Many speculators also moved into this activity and bulbs sometimes changed hands over 10 times per day. This, despite everyone knowing that the intrinsic value of the tulip bulb was ephemeral since the bulb was a fast-depreciating asset.

The buyers had the conviction that they would be able to sell the bulbs at a higher price. Thus, the perception of risk was limited. This went on till February 1637 where on one particular tulip auction, there were no buyers. Only then did the risk become real for the sellers. Prices were soon down to a fraction of what they had been, resulting in financial ruin for untold thousands of spectators. This started a shock that reverberated across Holland. This was the first known instance of a bubble.

Startup teams often begin to ignore risks related to their technology, particularly when they are too close to the technology itself and begin believing their own spiel. The onus is on you, the business driver, to take a step back and see the competing companies and, even more importantly, the potential customers and their interest.

There is also the matter of the difference between the technology itself and the product or solution that it facilitates. Technology teams often perceive no difference and again, therein lies your value.

5.32 Equity vs Upside

During the founding of a company, there is sometimes lack of adequate funding available in the founding team. This is particularly so for countries where a higher amount of cash has to be shown in order to start a company. In Switzerland, this is CHF 100,000 (about $100,000). The core team thus invites additional members like senior research scientists to join the team as founders. This can be a cardinal error (not in the religious sense, of course, that's another story).

There are many excellent reasons why the technology founders feel ethically compelled to share their company mostly with the scientists and professors under whose tutelage they have been able to get the technology to the point of potential commercialisation. The reason: these professors should get a slice of the upside when the technology is finally commercialised.

What is not fully appreciated are the challenges that a professor's involvement may entail.

5.32.1 Conflict of Interest

Scientists and professors work on multiple areas of research with frequent overlaps. So long as this is on the level of research, this does not pose any conflict. However, when research in any one area moves towards commercialisation, any overlap with other areas of research poses a risk for the company since it provides a backdoor entry to any competitor to access joint areas of knowledge, some of which may not yet be covered by patent. This happens if the competitor forges a relationship with the research entity by way of joint projects.

5.32.2 Limited Mindset

This component cannot be overemphasised. Professors, by their nature, tend to have a broad array of topics on which they oversee research. However, outside the research, most of them have very little understanding or appreciation of activities that are required to facilitate manufacture, competitiveness, commercialisation or managing market expectations. This can become a hindrance since the other team members, who are in the nascent phase of developing their ideas, become stymied by negative feedback based on ignorance.

5.32.3 Lack of Appreciation

Professors tend to be kings of all they survey. Their control on their fiefdoms tends to be absolute, frequently to the chagrin of their subjects. Due to this, they tend to have limited respect for ideas that germinate from those who are junior to them.

A professor's presence in the company can thus severely limit the capability of the other technology team members to vocalise their technical ideas. I came across a company quite like mine, which provided a good example of this. Even 5 years after the founding of the company, I was surprised when the technical co-founders still looked upon the technology lead (a professor) for ideas. This was in spite of the fact that while the professor worked constantly in the research lab, the other technology co-founders had been the ones building the commercial machines and processes with their own teams. However, when all the ideas were coming from one person, the company as an entity failed to institutionalise the way ideas were being generated, which percolated across the entire organisation. The company was still unable to get out of the shadow of the professor.

An effective option in such cases is to consider providing an upside to the professor in the form of stock options. This limits the professor's sometimes undesired feedback on the operational running of the company. With no formal role, the professor's focus also becomes limited to ensuring that the technology continues to be developed in the lab to facilitate flow-through to the company.

The upside for the professor is that he does not have to put money into the company to buy equity. Only when there is an exit option would he or she put the money and immediately cash out. On the part of the professor, not being a shareholder/founder would enable him/her to continue research without a risk of conflict of interest.

Takeaway *Choose co-founders with caution—being dumb can be excused, questions about loyalty cannot.*

5.33 Greed vs Greed

Like ego, some level of greed is healthy in founders. This helps them to be aligned to the practical vision of investors, which is that the endeavour makes money by being successful. However, sometimes too much of a good thing can severely impact the company's image with investors.

Scientists are driven by an expectation of entitlement. Sometimes in tech-driven companies, such people perceive that investors owe them something special to be "allowed" to invest in their ideas and technologies developed by them.

A case in point was a scientist with a focus on multiple technologies. Since the company's focus was to commercialise one technology, he took a stand that he should be allowed to separately commercialise other technologies unilaterally. This was understandable.

What was not as easy to understand was when he also took a stand that he wanted to have a sign-on bonus to join his own company. The investors tried to reason with him that since he had the shares in his own company, his upside was in the value created. Finally, when they did agree to give him a salary in his own company, he put another condition that he should not be asked to quantify the percentage of work for the company, since his main job was at his research lab. The final reason was for him to continue to provide consulting for other companies and investors evaluating other investment opportunities. The consulting may have been just as much for name recognition as for money, since scientists are driven by peer reviews.

It was just as well that these issues were raised after the investment. If they had come to light prior to the investment, the company would still be fundraising.

Takeaway *Ensure that the co-founders recognise when they can achieve wealth… it's after the company becomes successful, not with the investors' money.*

5.34 Scientists and Ethics

To us business drivers, the research done by scientists is sacrosanct and beyond reproach. After all, they are dedicated to the cause of furthering the knowledge of all humanity.

The reality is quite different. I'm not going after all scientists, but common knowledge today is that scientists are notorious for pilfering each other's work to make it their own. Apparently, this is rather well known and, strangely enough, also accepted as the price of doing science. They observe what other scientists are doing in their field, use scientific conventions to discuss each other's work and berate that of those absent and use this knowledge to further their own research. Further, they normally ridicule any research that goes against the grain of what they happen to believe in at a given time. Einstein was once told that a large group of 1000 scientists was signing a petition saying that his work did not hold any merit. His response was if his work really did not hold water, one scientist would have been enough.

This unfortunate tendency augurs well so long as the work remains in the purview of science. However, when this same science takes the initial steps towards becoming a commercial enterprise, copying ideas becomes a huge red flag because it impacts the freedom to operate.

A good example was the peel-off approach that our scientists initially used to create high-quality solar cells. On looking at the steps carefully, we realised that the approach used some knowledge that was proprietary to other scientific groups and was therefore covered by patents. So although our particular step was free of patents, the commercialisation could not be achieved without infringing patents. If we had continued in this direction, potential investors would have flagged this out during the due diligence.

But the real risk is never getting past the investors. Investors, after all, are trying to protect their interests, and after they invest, their interests become aligned to the success of the company. The real risk was moving towards production and being found to infringe a patent, thereby hindering our commercialisation. The entity owning the patent could then ask for half our kingdom and get away with it. The repetition of this point with industry examples elsewhere in the book underscores its importance.

Takeaway *Scientists define ethics differently. Assume and prepare for the worst, you won't be disappointed.*

5.35 For Those Who Come Later

When the startup begins, it only has the team of co-founders. With time, the company grows from the core team of co-founders to founders and employees. With the increase in the people, the structure of responsibilities has to be more clearly defined. This is because when the company has up to five people, everyone in the team knows everything and communication channels are transparent. As more people join, it becomes more and more difficult to share information with everyone.

As the company grows to between 10 and 15 people, communication of all key technology and business elements with the entire team takes longer and longer. This is what we experienced.

When we grew to about 15 people, the information sharing that we had with a much smaller team had not evolved from when we were much smaller. We used to have a meeting per week to discuss all key elements.

Since the entire team was now participating in these meetings, it took longer till we got to a point where these meetings took 2–3 h every week. Each person felt compelled to give detailed updates to showcase the amount of work they were now doing. At the same time, many of the other team members also did not find all the information relevant resulting in wastage of time.

We then decided to consolidate the meetings so that only the team leads met to discuss key points weekly. We then realised that the entire team did not always have a big picture of the strategy, resulting in misinformation that then resulted in nervousness. When you're running a startup where the revenue flows are uncertain and the industry is in turmoil as it always is, it doesn't take much to make the team nervous.

We then began to run formal meetings where the entire team could participate. At the same time, we began to formally run introductory sessions for new employees who joined the company. Although this formality seemed excessive at first, we realised that these new employees had not seen the company since the beginning, and for them everything was new. Thus, if the new employees did not know the background of the company, this alienated them from those who had been there since the beginning, effectively creating an exclusive club of haves and have-nots.

When the team grew to over 15 people, we noticed another change in the dynamics of the team. The level of interest that people had about the bigger picture when the team was much smaller diminished. More people began to simply be focussed on coming into office and doing the day's work rather than to know the details of how the company was planning to execute on its strategy. The focus at this point was to ensure that the new members felt like they were also part of the same team.

The company was transforming from a startup to a conventional company.

Takeaway *When communicating, keep it simple. People hear what they want to hear—depending on motivation and relevance.*

One Zurich-based technology startup that was building a strong team identified a young lady who was completing her graduation from Berkley. She had previously worked at Pixar or as she later recalled, "got her backside kicked by Steve Jobs". She must have been good.

On graduation day, she had offers from Google (pre-IPO), Intel and Yahoo. The founder decided to send her a return ticket. His offer: she could work for a month, and if she didn't like it, she could quit. The lady stayed on for several years and became one of their most valuable employees.

Another team member was an IP lawyer. Since the team recognised the importance of filing patents as a way to protect their know-how, they decided to look for an IP lawyer who could understand their technology. This was not trivial, since the requirement was for a tax lawyer who was also a geophysicist. They identified a suitable lawyer in Houston in Texas.

Through the conversation with the lawyer, the team convinced the lawyer that the company would have many challenges ahead. Additionally, recognising the attractiveness of *location Zurich*, the team made him an offer to join. This also gave the lawyer an opportunity to relocate to Zurich and gain international experience. So, instead of hiring the law firm, they hired the lawyer. Fast forward to today, where the lawyer's efforts on patents has resulted in the company having in excess of 85 patents.

5.36 Fired Founders

Sometimes, it is imperative to let a co-founder go, for the best interest of the team and the growth of the company. This is never pleasant—and is particularly difficult if the company already has employees and customers.

A co-founder who is asked to leave is likely to feel that he has been used and discarded and scorned once he is no more of value to the company. In this situation, since he is likely to have relationships both within as well as outside the company, anything negative he says about the company is likely to be taken seriously since he, by default, will continue to be perceived as being the voice of the company. This risks sending confusing messages to outsiders and consequently impacting the morale within the company.

A very effective way to mitigate this is by taking care of the ego of the founder. This founder can then be made an advisor to the CEO or special technical advisor to the Board. This ensures that he remains on-message, while at the same time being able to walk into the company with his head held high. His energy, which is undoubtedly significant—which is why he started the company in the first place—can be far more effective when aligned to the company than at loggerheads with it. If for nothing else, being on talking terms enable you to reach out to him for his signature for future rounds of funding.

5.37 Equity vs Options

Early employees often want to be treated on par with founders. This is particularly since these employees do not see a difference between the risks they have taken by joining a startup compared to the risk taken by the founders. Thus, whenever there is a discussion regarding sharing rewards, these employees often want to be given equity, however minor, for their loyalty.

This is an easy temptation to succumb to for founders, since a percentage here and a half percentage there do not seem to dilute the pie to any material extent.

The percentage of dilution however is not the problem, as we discovered during our fourth fundraising. Due to a complicated set of transactions between founders, a small number of shares of one outgoing founder ended up in the hands of a couple of employees. When we raised our subsequent round of funding, the founders also had the opportunity to get a small exit on the account of overachieving on our milestones. At this point, since the two employees were also shareholders, they were also required to sign the transaction documents.

When the two employees noticed that the founders were getting an exit by selling shares and they would not get the chance to sell shares but would get a bonus which was proportionally less, they felt they were being discriminated against and refused to sign the transaction documents. It took several hours of negotiations before the final signing to get them around. The situation was particularly fragile since a new investor was also coming in, and, if it appeared that there was a perceived sign of friction with key employees, this could unnerve the new investor. At this point, we were hanging by a thread between closing a really large round and going belly-up.

Fortunately, the employees came around and we were able to sign as expected by investors and desperately hoped by the founders.

That was a valuable lesson on why options are far better than equity. In the formative stages of your company, you do not want to be kept hostage to more unreasonable people than is humanly possible, given that you have likely started the company with a bunch of PhDs.

5.38 Dilution

One of the most important elements driving a startup's growth is ensuring that it has enough funds to commercialise. Advance payments from customers tend to be the cheapest form of funding that a startup can get, since no interest is payable on this money. The company thus runs on negative inventory and assets by investing in assets after the customers pay advance for the products. This is not uncommon in solutions that have relevance for the military or for technology that enables customers to have a significant global competitive advantage but is not often seen in other industries.

If the startup does not have the luxury of getting advances from customers, the only option is to get funding from investors. This is where the technical team's mindset about dilution becomes clear. So long as the discussion about transitioning research into real products for real people is going on at a theoretical level, the technical founders normally tend to be very comfortable. On practical terms, this tends to be slightly different.

Several years ago, when I began working with the technology team in order to commercialise the technology for my first startup, there was a great deal of excitement about the possibility of having their research converted into real products. Slowly, it dawned on them that by getting external investors to fund the company, these external people would own part of the company, and they would have to share their baby with outsiders. The founders would be diluted and no longer have full control over the destiny of the company. Suddenly, I perceived a pushback from the technical team.

The next option discussed by the technical team was to see if they could do more projects that could be funded by the government and European Union funds. This was not because it was the easiest way to get funds but because this was the only way the scientists who were the technical co-founders knew for getting funding.

When practical challenges like the months of waiting for approval of the government-based funding as well as the funding being only available for salaries were considered, the latter idea was rejected. The team then looked at the possibility of selling products in the market. There was this question of how to sell products that were absolutely years away from being manufactured… and the fact that the manufacturing facility was itself not in place.

Finally the co-founders agreed that the only option, while being the least palatable one, was to raise funds by getting investments in from investors and giving them equity. This, however, demonstrated the difficulty in motivating the technology founders to agree to dilution.

Takeaway Never underestimate the challenges in getting the technology co-founders to agree to anything en route to commercialisation.

5.39 Tech Driver Conflict

Many technology teams are led by individuals who have an interest in transitioning into becoming the business driver or even the CEO of the company. Few individuals can make this transition successfully because the mindset needed to drive the technology in the business is very different. There are exceptions—technology co-founders have driven some of the most successful companies; these include Microsoft and Facebook.

The concern is on two levels: if the technical co-founder plans to transition to the business side to drive the business, how is your work going to be defined as the business driver? The second concern is that the limited understanding of the technical person regarding business may become a bottleneck to commercialisation.

Strategic decisions within any startup are similar to strategic decisions of any large company; they take 10 % of less of the time and effort of running the company. If there is a conflict between who will make these decisions or the technical co-founder wants to be responsible for making these decisions, there is very less work for a business driver.

If you as the business driver get involved in a startup like this, there is a risk of a high degree of frustration. Additionally, the company will not really benefit from your business experience because the technology co-founder may end up making obvious mistakes as he learns to transition into the role of the business driver.

One solution may then be to ensure that you have equity in the company and then say that you will come in on a full-time basis when the company needs you. In the meantime, opt to support the growth of the company as an advisor. Although you will not be the driver of the company, as the official CEO, in this case, you will at least have the opportunity to get the future upside while diversifying your risk.

5.40 Peculiar Principles

If anyone tells you that scientists aren't strange creatures, don't believe them. Here's why.

One of the co-founders of Flisom was a professor who did not join the startup. He was not really involved with the technology, but had been a guide of the tech team. Due to a conflict with one of the other technology co-founders, this individual decided to sell his shares. There were two conditions: the first one was that his shares would be sold only to some of the co-founders he favoured. This was understandable. What was not as easy to understand was the second condition. He wanted his shares to be sold at the cost at the founding of the company, namely $10 per share; notwithstanding the fact that based on the value of the company, the shares could be sold to investors at a few hundred *times* the original value per share.

The principle behind who should get his shares, and more importantly, who not, was far more important for the professor than actually making money on his shares. This also reflects the challenges that business drivers as well as investors have in reasoning with scientists. They are often not driven by the same things that drive the rest of us.

Since the writing of this book began, the professor in question has sold his share in his *second* startup. This is a good example of investors investing in one technology while the professor monetises the second one.

5.41 Gaps and Hiring

Early on after the founding of the startup, it is important to identify the areas that can be suitably covered by the skills of the current team members. It is very tempting to give responsibilities to the team members since they are available. We've been there.

In the early stages of my startup, we had a particularly talented co-founder. Since we wanted the new employees to get exposure to his ways of working, we decided to have two of them report directly to him. After a while, one of the employees simply left the company. On inquiring with the second employee, we realised that the brilliant co-founder was also a control freak with an ego to match. He liked to take all credit while letting the employees take all the blame when things went south.

Being a small company, although we tried to rectify the situation, we also lost the second employee shortly after this, since the employee assumed that there was no way he would be able to totally avoid working with the particular co-founder. It was just as well that the co-founder realised he did not fit in the startup and soon decided to head back to the world of research—after teaching me an important lesson about fit and managing egos of team members.

A far more effective solution is to begin with the requirements and to then see which of the co-founders can fill these effectively. The remaining positions can be kept open. This can then be put forth to investors since it is assumed that they will contribute more than simply money. But more about this later.

The quandary of how to hire the right person is not an easy one to resolve. How, indeed, does one figure out if the person interested in a given position is fit for it. It has to be kept in mind that the work that you sign up for in a startup is likely going to occupy only a small percentage of your time, since things evolve so quickly.

Trying to find the right person for the job was no less important 20 centuries ago, when according to the New Testament, Jesus, who was looking for someone to fill the position of disciple, only asked, "What do you seek?" (Biblehubcom 2015) This question remains as relevant today, and if the answer is aligned to the vision of the startup, it can help in making the whole greater than the sum of the parts.

Takeaway *Keep a lookout for the ego; it's always lurking.*

5.42 Friction

Anyone who's seen a startup knows that the times when everything seems to be going well are few and far in between. More often than not, there are multiple issues, from mundane ones like overlapping responsibilities to gaps where no one is responsible to more critical ones like differences in opinion in the team regarding the vision of the startup.

One such case happened early on with my startup. When the team realised that the investors were taking longer to come on board, interest began to wane. At the same time, since no one wanted to be the first one to show that he was giving up, we continued pushing along. But as initial discussions with investors began—and quickly stalled—the recriminations began flying. Somehow, it became easier to blame others rather than try to resolve the underlying problems.

This is also when I realised the inadequacy of e-mail to resolve issues, since instead of helping resolve the problems, it made the arguments far more brittle and made individual opinions appear far harsher than they really were. Fortunately, we were able to come together and discuss the problems before too much bad blood had been spilt rendering the startup a non-starter.

Takeaway *Identify team-related issues early and work on resolving them. They won't go away. It's ego—not lack of funding—that's the primary cause for startup implosion.*

5.43 Diligence

One of the easiest things to overlook is why the technology team is keen on starting the company. Your assumption as the business driver is that they probably know what they're talking about and that the technology can do what they say it can. Your focus is then on the challenges relating to commercialisation and rapid replication and scale-up, with the capability of the technology and its differentiation compared to anything else that exists as a given.

But, this is not always a given.

Till you fully understand the motivation of the technology team, it is not wise to assume that the promises stated by them regarding the technology are real. This is in your own interest, since, after all, you will be dedicating the next few years of your life in commercialising this technology. It would be a pity if after the funding is in place and the company is en route to commercialisation that a fatal technology flaw comes up which impedes commercialisation.

There may be many reasons why the technology lead may not fully disclose the challenges or may understate risk.

The technology lead may find the idea of working in research onerous and "political". He may see the startup as an exit from this politics. As any founder will attest, a startup is rife with politics that has to be carefully managed. This is because there is no set hierarchy due to the rapid change and growth. This results in overlapping areas of responsibility and gaps. Since most people are big-company animals and thrive on being "responsible" for things, everyone is constantly stepping on other people's toes. This needs to be carefully managed to ensure high motivation.

Since you're banking on the technology, and by extension, the technology lead, the onus is on you to ensure that you know about his motivations and ensure that he is aware of the risks of a startup.

Compared to research, which may be a dead end, some members of the technology team may simply find the idea of entrepreneurship or owning a company more attractive. This is like being in love with the idea of being in love, rather than being in love itself. The former is even more dangerous than the latter, which itself is no walk in the park.

Takeaway Summary

1. *Tick the "stupid" things first; incorporation, equity, defining roles and responsibilities and authority will enable you to focus on the core task of making it happen.*
2. *The market will frequently put a higher perceived value on the solution than what the technology people imagine, but this will only be known once you get there.*
3. *Don't assume that the tech team has all the answers simply because they are the best in what they do. Your vision may be the only right one, simply because you have one.*
4. *Simple, elegant and criminal—if everything checks out, remember that it'll only work for you if the ethics line up.*
5. *As a business driver, align the right expectation with your technology team. Keep in mind that they do **not** understand your business vision.*
6. *Entrepreneurship shifts your perception... and perception is everything.*
7. *Being an entrepreneur is about the art of the possible. Scientists only understand the science of reality. Don't ever assume the technical team members will understand.*
8. *However bright your team, listen to your gut and never lose your nerve. Never forget, they are scientists and are clueless about what makes the world of commerce tick.*
9. *If the technical lead gives "constructive" criticism, it may be to ensconce himself from investors when targets are not achieved. Remember you succeed or fail together.*
10. *Be aware of priorities of co-founders who continue to work at the research institution. Know that their first love is research—the company is but a dalliance.*
11. *Even with a breakthrough technology, let no one convince you that it will be easy. The most challenging task is tuning the scientists' mindset to the company's future success.*
12. *Your business model will evolve. This doesn't mean the scientists' innovation is less relevant, it only indicates that the perceived value for customers is different.*
13. *There is such a thing as too much rocket science. When you're being enamoured by what the technology is, ask what it can do and how soon it can do it for real people.*

14. *The greatest value in an innovation is not breakthrough science but translating this science into replicable solutions.*
15. *Assume that technical team members will not appreciate the business elements of what makes a company and likely question the existence or relevance of it and of your efforts.*
16. *Ensure that the technology team has the right motivation to commercialise. Bind them legally to ensure no other spin-offs result. Drive comes from focus.*
17. *Don't assume that the technical team can see the same business vision as you, or their commitment is more than 9–5. That's what makes you the visionary.*
18. *Technology teams do not recognise that the scales are tipped in favour of the investors in the negotiation. Know that the investors are more equal than the founders.*
19. *Establish the vision and drivers of the co-founders early on and align expectations; this can mitigate much pain later, especially if the company becomes successful.*
20. *Communication with the technology team is paramount; as with good presentations, tell them what you'll tell them, tell them and tell them what you told them.*
21. *Reward senior technology leads with stock options, so that they get the upside without becoming stumbling blocks.*
22. *Be aware investors will require the technology lead's non-compete. Misalignment of expectations with the technology team will come back to haunt you.*
23. *Realise that a hierarchy is needed, since everyone can't know everything and decisions can't be made collectively. This painful medicine will ensure the patient's survival.*
24. *Hiring retired people is a high-value resource if they put systems in place, but if not managed well, this can cost much by hindering the agility of the organisation.*
25. *Learn about the motivations early. It may define whether you indeed want to get involved with the particular technology team, the technology notwithstanding.*
26. *Choose co-founders with caution—being dumb can be excused, questions about loyalty cannot.*
27. *Ensure that the co-founders recognise when they can achieve wealth… it's after the company becomes successful, not with the investors' money.*

28. *Scientists define ethics differently. Assume and prepare for the worst, you won't be disappointed.*
29. *When communicating, keep it simple. People hear what they want to hear—depending on motivation and relevance.*
30. *Never underestimate the challenges in getting the technology co-founders to agree to anything en route to commercialisation.*
31. *Keep a lookout for the ego; it's always lurking.*
32. *Identify team-related issues early and work on resolving them. They won't go away. It's ego—not lack of funding—that's the primary cause for startup implosion.*

References

Biblehubcom. (2015). *Biblehubcom.* Retrieved December 1, 2015, from http://bible-hub.com/john/1-38.htm

Data collated from company sources, Wikipedia and Reuters sources.

Wikipediaorg. (2015). *Wikipediaorg.* Retrieved December 1, 2015, from https://en.wikipedia.org/wiki/Tulip_mania

6

Patents: Whys and Hows, Protection Strategies for Your Innovation

Knowledge protected by way of patents is critical to the development of a technology company. This is the only thing that protects the knowledge of the startup and provides an effective competitive advantage. But there are several other excellent reasons for filing patents.

To begin with, patents build confidence among investors, for whom the greatest risk is that the technology founders or key employees may walk away. Although the idea without the founders may be worth very little, it helps the investors to hold on to some perceived value if the company has filed patents on its core knowledge.

Patents are also a good investment in case the company considers a trade sale at some point in the future. It pays to keep in mind the buyer's perspective when considering a trade sale. The buyer needs to justify to its board or to its shareholders that there is value in buying the company. Without patents, there is always a risk that the key people of the acquired company will walk away, leaving the buyer with assets of questionable value. Patents give assurance, however ethereal, that the buyer is holding solid assets that may hold value for the future. This assurance, in turn, makes it easier to make the deal go through in case of a trade sale.

Right from the time when you begin the evaluation of the technology, clarity about the patents held by the team is required. Normally, it is not possible for researchers to hold the patent ownership, since the research institution holds this. However, it's important to know that if they do decide to spin off their idea, they are given the licence to use the patent knowledge. This is particularly so if the names of the researchers are included in the patent filing.

© Springer International Publishing Switzerland 2016
A. Sethi, *From Science to Startup*, DOI 10.1007/978-3-319-30424-3_6

Different kinds of investors perceive patents differently. For VC or financial investors, the main focus is the exit from the company at a good multiple. Thus, they are most interested in filing as many patents as possible, since this makes for a good story for a potential IPO or trade sale, which would then give them a healthy exit.

For strategic investors the reasoning is different.

6.1   Back-Up

For strategic investors, the most important element is freedom to operate, and the value of patents is only to ensure that no other company replicates what the company does. This provides the company a sustainable competitive advantage in the market.

Strategic investors also consider patents as a fall-back strategy for investments that go wrong. A percentage of investments do not live up to the hype. For these, having a bunch of patents can then be considered as a safeguard since these failed investments can then disappear into the balance sheet in the guise of future assets and get written off when the management changes, thus allaying blame all around.

6.2   Exclusive Right to Use

Simply getting the right to use the patent is not adequate to ensure competitive advantage. It is important that the research institution also confers the exclusive licence to the spin-off. This is easy enough to find out since the rules for IP or intellectual property tend to be the same for all spin-offs of a given research institute. These research institutes are also becoming wiser about capturing some part of the future value of IP from the days where the founders of Cisco asked Stanford if it wanted to take cash or a percentage of the shares (normally 5 % in case of spin-offs) of Cisco. They opted for cash, which amounted to <$150,000 (Sam shead 2015). The 5 % (assumed) would have translated to a bit more at $22.5 billion in 1999 when Cisco's value was $450 billion.

6.3   FTO

This is quite likely something that most founders have never heard of. One of the most important things that patents provide is the freedom to operate. FTO, as it is also called, is one of the most important elements that investors will look at when evaluating the company for investment. The reason is simple—FTO ensures that the company has the right to do what it wants to do.

The concerns of investors may be well founded. There is only one thing worse than a company that fails to deliver on its commercialisation objectives, and that is a company that delivers but is not allowed to do so since it does not have the freedom to operate.

FTO will enable investors to find out if any component used during commercial manufacture is already patented by any other entity in the world. These components can include a new process or design of a machine that will enable manufacture or the output.

Even if all other things work well with the discussions with investors for funding, keep in mind that one red flag during the FTO can sink your ship.

There are some very expensive reasons why the FTO is so important. This is not only the case for young startups. Even large companies are not immune to the impact of FTO. In fact, the larger the company, the larger the financial impact can be if it does not have the freedom to operate.

Here's why not having patents can impact even successful companies. In 2002, NTP, a Washington-based patent-holding company, filed a case against Blackberry, claiming that its patents covered the technology used in Blackberry devices. Blackberry risked a shutdown of its services across the USA, on account of this dispute. To underscore the potential business impact, Blackberry had 12 million users in 2006, of which over 8 million were in the USA. Blackberry settled the 4-year dispute in 2006 by paying $612.5 million to NTP (Wikipediaorg 2015a).

Apple, one of the leading companies of our generation, has also succumbed to the FTO problem. Not once, but at least twice. In 2006, Apple agreed to pay $100 million to Creative Technologies over the design of its iconic iPod (Wikipediaorg 2015b). As recently as 2011, Apple is reported to have paid over $600 million to Nokia for technologies relating to the iPhone (Nytimescom 2015).

During the technical due diligence of my first startup, the lead investor hired two specialist companies for the purpose of the IP due diligence. Till this happened, our technical team lead had assumed that this would entail a 2–3 h interview with the resultant per-hour billing (rather than a 10 min meeting) since the poor lawyers also have to eat.

Our technical lead had in fact made such derogatory comments about the knowledge of the IP lawyers that we thought we would have to spend a significant amount of time in teaching them about the nuances of solar cells and the IP space in this area. Thus, when the IP firms sent us the questionnaire, our view was that this would be the easiest part of the due diligence. The reality turned out to be rather different.

With a five-page list of questions, it was clear that the lawyers not only meant business but also really understood the field of solar cells, as well as several ancillary technologies. They also had asked us several questions relating to specific machine designs for the process of commercial manufacture (that we hadn't yet thought of) since if there was any customisation of the machines required, they wanted to ensure that we did not impinge on any other entity's patents and that we had the FTO on all aspects of commercialisation.

As this due diligence continued, we gained a healthy amount of respect for the abilities of the lawyers. As weeks of this due diligence spanned into over 2 months, and my team was grilled on perhaps the 400th patent, we began to feel that this exercise would never end. The expenses also mounted, since we had agreed to pay for this effort. But finally, the day did come when the lawyers gave their report. They didn't indicate any red flags, but did say that in their opinion, considering the limited information provided by us . . ., given the current status of the technology . . . ., subject to . . ., subject to . . ., subject to! Lawyers never ever simply say "yes" or "no".

6.4   Patent Strategy

Just as important as ensuring that the team has the freedom to operate is a broad patent strategy for the future. Investors will ask for it, so a good time to start would be as soon as you identify the technology to run with.

A clear patent strategy will ensure that your company makes a conscious decision regarding the knowledge that will inevitably be created by the team. This will subsequently become a valuable asset in the future (Fig. 6.1).

Again, illustrating from my first startup experience, there were three areas where new steps were required towards commercialisation. These were the core area (process patent), secondary area (machine design) and ancillary area (future freedom). These are discussed below.

6.4.1 Process Patent

The core of the technology was the group of processes—these enabled the technology team to achieve higher results than what anyone else had ever achieved. In doing so, they helped the team to keep breaking their own world records over 12 years in a row. The competitors were using different processes and the big question was whether to file or not to file.

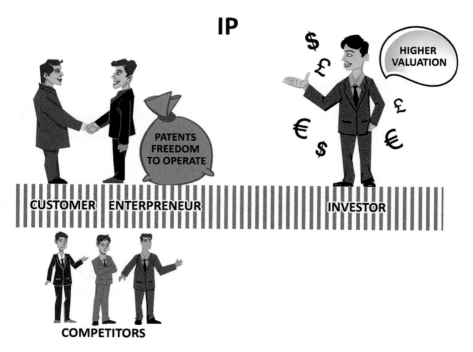

Fig. 6.1 Benefits of IP: FTO, increased valuation and edge over competitors

The risk of filing is always that when you write a patent, you essentially share all special knowledge in the patent—making it easier for someone else to replicate your technology. It only makes sense to file a patent if you are able to police this. Thus, if you are unable to check if someone is copying the knowledge provided in the patent, it may be better to not file.

Coca Cola faced this very dilemma about 120 years ago. The question on inventing the sugar and water drink was whether to consider protection by way of filing a patent or not. The forefathers of today's Coke may have had deep foresight, because they decided to protect the formula as a trade secret instead. The difference between patents and trade secrets is that patents normally expire 20 years after being filed. Trade secrets, however, last an indefinite period of time.

In our case, our special processes did not leave a signature on the end product. Thus, the only way to find out if a competitor was infringing on our patent was by asking them to open their machine and share information regarding the process details. Since our worthy competitors were rather unlikely to comply, we decided that we were not going to file patents for the core processes.

Takeaway *If your proprietary processes do not leave a distinctive signature on the end device, consider having trade secrets rather than patents.*

6.4.2 Machine Design-Related Patent

The secondary area of knowledge pertained to the machine designs for the machines that were needed to build and commercially manufacture these solar cells—these were very specific designs. Since these were more obvious by way of being visible and therefore also easier to copy, we decided to patent these designs.

Another reason for patenting these designs was that since we had the machines manufactured by external companies, this knowledge proliferated anyway. Having the patent on the machine designs enabled us to police them more effectively. This was because although there may be hundreds of flexible solar cell manufacturers in the world, there would only be a limited number of manufacturers building machines on which these solar cells could be manufactured.

6.4.3 Future Freedom

The third and the least strategically important component of the patent strategy was the future design options for the core machine. Additionally, the team also had add-on ideas relating to the process which we did not have the funding to pursue at this time, as well as design and process ideas for the noncore processes.

Each funding application required significant time and effort of the technology team as well as funding for the filing and subsequent annual fees. Since there was a significant financial outlay as well as manpower requirement for filing patents, at that point in our evolution, we decided that it would be adequate to have only the freedom to operate in these areas for the future. We thus decided to publish these in research journals and present them at scientific conferences. This put our ideas for the future in the public domain.

Once something is in the public domain, it is considered a prior art. No patent can be filed in respect of knowledge that is considered a prior art. We ensured that our knowledge would not be stolen, not by hiding it, but by making it public for all to see.

Takeaway *It's never too late to get lawyers' advice to make the patent strategy watertight, in the same way that it's never too late to start something new.*

6.5   Broad Versus Narrow

In the beginning of any startup, the lack of funds limits the filing of patents. That was the case with our team.

Before we formed our company, our technical team at the research institution wanted to file a patent to protect the knowledge generated. The first interaction with lawyers was a shocker, since the legal fees were almost ten times higher than the team expected. In an attempt to reduce the fees, the team decided to write a large part of the patent and only get it finalised by a legal firm before submission for the patent. As a consequence, the patent did not capture the precise knowledge that the team wanted to patent nor did it limit other entities from filing patents on similar areas due to the imprecise language used. That was an expensive lesson about trying to save costs.

Due to the lack of funds, young companies often only file patents for the specific knowledge that is at the heart of the competitive advantage. The risk in this is once you file a patent, the knowledge is out there. You then have to ensure that you are able to protect this from other entities that may try to replicate it. This protection can happen due to machine design or as a specific signature on the end product due to the use of the patented process.

There are some benefits of filing broad patents. One is that this becomes an effective red herring for competitors, since simply by looking at the patents filed by the company, competitors do not know precisely what process or proprietary knowledge the company is using if multiple patents on slightly different processes are filed. Freedom to operate is another obvious advantage of filing broad.

6.6   Vapourware

Another good reason for filing patents is to create a persona of technology or industry leadership. Given adequate financial resources, the benefit of doing this is to facilitate a swift exit strategy by way of selling the company if the business begins to go south. For technology startups, a delay in commercialisation resulting in the market having moved on or simply the inability to successfully manufacture commercially is the norm than the exception. In such case, the option to have an exit strategy that does not entail actually selling anything or something as prosaic as making a profit should not be ignored.

6.7   Design Versus Utility Patents

The above discussion relating to patents pertains to utility patents. These focus on functional aspects of the technology or product. Thus, they are more relevant to technology and are more comprehensive, but, at the same time, much more expensive to file as well as to defend.

A viable alternative is in the form of design patents. These are significantly cheaper to file, with cost in the range of hundreds of dollars. Design patents, as the name suggests, focus only on the design or ornamental component of the product. This can be a concern particularly if there is a risk that the technology has many design options to facilitate the same output.

A utility patent, on the other hand, would cover many different product variations in a single patent. It is much more expensive and can easily cost over $15,000 per patent and often significantly more.

The decision on whether to file utility or design patents depends on two factors:

1. Whether the most important attribute is the functionality of the technology or the design
2. Why these patents are being filed

If the unique design enables a particular functionality, a design patent is an excellent low-cost alternative. If the patents are being filed because they provide a perceived sense of knowledge capture during discussions with investors, as is frequently the case, a good solution is to consider having a combination of both utility and design patents, to reflect value and volume.

6.8   Liquidity Event

At the time of my first venture, I recall once having a conversation with a professor at IMD in Lausanne. He asked me what my plan was regarding patents. I stated that we were planning to file a few to capture the core knowledge that we had generated from our research.

His advice was simple. From the time that you start a company, you have to keep an eye out for a liquidity event. This is an event that generates liquidity for all the equity of the company. This can include an IPO or listing in the stock market. It can also include a trade sale, where a competitor or large company makes an offer to buy your company because it may fit into their strategy. As the company moves towards a liquidity event, a greater number of patents in the portfolio have a direct and positive influence on the valuation of the company.

Switzerland has many small companies with less than ten very highly skilled people. They provide a multitude of high-value solutions to clients. They remain small since the founders value their independence.

One such company based in Zurich had a focus on providing technology solutions for clients. These solutions included both IT-based solutions and specific engineering solutions. Along the way, they had created significant knowledge in key areas. One of their customers required solutions in the area of micro manufacturing.

As the company began to provide these solutions, the customer began to recognise the depth of knowledge resident in this small company. The customer became very interested in acquiring this knowledge and started discussions to acquire the company. After several rounds, the discussions broke off because the customer and potential acquirer realised that there were no patents and the company's knowledge was only in the minds of the team.

Since there was no patent capturing the knowledge, the prospective buyer realised that there was nothing tangible that they could acquire. Further, there was a risk that some other company already owned the knowledge in the form of a patent. The prospective buyer could thus open itself to litigation risk by scaling up a new area of knowledge without having full awareness of the freedom to file patent or freedom to operate. Needless to say, the deal did not go through, and the small company composed of technical experts missed the opportunity to capitalise.

This is not only in case of startups.

Nortel demonstrated just how valuable patents could be to a company. After going bankrupt, Nortel was still able to sell its 6000 patents for $4.5 billion to Apple and Microsoft (Peg brickley 2015). Not to be left behind, Google acquired over 17,000 patents and 7500 patents pending for over $12.5 billion from Motorola (Amir efrati and spencer e ante 2015). The reasoning for this was both to ensure that the acquirer companies had freedom to operate and to have the ability to countersue in case a competitor sued them. Since being sued can be a major distraction to a company's senior management, having a large patent portfolio is considered akin to a poison pill. Thus, if a company is able to countersue if it is sued, the cases go for out-of-court settlement to have quick resolution so that the executive management can focus on business.

Takeaway *Never exclude options! Remember that your investors are looking after their own interests, not yours.*

6.9   Evolution of Patent Strategy

In my first startup, although we began with only filing patents for machine designs, we soon realised that in order to have multiple options regarding business areas that we could operate in, we needed to revisit our patent strategy.

A viable business opportunity presented itself. This was to move into the area of manufacturing machines rather than manufacturing the solar modules themselves. The benefit of this approach was that as solar module manufacturers got larger, a very high level of investment would be required to build our manufacturing facility of the size where it would be able to compete on scale with the largest players—many of them based in China. The option of getting into manufacturing of machines seemed attractive since a significant part of the revenue of building a machine flows in up-front.

Compare this with building a solar module. Step one is to finish a pilot plant, demonstrating that it's possible to scale up. This pilot plant takes tens of millions of dollars. Step two is to make a scaled-up facility that requires hundreds of millions of dollars before the first solar module is created. The final step is to ensure that the quality of each module is what was expected. This is not trivial due to the multiple steps involved, each of which has customised equipment and own-designed process.

As soon as we started looking at the machine manufacturing business seriously, the first change was that of the approach to patents. Since the machines would be sold with the processes integrated, this was the right time to consider filing patents on the processes as well. Since the universe of machine manufacturers was limited, it would be easier to police the process patents.

Additionally, since the machines would be provided with the process already integrated enabling them to provide a given performance, the process could be in a black box because the customer was only interested in performance guarantees. The higher price of the machine could also be rationalised by customers based on the patented know-how, providing them with a higher perceived value. This approach motivated us to file more patents, since they clearly would have a monetary benefit if we were to ever take the route of selling machines.

Takeaway *Consider knowledge capture and the freedom to operate when formulating the patent strategy. This will evolve with any change in the company's route-to-market.*

6.10 Non-compete for Founders

From the time that the first investor invested in my first company, a major point was to have strong non-compete agreements for founders. This became centre stage again during the next rounds of funding since the investors had a huge concern that the founders would walk away with the knowledge in their brains.

To protect the knowledge, one of the main conditions preceding the investment was to have ironclad contracts with the founders as well as with all key employees. This was to ensure that they did not have permission to work in the same field if for any reason they quit working for the company.

Once the investment had been made and we were evaluating hiring people from competing companies, I brought up the point relating to non-compete that these technical people may have. It was then that I was told that in most jurisdictions, even if a company has an ironclad non-compete contract with its employees stopping them from working in the same field after they leave the company, most courts will side with employees and their rights to work. Particularly so, if this is the only thing that these individuals can do to earn a living.

6.11 Licence

Once it is determined that the research institution holds a patent, your startup has to ensure that you have the right to use. There are several components that can complicate this licensing issue.

6.11.1 Professor's Loyalty: To the Company or to His Craft

Professors and lead scientists working at research institutions often get involved in starting companies. However, they continue to do their research in the confines and safety of their institution. This becomes tricky if the professor's ambitions are stronger than his sense of commitment {read ethics} towards the company.

The professor may keep the option to license the technology to other companies, to the detriment of his own startup. When a professor is not fully involved in a startup but still owns a slice of it, he may consider another licensing of the technology if the startup seems to be taking longer than expected.

Since startups always take longer than expected, and professors always require additional funds to run their projects which will generate interesting research output which in turn will get published and get peer reviews, the non-exclusivity of the licensing can become a weakness of the startup and will be perceived as such by the investors.

Our investor situation was special. Having received the first round of investment from investors without preconditions, the technology lead was confident that there would be no requirement from future investors for sharing all the opportunities arising from the technology being commercialised. The upshot was that when the next round of investors came in, his view continued to be that he should have the right to separately continue research on and subsequently commercialise other overlapping technologies. Since he also perceived licensing opportunities from these, he was loath to give it up, in spite of business and legal counsel confirming the investors' view.

Now investors tend to be very clear that they want 100 % commitment from the founders to transition the technology to successful commercialisation. Finally, the technology lead agreed to give the right to the investors to have equity in any new spin-off created by him equal to the investors' equity in the current company.

Although the spin-off never happened, the other co-founders felt that they had been shortchanged by not getting equal equity in a possible spin-off, consequently degrading their trust in his ethics and his sense of fairness.

6.11.2 Who Paid the Licence Fees?

Researchers frequently have a limitation on funds required for payment of patent filing fees. In such case, they sometimes ask an industrial partner to pay the fees with a licence to the university so that they can continue to work with the patented idea.

This is a risky approach, since you could be creating your own competitor, especially since your startup may get the licence from the university but may face difficulty to sublicense. If your startup needs to go back to the industrial company {read competitor}, they will want to get their pound of flesh, and this will be a more expensive proposition than not filing the patent and simply publishing the knowledge.

6.11.3 Exclusivity

The value of the licence is in its exclusivity. The motivation of the university or licence-owning authority differs from the interest of the startup in this respect. The university would like as many entities as possible to have access to the licence so that the innovation can reach end customers and make a positive difference due to its usage. However, the value of the licence to the startup depends on the exclusivity of the licence. It is in the interest of the startup to negotiate the best possible conditions, including but not limited to exclusivity of the patent.

6.12 Licensing from the Research Entity

Different universities have different levels of experience regarding licensing of technologies. Thus, if the university is convinced that the startup will use the content of the idea covered in the patent, it is very likely that it will give exclusivity for commercial use to the startup. This is particularly if the university researchers who worked on the idea become part of the startup.

It is important to push for an irrevocable licence (although the university may not give this), since it may want the commercialisation right to revert back to it if the startup closes. The terms of the licence provided by the university become important for investors as well as to the startup closer to commercialisation.

There are several things to keep in mind while negotiating a spin-off agreement. If you're involved as a business driver, it is much easier to agree on points that will have a significant impact in the long term on the valuation of the startup as well as aligning the motivation of the technology team to the startup.

6.12.1 Right to Sub-licence

The university or the research foundation may want to control the licensing of the technology only to its spin-off companies. The university may thus not want to give the spin-off the right to sublicense the technology to *its* spin-offs.

The implication of the licence being limited in this manner has to be carefully thought through by the startup. As its business model evolves, the startup may decide to license its technology to another company instead of manufacturing the solution itself. Alternatively, the startup may decide to sell turnkey manufacturing systems rather that the product—as mentioned earlier. This will require a right to sublicense.

If the right to sublicense is not included in the original licence given by the university, getting it later can be significantly more difficult and cost a lot more by way of additional royalties in the form of percentage or revenue, profits or equity of the startup.

We began our company with a view to commercialise flexible solar cells. Along the way, we realised that much of the equipment that was required for making the solar cells was not available. Since we knew how to make this, we began designing and custom building the equipment. This opened another opportunity to move back in the value chain by considering manufacture of equipment rather than solar cells. Capturing IP on custom equipment design is important since it further blocks the competitors from catching up. Additionally, there is always the option of hiving off part of the activity that is noncore. So long as you have the IP on this, you always have the option to monetise.

6.12.2 What Else Is Included?

The spin-off agreement is an excellent opportunity to get equipment and machines transferred to the startup, especially if they have been used exclusively by the researchers involved in the idea of the startup. The startup can effectively put forth the argument that the equipment may not be of much value to the university since the researchers are now going to be working in the startup.

This has the benefit of reducing additional expenditure that would otherwise have been incurred in procuring the equipment and, more importantly, the loss of time in ordering and the time lost in the delivery cycle. Most importantly, if a particular machine has been used in creating the prototype or solution that the startup plans to commercialise, having access to the original equipment used to make the prototype becomes an excellent reference point.

6.12.3 Working at or Working with Technology

In many universities, the university is deemed to own the technology if you are working with technology. Working with the technology implies innovating. In this case, you require a licence to work with this technology.

However, if you are working at the technology, you do not need a licence from the university. For instance, if you are trying to improve the performance of the machine, it is not considered as an innovation and a licence is not required.

6.12.4 Right to Use Infrastructure

Universities normally provide free and easy access to infrastructure owned by them, for those working at the university. This can include not only space for offices but also a pilot manufacturing facility, with all the frills including furniture, meeting rooms, as well as other components required for pilot manufacture and skilled people. When a startup spins off from a university, it makes sense to include this in a spin-off contract, since it can save a startup not only money but also the administrative hassle of getting the logistics sorted out, enabling the team to focus on the important task of commercialisation of the idea.

Universities frequently have space for spin-off entities, and this can be made available for a period of 2–3 years. Sometimes all you have to do is ask. It can be a logistical advantage to access space for offices and pilot facilities if the university provides these, as otherwise, the time and effort taken to sort out these components this early in the evolution of the company can be a distraction for the team, particularly since these requirements are likely to change depending on how fast the company scales up.

The agreement with the university is also an excellent time to include additional components, particularly if they do not cost the university anything. These can include the machines that the researchers use for initial prototypes and pilot research.

More importantly, the agreement can also be a very effective way of ensuring that the knowledge created by the researchers who are now the co-founders is captured exclusively for the use of the company. This mitigates the temptation of researchers to try and spin off another company with a part of the technology that the investors may not be able to capture subsequently when they provide funding. Keep in mind that the university often does not know precisely what the researchers are involved in.

As a business driver, your ability to keep the researchers focussed on the commercialisation of the core technology without getting distracted is key. This happens easily enough. All technology leads, particularly those coming out of university research, have more than one iron on the fire. These researchers do work on multiple technologies or different approaches to solving technical challenges. Your biggest concern in this regard should be to ensure that all their research is clubbed into the same company and that they do not have any motivation to commercialise any other technology.

My own case illustrates this point. The technology lead at my debut startup was involved in multiple technologies and held world records in several. When we started our company, his only focus was to commercialise. However, as we proceeded with the negotiations, he realised that this could be an opportunity to segment the various technologies and start multiple companies. My responsibility, on behalf of the hapless team, was to ensure that all key technologies were included so that the technology lead did not have any motivation to start another company since this would have distracted him from the startup where we were involved.

IP can play a key role in ensuring that all possible distractions are eliminated for the technology team. Even if a parallel technology or new technique is not covered in the original mandate of the startup when investors come in, this can be included if a patent is filed by the startup.

On forming the company, our original focus was the manufacture of flexible solar cells. However, our technology was as relevant for rigid solar cells. Although this had not been included in the original mandate of the startup and the investors had also stated that the exclusivity of the co-founders was for flexible cells, we slowly began to file patents on rigid. This mitigated the chance that any of the technology co-founders would begin focussing on rigid and walk away, leaving the rest of the stakeholders in the lurch.

This strategy can safeguard you by mitigating distractions and ensuring that the technology team focusses on making your startup successful, rather than creating yet another one. You don't want to be backing the wrong technology or one in which the technology lead loses interest.

6.13 Licensing: The University's Perspective

For a good licensing agreement, it's particularly useful to know the university's perspective. This leads to awareness about what the university can give as well as what it is possible to get in return. There are, for example, certain elements that do not cost the university anything but can be hugely valuable for the startup. These include office space or connectivity, as mentioned above. Universities also normally pay the patenting fee, which can easily exceed 20,000 dollars per patent including the legal fee, even if the patent is filed for a handful of countries. This is advantageous, not only because it reduces the outflow of the startup in the initial stage but also because even before the startup is founded, the team can ask the university to file the patent. Since most patents are time-sensitive, they have to be filed before someone else files them. The university can thus file and subsequently license to the startup.

The university also has some constraints. Knowing what these are mitigates heartache by trying to negotiate something that is non-negotiable from the university's perspective. One is a transfer of IP. Normally, the university prefers to give exclusive licence to the IP rather than outright transfer. This is because in case the startup goes bust (it happens), the university is then able to transfer the IP to another entity for commercialisation. The university's interest is to ensure that the knowledge generated is used to improve the quality of lives of people and the only way to do this is to ensure that it is commercialised, rather than remaining a research paper.

6.14 Spin-Off Agreement

It is important for the startup to ensure that that university is rewarded enough to do the licence exclusively to the startup. This can be done by giving a stake of the company to the university or sharing a slice of the revenue or profits. The second benefit of the spin-off agreement is that it ensures that the key technologies that may be of relevance in the future are incorporated in the startup.

From the university's perspective, adding one or two additional points to the agreement does not make a big difference, since the university will receive substantially the same thing in return. The additional technologies, if added to the spin-off agreement, can have a huge impact on what options the startup has in future. Some of these technology options can be sold by the startup together with the IP even if the startup does not foresee using them.

Takeaway *It's beneficial to have options even if you decide to focus on one technology for your startup. You never know when it pays off.*

Incorporating additional technology options in the spin-off agreement also ensures that the technology co-founders have less motivation to walk away when the going gets tough. Remember, the technology guys are not the entrepreneurs; you are. They are far more likely to walk away in the face of uncertainty.

The spin-off agreement normally mandates what you give to the university in exchange for the licence to commercialise a technology. The options range from an up-front fee to ongoing royalty payments to equity.

An up-front payment or fixed future payments agreed upon are difficult to calculate properly since an amount that may be adequate for the university may be far too much, given the financial resources of the startup. The business model of the startup may also change resulting in the original licence not being as relevant as originally foreseen. A percentage of royalty on revenue or profits seems easy, but runs the risk of making the end solution much more expensive if the market subsequently evolves to becoming price competitive.

A percentage of equity or stock options is a reasonable alternative since it does not impact the limited funding that the startup has. However, since the startup gets diluted to that extent, a future consideration should include the first right of refusal on all new IP generated by the research in the area of focus of the startup.

For investors, it is important to know that even if the startup goes bust, they can still hold the patents for the perceived value. This conflicts with the interest of the research university since the university normally requires the patents to revert back in case of insolvency of the startup. This can and should be addressed during the formulation of the spin-off agreement.

The reason that research universities want the patent to revert back to them is because their focus is to ensure that the knowledge created in the university is used. If the patent does not revert to them, it will probably end up in the drawer of the insolvency court never to see the light of day. On the other hand, investors want the option to use the patent even if the startup goes bust.

A good compromise is to agree with the university that in case the startup goes bust, the investors will have the first right to use the patent. In such case, it may also be possible to ensure that the investors pay a certain sum, which may be shared between the university and the founders. Thus, if all else fails, the founders walk away with enough to consider starting the next thing. Going by the valuation and acquisition of patents in several large transactions by companies like Google and Apple, each patent may well be worth over USD 0.5 million. Thus, in a worst-case scenario where the only value of the startup is in the patents, you can ensure some upside for the founders if the investor walks away with this asset.

6.15 IP on Multi-country Projects

Researchers at universities frequently get funding from external sources such as government funding or even multi-government funding (like the EU). Several entities come together to form consortia for the purpose defined by the funding.

It is worth keeping in mind that many of the project partners tend to be corporates. The reason that they join these projects is not because they need the paltry funding provided. It is because this enables them to be aware of the latest developments going on in research and development.

Corporates are also particularly tuned to IP opportunities that may arise during these projects. Any IP generated during the project belongs to all the project partners. This gives rise to the risk of knowledge proliferation from research to industry. To safeguard against this, it is important for researchers to clearly define knowledge that they bring to these projects as belonging to them or "prior art", so that no other project partner can lay claim to this.

6.16 Patent Risks

Filing of patents poses as many risks as not doing so. These risks can cover different elements of the technology and business as discussed below.

6.16.1 Process Knowledge Proliferation

Filing a patent implies stating what you have that's special and covers both processes and products. This makes it easy for someone to copy what you have or what makes it special. The law of the land protects you in this respect.

Problems arise when the patentable knowledge cannot be distinguished in the end product. In other words, the special process does not leave a signature on the end product. The patent thus risks being copied without the patenting firm being able to police and protect the patent. After all, it is difficult to get your competitor to open his machines for you or show his process.

6.16.2 How Much to Tell

When filing patents, it is always tricky to know precisely how much to share. If you share too much, you make it easier for your competitors to copy. If you share too little, it may not offer adequate protection since a competitor may file a patent using your work as a base.

6.16.3 Reverse Engineer

Today, almost any product can be reverse engineered due to the advances of technology. A whole subsector has developed for healthcare, called generics. As soon as a product goes off patent, the generics, which, in the case of medicines, are medicines with the same chemical constitution, are made by these companies at knocked-down prices. These companies do not have to invest billions in R&D to invent new molecules. This is all possible because they can reverse engineer to constituents from the end product.

It is thus particularly important to know how to capture knowledge in a patent and, indeed, whether a patent should be filed for any given piece of knowledge.

6.17 Risk Mitigation

There are some simple steps to mitigate risks arising from patents. In case the patentable knowledge pertains to processes that do not lead to a signature on the end product, it is better to avoid filing a patent and have a trade secret instead. In such cases, patents make sense if the startup considers moving back in the value chain into manufacture of machines that will eventually make the products.

My startup team had a significant amount of knowledge in the area of processes used to make very high-quality solar cells. This knowledge was initially a trade secret since there were many companies, particularly in China, trying to emulate our work. Policing all this would take effort, particularly if we were unable to identify if our particular process had been used.

Subsequently, we considered moving into the equipment manufacture area. With this, we then decided to patent our knowledge on the processes since they were then incorporated in the equipment design. Policing this was much easier since there were only a handful of machine manufacturers globally and designs were essentially publically available information. Since no machine manufacturer wants to have a lawsuit relating to patent infringement due to the reputational impact, this provided us with adequate protection.

By telling too little, there is a chance that a competitor may file a patent that builds on the knowledge covered in the original patent. This would then run the risk of the startup not having *freedom to operate* or freedom to commercialise its own special knowledge.

Since the risk of reverse engineering can never be fully mitigated, the best option is to file the patent that ensures freedom to operate, particularly when it relates to machine design or processes that very clearly lead to a specific signature on the end product. This done, the next step is to rapidly move towards commercial scale-up.

Takeaway Summary

1. *If your proprietary processes do not leave a distinctive signature on the end device, consider having trade secret rather than patents.*
2. *It's never too late to get lawyers' advice to make the patent strategy watertight, in the same way that it's never too late to start something new.*
3. *Never exclude options! Remember that your investors are looking after their own interests, not yours.*
4. *Consider knowledge capture and the freedom to operate when formulating the patent strategy. This will evolve with any change in the company's route-to-market.*
5. *It's beneficial to have options even if you decide to focus on one technology for your startup. You never know when it pays off.*

References

Amir efrati and spencer e ante. (2015). *WSJ*. Retrieved December 1, 2015, from http://www.wsj.com/articles/SB100014240531119033929045765099538214 37960

Nytimescom. (2015). *Nytimescom*. Retrieved December 1, 2015, from http://www.nytimes.com/interactive/2012/10/08/business/Fighters-in-a-Patent-War.html

Peg brickley. (2015). *WSJ*. Retrieved December 1, 2015, from http://www.wsj.com/articles/SB10001424052702303812104576440161959082234

Sam shead. (2015). *Techworld*. Retrieved December 1, 2015, from http://www.techworld.com/news/startups/ex-cisco-chief-jokes-stanford-should-have-taken-stock-not-cash-for-spin-out-fee-3518361/

Wikipediaorg. (2015a). *Wikipediaorg*. Retrieved December 1, 2015, from https://en.wikipedia.org/wiki/NTP,_Inc

Wikipediaorg. (2015b). *Wikipediaorg*. Retrieved December 1, 2015, from https://en.wikipedia.org/wiki/Apple_Inc._litigation

7

Investors: Choosing the Right Ones, Getting Them Interested

When the technology has been identified, the team is in place, the business plan is clear and you are willing to take the leap, the next big thing is to make the required funding happen.

There are risks here even before you meet your first investor. One big risk relates to how much money you should raise in your first round. When we started talking to investors about our funding, we calculated how much we really needed to complete our pilot and get to commercialisation. At that point my technical team told me that our requirement was going to be about $15 million. Although I felt that this amount was rather on the higher side, I did not have the conviction based on experience backing my statement. At the same time, the technical co-founders were very clear that this was the amount required. So when I started speaking to investors, this is the amount I said we needed.

Due to our outstanding technology, Flisom had won many awards and got meetings with some of the best investors out there. But as soon as they found out what our requirement was, they simply backed out. It took me some time to figure out that investor groups had certain sweet spots where they were comfortable investing. However, by then I had already conveyed to some of the biggest European VCs that we would not be comfortably moving forward with smaller amounts of investment. By then the damage had been done, and the investor groups probably perceived that we did not know the playing field and were going to be difficult to deal with.

After having multiple dozens of conversations with investors without success, we reduced our financial requirements and started from scratch all over again. And, we also discovered an easy way to reduce our financial

© Springer International Publishing Switzerland 2016
A. Sethi, *From Science to Startup*, DOI 10.1007/978-3-319-30424-3_7

requirements. Instead of saying that the money was going to be adequate to get us to profitability, we simply said that this would enable us to achieve key milestones which would continue to give us a lead compared to global competitors. And that is how we got the first term sheet.

With rare exception, businesses are all about selling or providing a compelling value proposition that customers will buy. There are always exceptions. Facebook is one. The service provided by Facebook is the network. The naysayers may well argue that Facebook does not sell to its over one billion users. My view is that the one billion users are the product that Facebook sells to its advertisers.

7.1   Pay to Play

When a startup begins, the first step towards financing is for the founders to put in their own money. This demonstrates commitment within the team, since all founders then have skin in the game. The importance of this element cannot be overstated.

An excellent example was a startup focussing on streamlining insurance solutions for auto garages. The founder approached me with a common problem. They were running out of money and the software solution had not yet been fully developed. It transpired that the key founder had put his own money, several thousands of dollars, to set up the company and the other two co-founders simply reached an understanding that they would all have 1/3 of the company each. Over a few months, they realised that the software would take much longer to develop. At the same time, they also realised that the fundraising was going to take longer.

The two co-founders who had not invested money to start the company began to lose interest. The founder who had invested the money realised that he was doing all the work of developing the software. Given this, it did not seem reasonable that he should be sharing the rewards with the others. This is a situation where many founders find themselves, since you don't always know how your bedfellows will behave when the going gets tough.

In the meantime, the founder's wife, who had done a small stint with his company and had to be laid off, was unable to tap financial support from the government for unemployment. His personal finances were now running low as well.

Taken as one problem, it seemed very complex. This person was now on the verge of chucking it all up and going back to a corporate job. On reflection, it turned out that breaking up the problem into bite-sized bits made it resolvable. The first step was to close the company and offer to buy the rights of the co-founders. This would then enable his wife to get government support till she found a job. Closing the firm would also motivate his co-founders to sell their rights to him since the perceived value of the rights on a dissolving firm was negligible. The final step was to start a one-man firm and hire people only on a stock-option basis, while keeping at least 51 % of the equity with him since clearly he was doing the work, and this would keep the decision-making clean.

While closing the firm seemed counter-intuitive, it enabled a clean break and turned out to be an elegant solution. Otherwise, had he received funding for his original startup, he would have been locked in to the other nonworking co-founders.

Takeaway *A startup is like a marriage—if the team does not get along in the beginning, things are unlikely to improve after the kids, the mortgage and dirty dishes hit the fan.*

7.2   Finding the Right Investors

One of the first customers that a startup has to sell to is the investor(s). The unique value proposition is sold to the investors in order to get them to put in the money.

There are various kinds of investors. At the same time, there is no right or wrong investor per se. The only right investor is the one whose interests are aligned to your vision for the commercialisation of the startup (Fig. 7.1).

Takeaway *Targeting the right investors is as important as avoiding the wrong ones.*

The major investor groups are discussed below. Private Equity investors (PE) have not been covered here as they only invest in growth capital once the business case has been validated by way of not only revenues but the first level of scale-up. PE funds normally have a minimum threshhold of 100 million per investment and have funds exceeding 20 to 30 billion.

7.3   Angel Investors

These are wealthy individuals who have either been successful with their own companies or are wealthy professionals like consultants or bankers. They may either belong to investment clubs or invest independently. The sheer diaspora means that they are notoriously difficult to target precisely. The amounts that

Fig. 7.1 Investor types and their motivations

they invest range from several tens of thousands of dollars to even low millions, if they come together as groups of angel investors.

The advantage of these investors is that they can make decisions fairly quickly as they don't have to get clearances and approvals from committees and/or report to superiors.

The disadvantages of angel investors include micromanagement. Since many of these individuals have made their own money and have been successful in their own professional careers, they automatically assume that they will be able to add value to the startup. This may end up being a hindrance since startups have a different buzz, and too much management can sometimes do more harm than good to this fragile entity.

Angel investors also tend to want greater oversight with how the startup spends money. Assume the angel investor's net investible worth is $5 million. If he invests $500,000, that's 10 % of his total. He is likely to want information about each amount over $20 K–50 K spent by the startup. Sometimes, it's just not possible to justify this as the amounts spent on machines, hiring people, filing patents, participating in exhibiting at international conferences and creating demos and prototypes are down to the best judgement of the founders, rather than something that has very strong and defendable reasoning.

Angel investors have another curious attribute. They require very strong and credible references if they are to consider investment in the startup. A cold-calling approach seldom cuts it. Although associations including venture capital associations are present in most countries, they only provide contact information of some angel investors, while still not resolving the problem of cold-calling.

A far more effective approach is to get them to call you. Identify the buzz in your technology—there's got to be one. This implies identifying the potential impact of your technology in the broadest terms possible. The technical team cannot do this—they are too focussed on what's immediately doable, not what is possible and definitely not the global impact of what's possible. To repeat a cliché, those who make it big are the ones who believe they can.

Once the impact has been identified, get it written about in news media. In case you've never done this, it's good to keep in mind that the media is also looking for things to write about and a pitch on the global impact possible with the technology could get you there. Plus, it doesn't hurt to get some practice in making pitches since you can expect to do this for at least the next half decade, as the commercialisation of your startup accelerates.

The second option is to apply for awards and sponsorships. This is less for the money and more for the network and credibility. The entities to target are foundations, which are non-profit in nature. In many countries, the awards for entrepreneurship and startups are well known, and there is increasing awareness about them. Another option to find out about such awards is through technical universities or MBA programs, since this is where entrepreneurship conventionally begins.

These awards, however small, get you written about in the press and help in attracting angels. A particularly important and often ignored option is to have access to the details of the audience during the recognition or awards ceremony, if you do get recognised. Get the organisers to provide a list of invitees with contact details. If you've been on stage getting the award, you can be sure they'll remember you.

7.4   VCs

Venture capitalists or VCs are the most commonly known form of investors for startup firms. There are many advantages of going to them, at least in the regions of the world where they have a presence. VCs have a very good idea about what it takes to take an idea, albeit a particularly outstanding one, and help the team in converting it into a world-class company.

VCs are particularly strong in enabling aggressive scale-up and pushing a startup team to perform more than it thought it was capable of. VCs can also help in identifying weaknesses in the team and augmenting with the right skills, whether from their own firm or via their network. This is important because very seldom is a startup team complete. Another reason that VC investment is called smart money compared to angel investment is because VCs have strong global networks and know how to exploit them to help the startup in scaling up, including finding suppliers and partners and reaching customers.

One of the problems of VCs is the size of investments. Due to a combination of speed of return and larger bet size, VCs are slowly becoming access points of the few, rather than first points of investments of the many. The increasing speed of returns from startups like Facebook, LinkedIn and Twitter, where the main strength is go-to-market rather than technological advantage, results in VCs only looking for go-to-market opportunities rather than real innovation-driven investments.

Although IT-driven or go-to-market-driven opportunities help get the market closer, the sustainable impact of technology innovation-based startups cannot be questioned. You will likely agree, particularly if you are driving one.

The larger bet size pertains to the amount of funds that VCs are able to raise. Up to the late 1990s, the average fund size was in the range of $100 million. VCs then considered investments of $1–2 million, with follow-up rounds of another few million. Now, with average fund sizes of $300–500 million, they have to invest larger amounts in fewer startups, since they are unable to manage more than a certain number of companies in their portfolios.

Since there are many startups that only require amounts in the range of $1–2 million in their first round of funding, this puts the VCs out of reach for them.

Another reason why VCs are not everyone's cup of tea is because VCs only understand money and risk. This can have a couple of implications. VCs have no qualms in investing in competing companies, so that they may have the option to cannibalise one in order to ensure the success of the second. Although this is good for the VCs, it is not always so for the cannibalised startup, particularly if this is yours. The second risk is that since VCs only focus on exits, they are quite likely to walk away if for whatever reason your startup seems to run into delays in achieving milestones or, worse, if your startup's sector becomes less fashionable.

With my first startup, we experienced this—although from a slight distance. After discussions with multiple VCs, they decided to invest in competing companies since they showed more aggressive timelines to commercialisation. This was at the time when clean energy companies were considered the next big thing.

In this beginning, this gave us tremendous heartburn since our conversations with strategic investors seemed to have no end. However, the payback came some time after both our competitors and we got funding. The market for clean energy began to look for results. Since no results were forthcoming, the VCs began to put pressure on the investee companies. If you're running a startup, you may know that too much pressure can only make things go wrong. Since the VCs did not immediately see the x-times return on their investment, they began to cut their losses. This in spite of the fact that several of our competitors had done outstanding work and really had the potential to become industry leaders and make it work, given more time.

In a twist of fate, it was only those companies that got investment from Chinese investors or from strategic investors that were able to go on. Since we were backed by the latter rather than VC investors, we lived to see another day.

An important attribute of VCs is that since their only business is investment in startups, they have a process that takes a certain amount of time. It's good to know the time upfront since trying to rush it may be a fruitless exercise. It's also good to know what factors to negotiate on. A veto right, right of first refusal, tag along or antidilution rights are not something that VCs would provide. If co-founders are unable to agree with some of these, VCs are not the best investors for you.

Takeaway *Know what you want and whether VCs can help. If it doesn't fit, find other investor groups. It's not only about just the money.*

7.5   Strategic Investors

Strategic investors are companies who invest in startups as a way of externalising their research efforts. Their interest is thus not to sell their stake and make a good return on their investment but to eventually buy and hold a majority of the startup.

These strategic investors would normally consider the solutions of the startup as either complementary to their own, a technological extension of their value proposition, or providing higher perceived value to their products and services.

One thing to be aware of when discussing with strategic investors is that they take an extremely long time to make a decision. My experiences bear this out.

We began to discuss a possible investment with our current strategic investors in 2006. After much back and forth, we finally were able to get a term sheet in late 2008, by which time almost our entire team had been replaced by new faces. It took another year (that's right, 1 year) to convert the term sheet into a set of transaction documents.

Our lawyers were very surprised at the size of the term sheet, which was in excess of 20 pages. The real shocker however was when we received the transaction documents, which were over 400 pages. The lawyers told us, this looked more like a takeover of a multibillion dollar company with multi-geography operations than a sub-ten million investment. But this should not be a surprise since where other investors like angels or VCs are looking at an exit in 3–5 years, strategic investors have to look at a timeline of 10–30 years and incorporate all manners of contingencies and commercial rights.

An important factor when dealing with strategic investors is to ensure that there is an executive sponsor from the investor side with oversight on the investment. In the absence of this, you run two risks. The first is that this could be an initiative of a mid-level manager within the investor group. In such case, this investment may never see the light of day. The second risk is that the manager may move and your discussions with the investor would simply cease to be.

We experienced this first-hand with a major South Korean conglomerate. They evinced great interest in our company and even came over for a due diligence. However, they kept postponing our meeting and presentation requests to the senior management. Finally, we found that not only had the senior management not given the green light for this specific investment but that the senior management was simply not aware of the discussions between their mid-level management and our startup.

From the perspective of the mid-level management of the strategic investor, these were simply exploratory. More dangerously for us, they were running parallel preliminary due diligence processes on several competing firms around the world in order to figure out the advantages and weaknesses of each. Since we were not aware that they were also discussing with our competitors, we provided some information about our company strategy that we would have hesitated to share with the market.

We later heard that this investor invested rather a large sum in one of our competitors. When we once had the opportunity to meet with the senior management during a conference, they appeared to have no idea about our company, world record notwithstanding.

Our only saving grace was that our competitor ended up getting the investment by promising too much too soon, and reality caught up with them to the detriment of their investor.

Takeaway *Insist on discussions with executive sponsors; ensure that the investment discussions are in their system; and be patient.*

7.6 Sovereign Funds

Governments of countries frequently set up funds with the express purpose of actualising the strategy of the country in a given area of science, technology or business. This may be to provide employment to its citizens or spur research activity in an area of technology considered in the strategic interest of the country.

A few years ago, Middle Eastern countries started setting up sovereign funds with a view to diversifying out of oil wealth and oil-proofing their economic development for the future. This funding was provided to startup companies focussing on clean energy. Russia has a sovereign fund to attract nanotechnology-based companies as well as to provide employment to its deep pool of engineers.

A couple of factors define these sovereign funds. The funds are of relatively large size and average $10 billion. The decision-making is less tuned towards making immediate revenue and more towards satisfying the criteria defined in the policy. The size of each investment also tends to be rather large, ranging from several tens of millions to hundreds of millions of dollars.

Another attribute of these funds is that it takes a relatively long time to get this investment, due to the procedural nature of the fund. However, if the startup has a likelihood of fulfilling the criteria for the investment, it can be worthwhile to apply.

7.7   Family Offices

Very wealthy individuals frequently create family offices where professional wealth managers manage their incredible wealth. This wealth normally tends to be in billions of dollars.

The investment criterion tends to be broader than that of pure financial investors. This is where startups can exploit opportunities to get investment. Depending on the size of the fund, the individual investments can be of a relatively large size. Additionally, the timeframe of investments tends to be much longer than that of financial investors and can exceed 5–10 years.

Unlike financial investors, accessing family offices is not simply about sending an e-mail. References are key to reaching the decision-makers. Some of the most effective references are the ones who don't have a business motive to making it happen. Some of the really important ones are professors of business schools. Professors have incredible access to very wealthy individuals and families because professors write business cases about them, which is more a quest for knowledge rather than trying to tap the wealth.

Business cases serve the professors because this provides them greater respect in their peer group. These same business cases serve the wealthy individuals since this enables their stories to be told. One hand thus shakes the other.

In addition to having the right references to accessing the family offices, it is also as important to the areas of focus of family offices and what they expect. A financial return is not always the most important element. In our case, professors enabled us to meet the family offices of several very large investors with wealth exceeding ten billion dollars. The criteria ranged from continuing to maintain our head office and R&D in Switzerland to creating employment in Switzerland in addition to having a healthy return.

If we see it from their perspective, a $25 million investment from a ten billion dollar fund is relatively small. Even if we manage to convert this from $25 million to 100 million, it is still only 1 % of the total fund. Thus, the impact on the total wealth of the family office is limited. It is for this reason that other criteria become important and need to be emphasised when pitching to these funds.

Family funds have another advantage. Even if times are bad for the economy, they still have the capability to invest further and in larger rounds. First Solar, one of the key players in the global solar industry, is a prime example.

First Solar is the first company in the world to commercialise thin-film solar cells. These solar cells are about 100 times thinner than conventional solar cells that are based on silicon wafer.

First Solar got its funding from the family fund of the Walton family—owners of Walmart. The Walton family provided multiple rounds of funding, exceeding 200 million dollars by some estimates. This was through the dot-com boom and bust, where other forms of funding had almost dried up in Silicon Valley and beyond. The result was that First Solar became the second largest solar company in the world and at one point was among the top ten most innovative companies in the world.

Every innovative technology has the opportunity and has the capability to get there. It takes vision, a dollop of luck and support of investors who believe in the vision and have the financial muscle to get you there.

7.8   Foundations

Frequently, wealthy individuals create foundations with their wealth that can be used for the betterment of society or for investment in causes that they want to propagate. These foundations continue the work of the wealthy individuals through investments or donations in perpetuity. These foundations sometimes have a set amount of funds that they disburse each year as a donation without any expectation or return.

Foundations are an excellent way to attain funding for startups. They are similar to family offices in many ways. However, they are also very different. Being aware of their idiosyncrasies can improve the chances of acquiring funding from them.

Foundations are similar to family offices in that they are long-term investors and will seldom ask for a return within a period of 3 or 5 years, unlike financial investors. Since these foundations invest within their remit, it is relatively easy to identify foundations within your sweet spot as well as those that will definitely not fit. The ones in the grey area can be a second priority where it doesn't hurt to take your chances.

Foundations are unique in that they sometimes do not seek a return on their investment. From their perspective, it's simply a donation to a worthy cause. They may not even want their name associated with the investment. It is therefore particularly important to ensure that you are aligning yourself very carefully to the requirements of the foundation.

A good way is to get someone from the foundation on your side by pitching to him and getting his feedback. If you've never pitched to foundations, this feedback is worth its weight in gold, since their criteria of investment are almost totally different from those of other investors. Strangely, financial investors don't like foundations for exactly this reason. Whereas financial investors focus on monetary return to the exclusion of everything else, within a given timeframe, foundations focus on the difference that a technology can make.

The main challenge with foundations is not so much contacting them but getting them to take you seriously. For this reason, it is particularly important to establish credibility before contacting them. If you are recognised in any forum, identify the foundations that may be aware of the forum or better still may have been represented in the audience. Then follow up and get a meeting. You're now halfway there. Now it's yours to lose.

7.9   Low-Interest Loans

Countries, states or local regions frequently focus on particular sectors to drive growth. The financial vehicles chosen to drive this growth are the government-owned banks.

These banks often have the mandate to provide soft loans to innovation-driven startups. The assumption is that your startup is innovation driven or brings something unique to the market, be it the business model, technology go-to-market or customer access. In such case, it's likely that it will fit in at least some of the criteria.

These soft loans can have requirements ranging from specific employment generation to keeping the technology local, or doing the scale-up locally, again with bank financing. So long as the loans do not ask a guarantee of personal assets, it is worthwhile to consider this financing.

An important factor that helps to determine whether to go for loans or equity is the certainty of return within a given timeframe. If the certainty of revenue and profits is high, a loan will reduce dilution of the initial equity holders. This is because after the payment of the interest on the loan, the additional profit generated by getting the loan will accrue to the equity holders. If however, the certainty of revenue and profits is low, it is better to get investors against equity. This is because a loan will force payment of interest, curtailing the financial resources of the startup, whereas equity holders will have to stick with the startup when the going gets tough and only get a return when the company makes profit.

7.10   Getting Through to Investors

The best way to get to investors is to let them find out about you and then to contact you. These options will not only enable your startup to get noticed by the right investors but also provide precious initial capital—the lifeblood of an early stage enterprise. This credibility also helps in strengthening the subsequent valuation discussions with investors. There are some easy ways to do this.

7.10.1 Awards

Awards and recognitions not only help the startup to build up credibility and a brand name but can also provide initial funding. Depending on the country, this can go from thousands of dollars to over a hundred thousand dollars per award.

These awards can also include additional non-monetary support that can help the startup to strengthen areas that are weak. This form of support is sometimes provided by consulting companies and state-owned banks. The stakeholders can then be motivated to help the startup in opening doors and attach their credibility in doing so.

There is a benefit of getting these companies involved. It is simply that when external entities recognise the startup, they indirectly become stake-holders. These entities will then put their own resources and open their net-work to ensure that the startup does not go bust. This is particularly if the companies providing support as part of the award also advertise that they are giving support.

From consulting companies, the highest value added tends to be the open-ing of doors of specific investor groups in different geographic groups. That said, these companies will not normally open doors to these investors. They have to be coaxed into doing it. Frequently, these consulting companies oper-ate in different geographies where one hand does not know what networks the other hand has. In such a case, it is easier to pinpoint not only geographies but also specific customer groups.

My startup received one particular award where an international consulting company also provided support. Since we were looking for sovereign funds, we decided to inquire about the consulting company's relationships with the royal family in Saudi Arabia. Since there are over 5000 princes in the Saudi royal family, it is rather important to know who the most relevant ones are.

The consulting company's regional office was not only able to help nego-tiate the labyrinth within the extensive royal family but also in initiating a conversation with the investment fund of the appropriate royal. Although the discussions came to naught, it taught a valuable lesson—it's better to get a "no" from a potential investor than try to reach the right investor without the right network. Time is your most limited asset since there are so many investors out there, and the standard paradigms often don't work in accessing them.

Consulting companies also help in validation of financial models. This does not mean that investors will pay any heed to the financials provided by the startup—it only means that the investors know that the startup has done them using commonly agreed principles. As President Eisenhower once said, "In preparing for battle I have always found that plans are useless, but planning is indispensable".

State-owned banks also frequently get involved in national awards to startups. This can bring a very high degree of credibility to the startup. An award involving state banks can also open doors to state-owned strategic investors and customers. Although strategic investors take a long time to make investment decisions, the stamp of a state or national award provides access, which is the most difficult thing to achieve for a startup.

State-owned banks also have a negative attribute—very seldom does anyone ever take any initiative to help a startup—even after the startup has been recognised by the bank. The startup therefore has to lead the entire process of getting the bank to facilitate introductions to affiliates and convert them into strategic investors or customers.

The effort of converting state-owned affiliates of state-owned banks, although very slow and arduous, is worth its while because, although it takes a very long time to convert them into investors or customers, they do not have multiple conversations with startups. Thus, if they begin to have a conversation with you, they are unlikely to have a parallel conversation with your competitors.

When applying for awards, it's important to understand the perspectives of the jury and to have regional sensitivity. The example below illustrates this.

A Swiss technology startup won the European business plan competition in Rotterdam and qualified for the world championships in Singapore. They presented to the jury, with typical Swiss understatement of their accomplishments. They already had a customer and revenue at this time, and the value and uniqueness of their solution had been demonstrated. But another startup, an American one, presented a pill that had the ability to reduce obesity. This company also showcased X-rays to showcase the viability and functionality of the solution and also had a medical doctor who confirmed the way it would work. The second company won the award and the cash award of $25,000.

That evening, as the teams relaxed around the pool, the winning team professed surprise that the Swiss startup had revenues and a proven solution with a concept. It so turned out that the only thing that the winners had was a PowerPoint presentation.

This illustrates the difference between the mindset of startups from different regions and the importance of aligning to expectation levels of investors from those regions.

7.10.2 WEF: An Alternate Reality

A year after I started my first company, the buzz about alternative energy was beginning. The following year, this buzz had reached its crescendo. Since the co-founders were fundamentally researchers, the uniqueness of their research was that they had held the world record for the highest conversion of light into electricity on flexible solar cells.

Although when we began the company, the main driver was to commercialise flexible solar at a low cost rather than the world record per se. The recognitions and awards began when the world realised the importance of low-cost clean energy without the risk of a Fukushima or Chernobyl. It was about this time that I received a call from the World Economic Forum telling me that on behalf of the company I had co-founded, I had been invited to receive the Technology Pioneer award granted to individuals commercialising technologies that could have a meaningful impact on humanity. When I realised that this was not someone trying to sell me something, my reaction was amazement. I had always heard of the WEF as the place that the people who had arrived on the global stage were at.

A short month hence, I was in Davos attending the WEF for the major part of a week. On the first day, I was walking down a corridor when I bumped into someone. After apologies on both sides, I saw him heading to meet the leader of Israel. It suddenly struck me that this was the then Palestinian leader and they were here to meet each other! Something unthinkable in the public domain given the Palestinian conflict. This truly was an alternate reality.

Individuals who had been recognised at Technology Pioneers in earlier years included the founders of Google, among others. At one of the sessions where the current pioneers make their pitch and alumni coach and challenge the current Pioneers on what lies ahead, Michael Dell of *Dell* had asked me a couple of questions about the potential of our solutions on their laptops. I knew he was interested. At the cocktails at the conclusion of the session, I saw him again and when he saw me, he stopped momentarily. It just so happened that at that very moment, I was in the midst of a conversation with Larry Page of Google, where Larry was sharing nuggets regarding growing pains he had experienced in entrepreneurship. The moment passed. I didn't see Michael again.

But perhaps it was just as well, since it was Michael Dell who, when asked in 1997 what could be done to fix Apple, had said, "What would I do? I'd shut it down and give the money back to the shareholders" (Cnetcom 2015).

The exposure to these individuals who have become legends of the new generation truly opened my eyes to what makes them special. It was the strength of their personal convictions and ability to perceive obstacles as stepping stones. It is in this way that they are able to distort reality to align to their own vision, as was first said about Steve Jobs of Apple.

The relationship of the awards to investors is that these awards not only give credibility but also open a vast network. It's like being from Harvard or McKinsey. Once you've been there, you're always an alumni and the network will always open doors. And it's the small awards that open doors to bigger ones and finally to funding.

It was at the WEF that I was grilled by a very senior executive of the company that finally invested in us. Within the first five of minutes, he had understood our technology-related challenges. He spent the remaining 40 minutes in tearing our strategy to shreds. I found out much later that the grilling was not so much about the go-to-market of the technology but how I reacted under pressure. I must have passed, although at the time it appeared more likely that I passed out.

One of the most important things about these awards and recognitions is to prepare the takeaways and networks prior to the big day. This enables you to know who to network with. It is as important to follow up immediately after the award since there are likely to be key members in the audience who can open doors.

7.10.3 Speaker Opportunities

An excellent opportunity to gain credibility is to grab opportunities to be a speaker at events. This enables you to hone your pitch, since in larger gatherings, it is much easy to field questions because no one has the opportunity to dig deeper, and the questions remain relatively superficial.

That I had never been a particularly adept public speaker would be to understate facts. My hands would become clammy and I would get cold feet. My only saving grace (there was one) was that when I was extremely nervous, I would yawn. This would give people the impression that I was particularly comfortable with the situation, as though I gave presentations every day to build an appetite before meals.

One of my more interesting speaking opportunities was when I was invited at an event under the auspices of (his highness) Sheikh Mohammed bin Rashid Al Maktoum, the emir of Dubai. It was difficult to figure out who was who, since the audience comprised largely of people wearing the Middle

Eastern garb of flowing robes. At the conclusion of my talk, one such man approached me about our work and his interest in buying our products. On my inquiry, he casually mentioned that he was the defence minister of Iraq.

For reference, this was in the thick of the Iraq war and the US military had a very large presence in Iraq. My immediate quandary was whether he was representing the US-supported Iraqi defence ministry or whether he was part of the Iraq that was slightly upset at the US invasion.

I saw visions of my being pursued by the secret service organisations of Western nations. Although I had hoped for interest from investors and customer leads resulting from the talk, this was not exactly what I had in mind.

That said, speaking opportunities are easier to find than awards. The clearest opportunities are in the university domain. All management and technology universities require their students to get exposure to entrepreneurs and entrepreneurship. This can also benefit you since the professors can open valuable doors. And when you begin your journey as an entrepreneur, you need all the well-wishers you can get.

7.11 Back to School

Many MBA schools invite startups to come in as case studies of how creativity within a startup happens. This is an excellent source of good quality, if distracted, expertise.

Young students doing their MBA or relatively experienced executive eMBA students in top MBA schools globally are supposed to do projects where they work closely with startups as part of the entrepreneurship modules. The students can bring value by either validating the work that has already been done or do some work to progress the commercialisation process.

I consider this intellectual manual labour. The tasks given to them have to be spelt out very precisely to ensure valuable results. It should also be kept in mind that these MBA students, although very bright and driven, are only doing this as a project to get good grades. They will seldom get original entrepreneurial thinking to the table. If their experience and skills can be properly aligned to the specific tasks, they can save the startup significant effort and money.

We were selected by IMD, a top MBA school based in Lausanne in Switzerland. They threw a group of executive MBA students on our way. Now in a startup, there are many assumptions and convictions of the founders. We were no different. When a bunch of really bright individuals with management experience began asking us questions, our initial reaction was to question many things that we were doing, since there was no empirical evidence to support our decisions.

Slowly, it dawned upon us that there was a good reason that they were shadowing us. While they had management experience, they were missing a key element to being true leaders—the capability to lead with a vision and having an entrepreneurial mindset.

Being so focussed on making the future happen, it took some time to realise that entrepreneurship was what these executive MBAs were here to learn. From that point, we were more self-assured and tried to share the propensity to risk and the focus on making it happen to these individuals. In doing so, we were also able to get much more from them and strengthened our positioning using their cumulative experience.

Since we were relatively new on the block, it was also good to get different perspectives: one of the students worked with the Swiss Stock Exchange and others were in entrepreneurial teams or in the investment arms of large corporates. Perhaps, it was the understanding about corporate investing that subsequently enabled us to close our investment with corporate investors. In a way, it was this that enabled us to survive to see another day since corporates, unlike financial investors, have a more long-term vision and the patience to support the startup through hiccups along the journey to commercialisation.

Takeaway *Take away learning whenever you can, you never know when it pays off.*

7.12 Investor Identification

Within each investor group, and particularly for financial investors including VCs, it is important to identify the likely investors, since each contact takes time and effort.

Depending on the investor type mentioned earlier, the process has to start with looking at the focus sectors of the investors. This is normally easy to find. The next step is to see if the investor has made any similar investments. If the investor has invested in your competitor, it is less likely that they may also invest in your startup.

In case the investor still evinces interested in you, it may imply that they have a portfolio approach. This means that they would like to have several investments in different technologies or business models in the given sector, since they may not know which one will eventually succeed.

There are two risks of the portfolio approach. The first risk is if the investor invests a small amount of money in your startup, this may be to facilitate knowledge transfer to their larger investee company. The second risk is access.

Investors provide access to customers and other partners that can accelerate the commercialisation of the startup. If your investor has multiple startups, these resources get distributed and your startup receives a small share.

Most VC investors follow the portfolio approach, where they invest in multiple companies in competing technologies addressing the same market. Strategic investors are different—most times—a strategic investor will invest in only one company. Therein lies your advantage.

7.12.1 Fund Requirement

If the investment required is up to a million dollars, it is not worthwhile to go to larger financial investors like VCs or even strategic investors. Investors who have very large funds cannot afford to manage hundreds of startups. It is thus better to look at an angel investor or small VC investors whose fund size is in the tens of millions.

Foundations could also be an excellent option, since their mandate is to provide funds, sometimes as grants to deserving startups. Many startups don't consider this, but this is as close to free money as possible, since foundations don't dilute the equity if this is a grant, and otherwise have very soft criteria that the company has to follow. Mostly it deals with ethics rather than a rush towards profit.

If your requirements are in the range of a million to five million dollars, you are better off going to a VC investor. Even here, the investors that could have interest would be the ones with funds of up to $100 million to $200 million. Family funds could be a viable option, particularly the ones that have a focus on your category.

Closer to the $5 million level, strategic investors could also be an option. It has to be kept in mind that strategic investors take a very long time for decision-making. Hence, they may not be viable for early stage investments. If a strategic investor does invest, keep in mind that they are not yet aligning their internal strategy to your solution but are more likely doing this as a risk investment. Only if your startup delivers on the pilot and becomes ready to scale up after de-risking the manufacture is the strategic investor likely to consider you as part of their strategy.

If your requirement is in the range of $5–$15 million, you are definitely in the sweet spot of the larger VC investors as well as strategic investors. VCs would however like to have a short time horizon for the investors compared to strategic investors. At the same time, VCs are more likely to help you to monetise than strategic investors.

Family funds can also be good investors at this time. The investment criteria tend to be far more subjective compared to VC investors. It's particularly important to be introduced rather than cold-call. In addition, it is imperative to ensure that the focus of the fund is aligned to the business of the startup. If a respectable VC or strategic investor considers taking the lead on the investment, a family fund can be an excellent combination since this can protect the rights of the minority (read founders) shareholders.

For anything over $15 million, you are now in the sights of strategic investors as well as a consortium of VC investors. Beyond this point, it simply becomes too large for one investor to pick up.

A very good approach is to try to get different investors lined up and get a consortium of strategic and VC investors. The benefit of this combination is that VCs will try to multiply their money on exit, thereby maximising the value of your equity. At the same time, strategic investors bring a very important attribute, patience.

Patience, as any entrepreneur will confirm, is the most important element since milestones have a tendency of slipping. Payments from customers get delayed. In fact, all the things that can go right get delayed and all things that can go wrong happen early. This is where strategic investors show their value, since they have a very clear focus on insourcing technology of the startup and commercialise. Strategic investors also recognise that these delays happen. Thus, if your milestones slip, or if you need more money to get there, strategic investors are more likely to cough up.

In a tough environment, VC investors also like strategic investors as that then enables VCs to have a clear exit by selling their stake to the strategic investor. VCs also know that once a strategic investor comes in, he's likely to go on supporting you.

At amounts of over $15 million, another segment of investors that becomes relevant is sovereign funds. Their criteria tend to be subjective, and it is important to have awareness about what they require before applying for the funding. The time required to get the funding tends to be even longer than that of strategic investors and ranges from 6 months to over a year. An introduction is quite important but not imperative.

A bonus of accessing sovereign funds is that they are able to enable local banks and financial institutions to jointly participate in the funding. They are thus able to create their own consortia. And consortium building, as the next chapter will demonstrate, is no trivial matter.

7.12.2 Risk Profile

If your startup's risk profile is high, it is always better to get investors to share the risk. However, if you have a very high degree of certainty that you will be able to start getting returns from your startup early, it's better to go in for loans.

The way you can share your risk is by getting investors to invest in equity of the startup. Thus, if there is a delay in getting to a positive cash flow, they can't put pressure to get their return. If the risk is low and the cash flows in a short period are assured, it is better to get the funds as debt or loans. This way, you capture the upside potential and value generation and limit the downside by way of dilution of the startup.

7.12.3 Timing of Funding

One of the things that entrepreneurs miscalculate is the time of the revenue. At the same time, their limited experience results in not considering some expenses or being too conservative about them.

Entrepreneurs are inherently optimistic people; otherwise, they would stay with their safe jobs in big companies. This optimism often leads to assuming that revenue has a higher probability of happening, or even more dangerous, that it is likely to happen earlier than it does. Entrepreneurs, knowingly or otherwise, forget about things that can delay revenue. This is similar to trying to lose weight. When you're asked to remember what you ate through the day, you're more likely than not to forget a few items that you munched on. On the other hand, you're never going to put items you didn't eat on the list. And so the grams creep on.

Most startups don't go bust because the ideas are inherently bad. They go bust because the company runs out of funds. The cash flow is therefore critical. Something as simple as a waiting period for cash to come in after you provide your solutions to initial customers needs to be considered carefully. Be conservative. Like they say, it's better to be one hour early for your flight than a minute late. And so it is with cash in the bank.

Optimism is great when you're talking to investors about the potential for your solution and the size of the market to be addressed. However, when it comes to cash, raise much more than you think you'll need. Even technology co-founders can underestimate the requirement for cash for machines or processes, mainly because they are used to fabricating tools and making their own machines when they are in the lab environment.

When we closed a large round of funding, the team's initial focus was to pinpoint milestones and begin working on them. After receiving the bids for the machines required for the pilot, one technical co-founder said they seemed too expensive and that he could make them for <20% of the amount quoted. We thus took the approach of building our own machine. This was precisely the wrong approach, since it took much longer to build our machine, and we had to go up the learning curve when things didn't work.

Takeaway *Once you get funding, focus on delivering. Change the "can be done cheaper in-house" research mindset to "get it done fast and professionally" commercial mindset.*

7.12.4 Prioritisation

The prioritisation of investors normally relates to VC investors, since if other investors are in the sweet spot of investment, they can be accessed in parallel. The reason that prioritisation is important is because it takes a lot of time and effort to respond to investors' queries. At the same time, it is important to keep them engaged once they become interested.

Several important elements need to be kept in mind when accessing VC investors. Since there are so many of them, it's a good idea to prioritise. The best VC investors are the ones that challenge the company and the team to achieve more than the founders thought possible. This is done by ensuring that the company is able to address the most important customer segments and by opening the necessary doors to facilitate this. Top-tier VC investors have very substantial networks and will facilitate this.

If a given VC has had a number of funds in the past, it implies that the VC has a good network with potential customers and partners. The successes of the startups that the VC has invested in are also an important attribute of the quality of the VC.

An important criterion for whether a given VC is suitable for you is by checking whether the VC has invested in a competing company. If the risk of knowledge proliferation is very high with the competing company, drop the priority of this VC. However, since most VCs have a portfolio strategy when investing in a sector, it's not in your own best interest to be paranoid.

The funding cycle of the VC is also an important element in determining whether he is likely to invest. Normally, VCs raise funds for 8–10 years. At the end of this period, they have to return the funds to their investors. If the VC has already invested a large amount of the funds available or if they are late into their own funding cycle, they are unlikely to invest.

The funding cycle is similar to applying to MBA before the first closing of the applications. You definitely have a better chance of getting in. But, if you apply on the final closing of applications, you need to be significantly better than the other candidates who applied earlier for the MBA school to knock another candidate off the list.

Another important element of prioritising investors is geographical focus. We once contacted a top Silicon Valley investor who did not have a presence in Europe. Since our business was within their area of focus, they had a lot of questions and we of course spent time and effort in responding. Finally, they said they might consider co-investing if a local lead investor could be found. In the meantime, we had provided information that could be used to strengthen a competitor in this increasingly global business.

Takeaway *When initiating discussions with an investor, ask whether they can consider taking the lead or being the only investor. The answer can save you much heartache.*

7.12.5 Diversify Discussions

A friend of mine started a company with a high fund requirement due to regulatory purposes in his industry. The requirement was €25 million for the first round, a very high number by any standard. He got into intense discussions with a very wealthy individual who had already made his billions.

Since the discussions were directly with the wealthy individual being the investor, there was no specific formal process. In the midst of the discussions, the investor suffered a heart attack. The entire set of discussions, which had been ongoing for several months, got delayed by a month. Since he had a great degree of confidence in the wealthy investor's capability to invest, he had omitted to have parallel discussions with other investors.

When the wealthy investor recovered, his priorities changed from getting a return on his investment to wanting to make a difference with his money. While this was probably a good thing for several charities, it was less so for the startup, since the business plan dealt with the prosaic reality of making a significant return and less so towards making the world a significantly better place.

And so my friend went back to working in the extremely well-compensated industry focussing on the acquisition of distressed assets and left another dream in the dust.

7.13 Geographical Differences Between Investors

VCs in different parts of the world look for different attributes in companies.

When we began talking to the US-based investors, they kept telling us that we were not going to be competitive enough. It was later that we realised that the US investors were reducing the milestones that we were providing by 1/3 to 50 % and increasing the cost by 50 %. Since our team was predominantly composed of scientists, they tended to be conservative as well.

When we said we would be able to achieve certain milestones in 3 years, the US investors felt we would take 4–5 years to get there. At the same time, being very light on marketing and business became a huge disadvantage for us, since US investors like the strategy for going to market early on.

When we began talking to investors in Europe, they took much of what we stated at face value. This included the things that we believed we could achieve and the funds required to achieve this. They understood that so long as it was a breakthrough technology and the market was moving in this direction, it was okay to focus more on taking the technology out of the lab before the company began focussing on marketing and business development. A typical attribute of European investors is that they look for deeper and more mature technology and less spin.

Just as there is a difference in investors based on geography, there is also a significant difference in the startups based on geography. US-based startups are earlier stage when they get funding and therefore have a higher degree of technology risk. It is common for startups with hundreds of millions of dollars of funding to change technology focus since, from their perspective, technology is merely the enabler, which is one component of the business.

European startups have a much higher survival rate compared to the US-based startups. At the same time, for the startups that get towards commercialisation, being US-based enables them to get to the market faster since go-to-market is a huge focus. Thus, they scale up faster once the concept is demonstrated. European startups have a very clear focus on strong technology, and technology is considered to be the entire foundation, rather than simply the enabler, for the business.

7.14 Reason for Fundraising

An important question that any startup needs to ask is not only how much money is required but why the money is being raised. The answer will enable you to identify the investors that better fit the funding requirement. Early on in the fundraising process, this seems like a moot point, since the only thing that a startup can imagine is having money in the bank.

Investors who are aligned to your vision of how the technology can best be commercialised and are willing to open doors to enable that are truly the angel investors. But there are also other investors who invest in certain sectors just because other investors are doing it.

If your investor's timeline for exit is not aligned with your own timeline, this can result in undue pressure to deliver in unrealistic timelines. In a worst case, the investor may force you to take the product to the market even when it is not fully developed to facilitate their exit. This may be a good strategy for the investor since it increases the perceived value of the startup. However, for the startup itself, this destroys value since the founders are left holding the remnants of the reputation of the startup long after the investor has exited.

Investors can also force the founders to sell the company because they want to exit. If you read the fine print, you'll realise that this is one of the rights of the investors. It's called "drag along" and it's a standard clause in investor agreements.

If the funding from investors comes in the form of tranches, this becomes another way for investors to reduce risk in case the startup is unable to achieve key milestones. But it is also likely that the market seems to change and the investors lose their conviction. In such case, even though the startup may be overachieving on its milestones, the investors will refuse to invest in future tranches. In legal agreements, this is reflected when it says the investors have the option to but cannot be forced to invest in future tranches.

The right investors also provide credibility to the startup and attract other investors in future rounds. Since a startup always needs more money, more so if it's successful than if it's not, it's good to be aware of potential investors and how they can be motivated to invest.

A Harvard Business School study on the size of startups found that the larger the startup by way of employees and investors, the more stable it became and the more resilient it became to closing down. This is because of the reputational damage to the stakeholders if the company closes down. This holds true when the company's products are ready and the most important elements to ensure survival is getting access to customers or route-to-market.

However, the inverse is true when the company is still working on the pilot and the technology is not fully mature. We saw this play out in the flexible solar cell business. American companies built large teams in areas like sales and business development while their technologies were not fully mature. Being in Europe, our mindset was conservative and we kept strengthening our manufacturing while keeping other areas like sales, marketing and PR very light. Eventually, in spite of having funding 50 to almost 100 times our own funding, many of these American companies could not survive their cash burn and closed down. We continued to take small but meaningful steps in manufacturing and lived to see another day.

Starting a company is a privilege, notwithstanding the blood, sweat and uncertainty involved. As entrepreneurs say, if they had known the amount of effort and frustration involved before they began, they would probably not have gone in for it. Having done it, they would not have it any other way. This is the reason it's so important to find the investor who will stay the course.

7.15 Your Positioning

You may consider it early or selfish to begin thinking about your own future within the startup when you are considering investors, but it is a fact that some investors like to replace business drivers and get their own members of the management team. While this may be good for the company, it may not be so for you, especially if you are considering the startup from a long-term perspective.

As the business driver, your role may be the most tenuous since the technology experts among the co-founders are likely to be required for far longer to make it happen. If you have the luxury of choice regarding selecting investors, it is important to get the ones who share your vision, unless you see yourself as a serial entrepreneur and see the startup as a stepping stone.

Among investors, VCs have long been the preferred choice. However, this is no longer the case. Before Internet startups began constituting a large proportion of startups, VCs were used to waiting for a number of years before expecting a return. However, with a larger proportion of startups coming from IT, the VC investors now expect a return in months or up to 2 years. For startups focussing on manufacturing or those driven by technology, this time period is simply too short.

Other investors like family funds or foundations are now very attractive alternatives since they have more patience and are comfortable waiting longer before they expect a return from their investments.

7.16 Valuation

Valuation is the pre-investment value of the company. The reason this is so important is because it determines how much of your company the investor owns after he invests the given amount of money.

Planning for a high valuation is like planning for admission into Harvard for your MBA. The process of planning starts long before you actually apply.

Each of the points below increases the valuation of the company. Several of these can be accomplished without any advancement in the technology or financial investments. But since these are important for investors, they are worth considering (Fig. 7.2).

7.16.1 Idea

There are certain easy benchmarks to determine the valuation of a startup. If it's just an idea, it's mostly worth just about as much as the paper it's written on. This is notwithstanding whatever you hear to the contrary, including eBay and Google being started that way.

The success stories are the exceptions and hide the fact that there are probably a bunch of PhDs or folks who dropped out of college half way to pursue their idea. The reality is that every MBA student has a repertoire of ideas that can be written down on the back of an envelope, but which will never see the light of day.

The reason the idea itself does not have more value is that if it's only one person with the idea, there is a high probability that you could change your mind about doing this full time. Additionally, investors also perceive that if you've been unable to convert more people to working with you on the idea, either the idea itself is not very good or your selling skills are the pits. In either case, it's a bad investment.

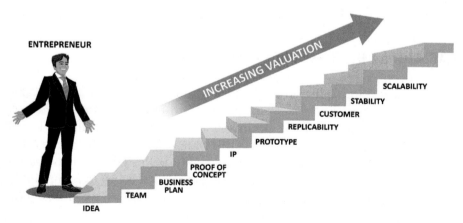

Fig. 7.2 Determinants of valuation

7.16.2 Idea + Business Plan

If you've prepared the full business plan documents, including the executive summary, the presentation, the business plan and comprehensive financials, it tells the investors that you are fully dedicated to the idea. It begins to have a certain perceived value. This is still worth in the tens of thousands of dollars.

7.16.3 Idea + Business Plan + Technology

Assuming the idea is backed by technology, this idea suddenly gets a certain foundation. If you have patents, this definitely increases the perceived value of the company as investors now feel that your idea is defendable. In a high-growth market, protection of an idea can itself be worth a significant amount of money.

This protection becomes the barrier-to-entry for other competitors who may want to enter the same field. Investors realise that if you've been able to do the hard work of not only getting the idea, but having a patent to protect it—yours now has less chance of being a half-baked fantasy. This may now have a perceived value of up to 100,000 dollars.

While it is difficult to value a particular patent, two recent cases give a reasonable indication as to the value of patents. When Google purchased Motorola's patents and when Apple and Microsoft purchased Nortel's patents, the average price per patent was between $500,000 and $750,000. The lower price included the patents pending. If only the price per granted patent is considered rather than for patents pending, the average price per patent was approximately $750,000 (Economistcom 2015).

7.16.4 Idea + Business Plan + Technology + Team

If you have a team dedicated to the idea with the technology, the idea may now begin to have a life of its own. This can now have a ballpark of around a million dollars. Thus, if an investor invests a million into the company, he will end up owning half the company. At this time, you're probably already fully involved in it with funds from friends and family. Before getting an investor, it is a good idea to do some of the other things provided below to pump up the pre-money value of the startup. Alternatively, a better option is to invest more time working on the idea to get it to the next level (also provided below).

7.16.5 Idea + Business Plan + Technology + Team + Prototype

The next step in the progression of the idea is having a prototype. This not only enables you to increase the perceived value of the startup, it is also the all-important step of showcasing that your idea is something that can be done. You're now likely to get taken more seriously by angel investors. At this time, your perceived valuation is likely to be in the range of a couple of million dollars.

Thus, with a startup that has a team, a prototype and a patent, you could justify a company valuation of up to two million dollars. If the market is significant enough and your competitive advantage sustainable, this figure could go up to tens of millions of dollars.

7.16.6 Idea + Business Plan + Technology + Team + Prototype + Customers

The most important element that influences valuation is paying customers. If customers are willing to pay for the solution, this demonstrates that there will be a market for the product. If the solution is not yet ready, the fact that customers are interested in paying for the solution on a pilot basis when it becomes available provides confidence to investors. And additional confidence translates to closing a deal with an investor or improving the terms of the deal. Beyond this, the valuation depends on the size of the vision that you can show to the investor.

The question that most startups face is how to increase the perceived value of the company without actually having a product. The increase in the valuation is particularly important in the initial stages of the startup since this is the time when you have complete freedom to drive the company forward in your vision without the encumbrances imposed by investors. The valuation is also important since the higher the valuation, the lower the proportion of the company that you'll have to part with to get the initial funding from investors. This perceived valuation holds true through the life of the company.

Let's assume you have an idea, a technology, a business plan and a team. The team is probably working in their own research or corporate jobs as it's frequently useful to be able to afford something to eat even the team aspires to have their own startup! At the same time, it's not possible to take any big steps like having a prototype or setting up a pilot plant. These things take time and money. After all, that's what the initial funding is for.

Beyond this, the valuation of the startup can be increased if you have suppliers who are able to provide raw materials, machines or the components that make your solution. It has to be kept in mind that these do not require advancement in the technology or investment in building IP, prototype or a pilot facility.

7.17 How Much Is Enough

It is commonly understood that raising too much money can be a trap. The reason is that for additional money, the startup has to make aggressive promises to investors. As soon as the funds are in the bank, the clock starts ticking. Before you know it, you're running behind in your milestones. And so the pressure from investors to deliver begins. With this, rash decisions are made which the startup lives to regret, since the consequences follow, unless you are lucky enough to exit in the meantime.

But a more important distinction is between how much the technology founders think is enough and how much is actually enough for the startup. In Flisom, we were in the midst of our scale-up and asked the technology team how much they though we would require for equipment and other consumables. They provided us with a fund requirement of $25 million. We began discussions with investors with this as a basis. Part way through the discussions, we realised that the money had been calculated only up to the installation of the machinery. Although this was an important element for us, it was irrelevant for the investors. Their interest was in the deliverable with the funding, since this would enable them to showcase a greater perceived value of the company to their board as a result of the investment or higher valuation for future rounds of funding by new investors.

The difference between the setting up of the new equipment and the deliverables with this equipment was almost a year and entailed running cost including salaries, consumables, service and maintenance and other administration cost. The final amount we ended up raising was higher, much higher. The investors could have baulked and walked away. They did not, but it wasn't easy.

7.18 The Finance Mindset

Startups often underestimate the challenges of managing the money once they get it. This is particularly the case with technology companies, which have been run by their technical founders since inception and have grown organically. Although the companies may be a decade old, the mindset is that the finance is about ensuring that there is enough to pay the employees and some for the R&D required for organic growth.

When larger investors look at the company, particularly for rounds larger than $5 million, their concern is regarding the actual financial requirement of the company. This is because no investor wants to go to his board 3 months after the money is raised, to say that the company actually needs 30% more, because the company forgot about the additional expenses of setting up international offices or higher legal fees or expenses relating to marketing or business development.

Other than the challenge of having to go to your recent investors on your knees for this additional funding to achieve the agreed upon milestones, you end up with additional conditions that can be onerous at best and can result in steeper dilution of the founders' equity at worst. Additionally, this can also impact the credibility of the founders as management of the larger company.

An effective way to mitigate this is by identifying a CFO. This could be a person who may be hired by the startup with the new funds. But this person could also help the company to do the financials or at the very least, validate them when the startup goes to investors.

Once the investors invest, they also like to speak to someone who speaks their language. This finds the technology founders completely out of their depth. The reason for this is that investors like to see their money working for the startup when it is not being used. Common optimisation techniques include planning for the fund requirement and currencies in which the funds are to be utilised, in case of international machinery acquisition. In this way, in case your currency depreciates by 20% compared to the currency in which the machines are to be procured, you're not negatively impacted.

The financial person can also get the funds to work by converting money into fixed deposits for the period that the funds are not required. The interest can easily pay for salaries of a couple of headcounts. Last but not the least, it helps to have a person who acts as a buffer in case there are financial challenges that the technical team may be ill suited to.

Investors have only two major questions after they provide the funding. One relates to milestones. The other is the cash situation and how it's being utilised. It thus makes sense to have someone on the team who can relate to what customers are talking about, since you will most likely need them for future rounds. It never hurts to make nice with people with the money.

7.19 Credibility: And How to Get It

There are certain things that can increase the valuation of the startup or increase your chances of getting funding. One is an advisory board or a group of advisors. This is much easier to get than one imagines. The most important step in the journey, as they say, is always the first one. In this case, the credibility of the first advisor will influence how easily you are able to get other advisors of similarly high credibility.

Startups with experienced entrepreneurs try and get very high-profile advisors to add credibility to the company. At least one of our competitors in the USA got a Nobel Laureate to be an advisor. This, notwithstanding that the area of competence of the advisor was completely different from the area of focus of the company.

7.20 Valuation: The Investor's Perspective

With all the general trends in valuation mentioned above, investors will always look at reference points in the industry when arriving at a valuation. One reference point is the valuation of competitors in the geography of relevance. Since startups increasingly operate in a global environment, the valuation of the major competitors globally is of relevance. When using this as a basis, a competitive analysis of the startup's strengths vis-à-vis the competitors can become an excellent handle. If for nothing else, this is important because it pre-empts the investor pulling down the startup's valuation by stating that competitors are ahead, since this sends a message that the startup knows its value.

An argument of investors when deciding on a valuation is that the competitors are now stronger having received funding, whereas the startup's perceived valuation will increase partly due to the investment and brand name of the investor. In such way, both startup and the investor may have strong reasons why the valuation should be of a certain level.

However, the only defining valuation is the one at which the investor is willing to come in and the leverage of the startup. Only when the startup has other options can it negotiate from a position of strength. In other words, negotiation from strength only works when you are able to walk away. Since most startups do not have this luxury, the important thing is to close the round of funding, even at a lower valuation, since this enables you to commercialise. Even a smaller size of a much larger pie is much more than 100 % of a really small pie.

When investors look at valuation documents prepared by the startup or the financial advisors of the startup, it is not to see the valuation arrived at by the startup. This is because everyone knows that it is possible to tweak all figures and arrive at whatever cash flow projections or valuation is desired. Rather, investors want to see if the financials, including the valuation provided by the startup, consider all appropriate assumptions and the methodology makes sense. This will tell them that you've thought through the process carefully.

We hired a global audit firm to prepare the valuation methodology and pitch to potential investors. When we began discussions with the transaction advisors representing one of the investors, they looked at the financials prepared by our advisors and decided to completely discount it all. In effect, they began the discussions on our financial projections from scratch and prepared the whole thing once again.

On inquiring why they had discarded our financials, they said we had omitted to consider the reducing cost of raw materials in the coming years, which would have reflected more competitive pricing in the coming years. If such an important element had been ignored, they felt the valuation in particular and financials in general could not be adequately represented. Thus, a seemingly minor omission could risk our credibility relating to our financial projections.

Takeaway *The devil is really in the details. Since you get but one chance with each investor, make it count.*

7.21 Bankability

This is the magic word for a certain class of investors who look for credibility prior to investing. These investors include banks and financial institutions as well as select strategic investors.

For example, if you want to instal solar modules, you go to a bank and ask for a loan to do so. The bank would like to know how the solar modules perform over a period of time. You would find it relatively easy to get this information in respect of conventional rigid solar modules since they've been commercially available for over 30 years. However, you would struggle to get the same information for flexible and highly efficient solar modules even though they're cheaper and as efficient, simply because they haven't been around that long.

Thus, everything else being the same, the flexible solar modules would not be considered bankable whereas rigid ones would. Investors for whom bankability is important focus more on improvements on conventional technology rather than something radically new. Knowing how important bankability is for investors being targeted by you and whether your solution ticks this box can save time and effort.

7.22 Going Public

Many companies feel that a sound alternative to going to investors discussed above is to get quoted on a stock exchange. This is what Daystar did in 2003.

Daystar was a company focussing on flexible solar cells. The management believed that the best way to raise money was to get listed which it did on NASDAQ. The company raised about ten million dollars (Nasdaqcom 2015).

What the company did not realise was that once you list on any stock exchange, the market determines your value. One disadvantage of this is that if you want to raise additional funding, you have to do so by way of secondary offerings. The valuation of the company is now already defined by the markets, so the company can only raise additional funding by providing a significant discount to the share price. Financial investors typically do not like to touch companies at this stage since the potential to multiply their investments by x-times is no longer available.

Going public implies that you can no longer control the valuation of the company and that it is now determined by the perceptions of the market. You can no longer control the story since not only is all the information covered by news articles and equity analysts, it is compulsory to submit periodic reports to the stock exchange authority. This takes the subjectivity out and with that the possibility of the valuation upside pertaining to the subjectivity.

The secondary offering can be a minefield since these are normally done at a discount to the share price at a given time. The size of the discount reflects the desperation of the company. Although a greater discount enables the company to attract a higher level of new investment, it sends a very negative signal to current shareholders who now realise that their shares are now worth much less.

The second problem for Daystar was that there was suddenly a huge amount of paperwork and administration required to comply with the regulations pertaining to companies quoted in the stock exchange. This put a drag on the limited resources of the management, which should have been focussing on getting the business off the ground and transitioning the technology to commercialisation.

The final problem for Daystar was that like all stock-quoted companies, it needed to provide updates on a regular basis to analysts who were following the company. The business of these analysts is to keep track of milestones that the company misses and promises that the company does not keep. Additionally, even if the company hits all its milestones, it can be pilloried if the market moves forward and the company seems to be getting left behind. This can be a huge and ongoing distraction for the company since any "sell" rating from an analyst can send the stock price plummeting. This in turn can have a negative impact on the most valuable assets of the company, its employees.

A combination of these factors pulled Daystar into a downward spiral where all that was required was additional investment and patience. This is an example of the result of going public too early when the company's products are not yet market-ready.

Ascent Solar (Wikipediaorg 2015) was another such company that decided to go public when it needed additional funds. The problem was that the company was still doing development and its products were not fully market-ready. Now there are certain industries where companies can go public without having a mature product and revenue. One such industry is the pharmaceutical sector. Here, the market is able to put a value on companies based on universally accepted norms reflecting the progress that the company has made depending on the stage in the approval process, even though the company may be projecting losses for the foreseeable future. Solar is not one of those industries.

Ascent went public in 2006 at an IPO price of $5.5. In the following 2 years, it raised its first of several rounds of funding in secondary offerings. At this time, Ascent raised funds at $8–$10 per share.

The market soon perceived the gap between milestones achieved and those promised. This immediately had a negative impact on the perception of the company. The shares began a downward spiral. This was in contrast to the achievement of key milestones by the company towards commercialisation. Since the company was listed in the stock exchange, there was very little control that the management had over how the company was perceived.

In 2010, Ascent's shares were being quoted at $6.5 per share. At that point, the company decided to have another secondary issue at $4.15. The discount was clearly to attract new investors. Post this investment, the stock continued their spiral downward since the original investors continued to get diluted due to the discount offered to new investors.

In 2012, Ascent raised money on a secondary stock offering. This time, the shares were being quoted at $1.8 per share. The desperation of the company was reflected in the price at which the new shares were offered, which was

$1.2. In spite of the company getting new contracts to sell its products that were finally coming to the market, the perception was very negative. In the meantime, notwithstanding the future of the company, the shareholders and early investors had consistently been diluted. Ascent had ridden on the wave of hopes about PV and found it difficult to live up to the perceptions created in the minds of investors. In 2014, Ascent did a reverse split, where ten shares got cumulated into one share, in order to comply with the NASDAQ minimum bid price requirement. At the time of writing, the cumulated shares were trading at around $0.1 per share. Brutal indeed, if you were left holding the baby.

If you are a private company funded by VCs or other sets of investors, your company valuation is not publicly known. It is thus possible to create an aura of exclusivity or indeed ride the next wave of perception and expectation. This can enable you to get funding from the next round of investors at a high valuation.

Interestingly, if you are in an area considered "hot" by investors, the valuations can be significantly higher than the capitalisation of publicly quoted competitors, even though they may be closer to market. In this sense, your pre-money value for new investors depends on how big your vision is since being in the black is not yet on the radar. Once the IPO happens, not only is the company tracked for performance solely driven towards revenue and profits but the market capitalisation is there for all to see. This makes it difficult to get additional funding at a premium once you are publicly quoted. The example of Ascent doing secondary offerings after its IPO at a lower price illustrates this quandary.

One thing that many founders perceive is that once the company is listed, they'll be able to sell their shares in the open market and exit. But in practice, investors like to ensure that founders have a lock-in period after the IPO, giving reality a chance to catch up with the company's valuation. Incidentally, investors have no such lock-in. Thus, if the company's business model is flawed or the company is not there yet with its revenue forecasts, it's more than likely that the company's shares are not worth much.

The second consequence of the company's shares getting diluted is that the founders' shares get diluted faster. Early investors often have antidilution clauses built into their investment agreements. Due to this, the founders' shares are worth very little, if anything, and at the same time, they have to work in the company due to onerous lock-in conditions like non-compete. These factors make it very unattractive to go public too early.

If the company is still privately funded, it is relatively easy to influence (manipulate?) public opinion or ride the wave of buzz and get the next round of funding at a nice bump in the valuation. The current investors have no motivation to share their (adverse) views, since they do want new investors to come in with more money at ever-increasing valuation and, if the current investors are lucky, enable them to get a quiet exit. It is also possible to provide key bits of news that can influence the coolness factor in order to get funding at a respectable valuation.

7.23 Crowdfunding

One evening, Shane Small and Elan Lee got together for a game of cards. They put a joker in the deck and whoever got it first lost. They called it BombSquad. After neglecting friends and family for a few weeks, they came up with a few rules. At this point, Matt Inman of *The Oatmeal* joined them and Exploding Kittens LLC (Explodingkittenscom 2015) was born. They went to Kickstarter.com in order to see if others found the card game they had created as compelling and with a view to do crowdfunding or crowd-sourcing. With a funding target of $10,000, they started well and kept going. Their funding target was reached in 10 minutes and overachieved by *10 times* in the first one hour. The amount raised at the end of the 30-day campaign exceeded $8 million.

The most remarkable thing about this was that the team did not have to commit anything to the backers other than a pack of cards. Effectively, no dilution. The age of crowdfunding had arrived.

After we began our startup and initiated discussions with financial investors, we had visions of investors trying to beat our door down, cheques in hand. This picture began to change after several rejections from investors. Although we always heard from people who saw as much value in highly efficient and flexible solar cells to charge their mobiles, laptops and homes as we did, we lamented that there was no way to sell shares directly to people. Clearly, we were not the only startup to think so.

With VCs able to raise ever-larger funds, it is becoming increasingly difficult to raise smaller funds for early stage startups. This is even more so if the startup is not in any sector that happens to have the buzz at a given point in time. We began our clean energy company before clean energy became a buzzword. At the time of writing, the buzz can be considered to definitely have fizzled out. The streets, as they say, are strewn with corpses of startups that raised money by riding the buzz without the technology to back them up. And clean energy continues to survive—and eventually will enable a cleaner world.

Crowdfunding is the solution to the conundrum faced by startups with good product ideas that simply cannot get funding from conventional investors. Although this is still in its nascent stages, companies with solid product ideas are able to get funding that effectively results in negative inventory. People pay money with which the company is able to produce the products that are then delivered to these people.

The benefit of crowdfunding is that the startup does not get diluted since only products are provided to the individual investors and not the equity in the startup. This is quite likely to undergo evolution since first mover customers know that they are taking a risk by buying into new and untested products. These customers also recognise that the company gets a bump in the valuation by shipping products out. Due to these reasons, this business model may evolve to provide some additional benefits to these customers/micro-investors.

The great advantage of crowdfunding is that it provides a route-to-market for new products. This is normally the biggest challenge for young companies. Once products are in the hands of a small number of people, this also provides confidence to investors. The other advantage is you get first-hand and prompt feedback about what particular attributes of the product are of the most perceived value to end users, since it is well known that many new products are used in ways that are different from those that the founders originally intended. The example of the colour of the solar modules by NATO rather than simply the efficiency, discussed earlier in the book, is a case in point.

The risk of going down this route is that if the products are not up to snuff, it can have a negative impact on the startup's reputation at a time when the company can ill afford this. However, this is definitely a sound alternative to tapping your own dwindling funds and at the same time finds out if the product will actually fly.

7.24 Interest

Young startups frequently get excited when investors say the startups seem interesting. "Interesting" is unfortunately one of the most ill-considered terms in the lexicon of starting a company.

When startup business ideas are shown to investors, their frequent response is that it is "interesting". This leads the startup along a garden path where it remains hopeful of securing funding from the investor.

When an investor first shows interest in you, it may appear foolish and a sign of desperation to push him towards making a decision. It is however fully appropriate to ask what the next steps and timelines towards closing the investment round are. These tough questions will enable you to know if the investor considers you *interesting* by way of becoming aware of new and emerging business models or as a startup competing with one he may have already invested in to gather competitive intelligence. Asking for a timeline to close really puts him on the spot towards putting the investment where his mouth is. It will also demonstrate your discipline regarding the timeline to the investors, which doesn't hurt you when you get to the next stage of discussing milestones. And as you'll realise, it really *is* about perceptions.

7.25 Event Organisers

Recognising a niche based on hopefulness, event organising companies try to invite these startup companies to events where they can hope to make a pitch of between 5 and 15 minutes in front of investors. These event organisers also charge fees from startups for the privilege of presenting to investors.

It's good to recognise that you, the startup, are the product and the investors are charged hefty amounts to attend as well. Asking the event organisers to sponsor your trip is fully justified since at a minimum, this will result in their having to demonstrate why attending this is of value to your startup. It's also good to be upfront about the value that your presence brings to their show, since it tells them that you know what the score is.

At events like this, the greatest value is in networking with the investors participating since this enables you to share your story with them prior to the meeting. When you meet the investors at the event, you gain an edge compared to other startups vying for their attention. The face-to-face meeting also enables you to take the discussion further with interested investors or, as importantly, knock investors that don't fit off the list.

Event organisers are normally loath to share this information prior to the event. In case you encounter such resistance, a good argument is that this will improve your chances of closing a deal with a participating investor. This can then become a very powerful reference for the event organiser. He's more likely to help you with the investor if he knows you can get the funding without his help.

Takeaway Summary

1. *A startup is like a marriage—if the team does not get along in the beginning, things are unlikely to improve after the kids, the mortgage and dirty dishes hit the fan.*
2. *Targeting the right investors is as important as avoiding the wrong ones.*
3. *Know what you want and whether VCs can help. If it doesn't fit, find other investor groups. It's not only about just the money.*
4. *Insist on discussions with executive sponsors; ensure that the investment discussions are in their system; and be patient.*
5. *Take away learning whenever you can, you never know when it pays off.*
6. *Once you get funding, focus on delivering. Change the "can be done cheaper in-house" research mindset to "get it done fast and professionally" commercial mindset.*
7. *When initiating discussions with an investor, ask whether they can consider taking the lead or being the only investor. The answer can save you much heartache.*
8. *The devil is really in the details. Since you get but one chance with each investor, make it count.*

References

Cnetcom. (2015). *CNET.* Retrieved December 1, 2015, from http://www.cnet.com/news/dell-apple-should-close-shop/

Economistcom. (2015). *The economist.* Retrieved December 1, 2015, from http://www.economist.com/blogs/babbage/2011/08/valuing-patents

Explodingkittenscom. (2015). *Explodingkittenscom.* Retrieved December 1, 2015, from http://www.explodingkittens.com/

Nasdaqcom. (2015). *NASDAQcom.* Retrieved December 1, 2015, from http://www.nasdaq.com/markets/ipos/company/daystar-technologies-inc-593356-36366

Wikipediaorg. (2015). *Wikipediaorg.* Retrieved December 1, 2015, from https://en.wikipedia.org/wiki/Ascent_Solar

8

Closing the Deal and Getting the Funding

You've come to the point where investors are interested in you. The interest of one investor invariably gives one the aura of invincibility. You *know* other investors are going to bite and at significantly better valuations. The first investor is only a validation of your conviction that this thing was going to fly and you're now in serious play.

Sorry to crash your party, but sometimes one investor is all you ever get. The startup world is strewn with corpses of companies that could have changed the world but waited for a better valuation.

Even investors recognise the impact of any delay once they give a term sheet. Be aware that they do this for a living and see smart people like you several times a *day*. The most common risk to investors is that you may shop around with their term sheet to get a better deal. Proceed with caution, since the investor world is much much smaller than you realise, and they do talk to each other, the NDAs notwithstanding.

Further, assuming you get the investment from the investor, this funding itself is not going to make you rich. On the contrary, it will only lock you in with a few peanuts by way of salary, till you actually deliver on your promises. Like in a new relationship, if the investor finds out that you were not faithful and did try to shop around with his term sheet, you will lose credibility when credibility is all that you have going.

© Springer International Publishing Switzerland 2016
A. Sethi, *From Science to Startup*, DOI 10.1007/978-3-319-30424-3_8

8.1   Consortium Building

You have a number of investors and one of them gives you a term sheet with a lower valuation than you expected and lesser money than you asked for. What do you do? Well, you have a number of investors who may be able to put in smaller amounts, so all you have to do is get them together, right? Wrong.

Consortium building is one of the main reasons why investment deals *don't* happen. As soon as you get two competing investors together, they do not strengthen based on the strengths of each investor. On the contrary, they exchange each other's red flags about the investment in your startup since they don't want to look foolish in front of their respective managements by missing out on an obvious reason why you subsequently did not succeed.

We had a similar situation in my first company. We had a number of entities interested, and one top European VC firm built its own consortium with another VC firm. They said they'd give us a term sheet with half of what we wanted and at less than half the valuation we had dreamt up. Our first reaction was to say that we had a strategic investor also interested in being part of a consortium and would introduce this strategic investor for building a consortium. Result: the strategic investor took too long to commit, and we didn't score with the VC firm since they took off their offer to invest without the strategic investor.

Takeaway *Don't assume you're smarter than investors. In particular, don't assume that you can get away by having a bigger ego than them.*

Consortium building is also a bit like getting your competitors together. Remember, investors are on the other side of the table till they invest. By getting your competitors together, you end up weakening your negotiating position.

What you want to do is to get more than one term sheet on the table. This commitment from more than one investor implies that they have already done their due diligence and that there are no red flags. In this case, getting them together may enable you to do two things:

1. You increase the amount of funding by cumulating the investment.
2. The second—and more important—you protect yourself since one investor may be inclined to take advantage of your position after the funding if he's the only investor.

Two investors counterbalance each other, so one investor will stop the second from any action detrimental to your startup and, by implication, to the value of your shares in your company.

It's important to understand how having one strategic investor can be detrimental for your startup. How does this happen? Assume that strategic investor or "SI" is the only investor. If you commercialise successfully, SI may use its veto rights into your startup to force you to sell to its affiliated company at a price lower than market price. SI may subsequently sell at a higher price, capturing more of the profit, leaving your startup a shell company. The other thing that SI can do is to make the investment unattractive for other investors. This is done by putting fine print in the legally binding documents giving SI certain special rights or veto rights on future decisions. Unless SI is willing to relinquish many of these rights, or share these with new investors who come later, the investment becomes less appetising for future investors.

This is where the option of getting a coinvestor, like a VC fund, comes in. For the VC, the benefit is that SI will very likely provide an exit route as your startup commercialises, since SI will want to own all the equity in your company. For you, the benefit is that the VC is clearly focussed on money maximisation, thereby ensuring that you will get the maximum value for your share.

Again, the most important thing is to ensure that both investors are committed. And even then, the use of caution cannot be overstated. At a minimum, consortium building will result in a delay in the proposed investment. You need to ensure that you have enough liquidity to ensure survival through this process.

Takeaway *Delay consortium building unless any one investor cannot commit to the full fund requirement. Remember there's no going back.*

Back to my story: soon after the VCs took their offer off the table, we were able to get some strategic entities engaged. In our wisdom, we decided to get them to start talking to each other. They exchanged red flags about us. Additionally, they tried to align to each other's timeline. Since strategic investors are notoriously slow moving, their discussion resulted in delays in the investment.

This was not all. When one of the strategic investors S1 decided to walk away, the second strategic investor S2 developed cold feet. They stated that they could only invest if we could get another strategic investor S3. We happened to be talking to another entity, S3, and got them to the table. This was our third try at building a consortium. S2 got us to provide deep industry analysis and insights, something we were able to do due to our expertise in the field. This finally resulted in a draft term sheet that became the basis for discussions.

Suddenly, the investor S2 decided to terminate the discussion without providing clear reasons. Naturally, this resulted in a great deal of nervousness for us as well as uncertainty for strategic investor S3. Very shortly after this, we read that S2 had gone ahead and invested almost $60 million to acquire a stake in a competitor in the USA. Things have come full circle because although the US competitor subsequently raised an additional $30 million and is quoted in the stock market, the company is valued at a tiny fraction of its value at the time of its IPO.

In case you were counting, I failed at least three times with consortium building.

One way that consortium building can work is when one investor takes a lead role and confirms its investment, including the amount, valuation and cornerstones. Other investors, who are also interested but do not want to lead the round, can then be brought in. These other investors may not want to take the lead for a multitude or reasons including lack of proximity, inadequate understanding of the sector or limited management personnel to directly oversee the investment.

So long as the potential coinvestors have no remaining red flags and are comfortable coming in under that same valuation and other conditions provided by the lead investor, a consortium is possible. However, even if all conditions are agreed upon, a consortium will result in more time being required for closing the deal. In geographies like the USA, the additional time may not be significant, due to their level of comfort with building consortia. In regions like Europe, the additional time can be 3 months or more over the normal time taken for closing the round.

Additional time will also be required if the various investors in the consortium include VCs, strategic investors or family offices. This is because in addition to the normal areas of conflict and overlap, different investors have different visions for their exit, additional capability to invest in future rounds and interests in strategic rights for commercialisation.

That said, having investors with different backgrounds does provide a better sense of balance. We experienced this first hand. During our fourth and rather substantial round of funding, we knew that this would be beyond that mandate of a single investor to do. Given the timeline for commercialisation and potential exits of the investors, we also knew that this would not be aligned to VC investors. The "only" investors that then remained included strategic investor groups and family offices.

We then got term sheets from the three leading investors, which included two strategic investors and one family office. However, the misalignment between the strategic investors and the family office was almost a bridge too far!

The strategic investors were more interested in the future commercialisation rights of the technology and how they would divvy up the spoils.

The family office was only focussed on the company retaining a presence in Switzerland, rather than having substantial interest in any timeline for return on the investment. The family office had a very large net worth. By investing a few tens of millions of dollars or about 0.5 % million of their net worth (as an example), if they got a return of five times in 5 years, that made it 2.5 % of their net worth. Only when we put ourselves in their shoes were we able to understand why their main driver was not the return on investment.

The investment of the family office was thus due to a belief in the sector and to retain the competitive advantage of Switzerland since the technology had been developed there. The involvement that they wanted was so low that they didn't even want to look at the legal papers, conditions, milestones and deliverables, so long as they got the right number of shares for their investment. It was only when we insisted that they take a board seat that they said they would consider it. That begins to provide a view of their understated approach.

Takeaway 1 *Don't assume financial return is key for all investors.*

Takeaway 2 *Investor alignment is key to consortium building. Let one take the lead so you deal only with one entity representing all investors.*

8.2   Time Is Critical

When starting up, there are so many things that need to be done that one tries to postpone the time when meetings with investors have to be organised. These include, but are not limited to, getting a crisp website, financials, look-and-feel of the presentation and even business cards.

This is also because you want to put your best foot forward with investors to create the best impression possible. There is however the risk of too much delay.

In my own company, I recall how we agonised over the colour schemes of our presentation and business plan, where we had extensive use of charts. We worked on the financials to the point where they were about 65 printed pages long, *in font 6*. That's how complicated we made it. Perhaps this was also due to the fact that we let loose a PhD in physics on the technical numbers. We then tried to do business and financial scenario planning and got some McKinsey suits in for that purpose on a moonlighting basis (yes, it's possible to do that).

In retrospect, the most important element, other than the differentiator of the business case, is the drive of the founders. In our first funding round with an angel investor, we were told that the reason for the investment was that the business driver was with the technical team, giving a sense of balance and a focus towards commercialisation.

During the larger second round of investment, led by a strategic investor, the investor's board was 50:50 on whether to invest. This, by the way, is pretty much the norm, since not all the individuals on the investor's side are likely to be absolutely in sync with the concept, technology and vision. The decision to invest or not to do so really comes down to 51:49.

In our case, the strategic investor's board's split was against us, since from their perspective, we were too early stage. This was because our requirement was sub-$10 million and their annual turnover was closer to $100 billion. What tilted the odds in our favour was our passion and earnestness. Through all the agonising work on the presentation and fine-tuning the financials, this was one factor that we had not accounted for: just be real.

Takeaway *Never underestimate that power of conviction. As long as you have conviction and excitement about your vision, there's no wrong way to present to investors.*

8.3   Easier to Say No

No One Ever Got Fired for Buying IBM. This was the old adage when there was a lot of uncertainty about IT. You were happy to pay more to IBM because you didn't want someone questioning an incorrect decision.

In the same way, no investment manager ever got fired for saying no to an investment. Technology co-founders often do not realise this, since their working lives are built on the premise that they are right, and the startup is founded on the outstanding work that they may have done. Investment managers on the other hand look for reasons why they should *not* invest in a company.

This is similar to the medical profession. My father, who was a doctor, once confided in me that he worked by elimination. No, not of patients in case you're wondering. He figured out the ailment by eliminating other ailments based on symptoms that his patients did not have.

8.4 Interested Investors

You're having a number of very advanced conversations with large and credible investors who are very interested. Let's read that again. You're having a number of *very advanced* conversations with *large and credible* investors who are very *interested.*

By "very advanced" you mean they have requested all the documents you have including the executive summary, the business plan, the financials and the "stack" or the presentation. They have also requested for some information that you don't have and have asked some very leading questions. Doesn't mean much.

"Large and credible" investors should imply first and foremost that they have the money to invest. Only when you have the luxury to have multiple term sheets do you start looking at the "large and credible" factor. If so, refer to the "investors" section.

"Interested" is probably as dangerous in the world of startups as "I think she's interested in me" in love. It covers all kinds of delusions and makes you feel that you're heading in the right direction just because you're moving. A bit similar to thinking a girl just winked at you because you only saw one side of her face.

Takeaway 1 *When investors ask for all the info that you can provide, they may only be building market intelligence to invest in your competition.*

Takeaway 2 *Interest doesn't mean anything unless you have a clear committed timeline for the term sheet and beyond.*

Technology people who start companies continue to have the mindset of arrogance that is part of the reason why they are able to do magic with their technology. However, a strong motivation to closing deals (as well as for subsequent success) is to not only share common goals and a vision but also to have the same pain.

If one of the founders has a strong back-up plan, or worse—a parallel revenue stream that he continues to exercise—he will have a vested interest in ensuring that the second revenue stream is not impacted. This is precisely what investors will want to curtail to ensure that the founders are fully committed. This sometimes results in an impasse.

One of our technology co-founders was involved in consulting activities on behalf of his university. This provided a good revenue flow to him in addition to his regular research-related activities. He assumed that the investors should not have anything to do with his other activities. As it turned out, this was exactly what the investors wanted to curtail, since by consulting for other companies, he was helping them strengthen their technologies, which meant he was fostering our own competition.

Because technology people have always prevailed during their careers that have resulted in breakthrough performance, they automatically assume that they will be on par with investors for the purpose of getting investment. Their assumption is that the investors will bring money to the table, but they will bring technology, making them at par. This is one of the biggest risks for the business drivers in a startup. Technology is an enabler but not the whole reason for the success of a company. Additionally, investors always have other options for investment. It is thus normal that the final transaction will be veered slightly towards investors and will not be on par.

8.5   Don't Let Go

Though the options available to us continued to dwindle and our available cash continued to shrink at an alarming rate, we kept our focus on getting funds from strategic investors—even though we had heard nightmares about the agonisingly slow pace of decision-making.

This focus was driven by the fact that our requirement was very large and the timeline for return so long. We persisted with our discussions with our strategic investors since we knew that our fund requirement was likely to be north of $100 million. And this was only to complete the pilot plant.

This focus was due to the dog-headed conviction that we *had* to make it happen, however slim the odds. This conviction in the face of insurmountable odds comes only to those who run their startups because there are times when you have no option but to believe. And that's the reason entrepreneurs are diehard optimists. That's also the reason a startup never has problems—only challenges.

At this point, our discussions with strategic investors had been ongoing for almost 3 years. When they tell you that strategic investors are slow moving, believe them. And if they take time to make their decision, or if they decide to walk away for the current round, keep the relationship alive. Contrary to what you may believe, your current fundraising round is not likely to be the last one, and it's easier to build on an existing investor relationship than to build a new one, even if the investor has not invested in the earlier round (Fig. 8.1).

Fig. 8.1 There will be many rounds before the circle is complete

One of the three strategic investors finally stepped up and confirmed their firm intention to invest a substantial sum. This suddenly put pressure on our current strategic investor, which had, till that point, invested only a fraction of this amount. With positive indications from two investors, we escalated the investment decision with the third investor with renewed confidence as we knew we were negotiating from a position of strength. Previously, in the absence of any firm indication from the current investors, the third investor had been doing the due diligence for almost 1 year.

Now the point with strategic investors is that they are frequently very large. Our strategic investors had revenues in excess of \$100 billion. Thus, from their perspective, once the decision to invest was approved, the quantum of investment was less of an issue, compared to financial investors. On grilling us about the financials, the investors realised that although we were asking for amount X million, our real financial outlay was likely be closer to amount $X + Y$ million. In the final meeting to convince the third investor to join the round of X million, they not only confirmed their intent to invest but also stated that they would like to raise the size of the round to $X + Y$ million. From having <\$1 million to the prospect of a bit <\$100 million took less than a week—and seemed like a lifetime.

Takeaway *Never let someone else's advice supersede your conviction, particularly if he's not been there.*

8.6   Priorities

When planning to contact investors, it's good to prioritise based on which investor can bring the maximum value to the startup. At the same time, it's good to contact some investors who are not in the Ivy League. The reason is that however much you have prepared your documents, you will be rough around the edges when you first begin talking to investors. It will take some time to prepare the right responses to their questions.

This is similar to your reasoning when you interview with the banks of lesser consequence before you interview with Goldman Sachs. You want your line of thought to be seamless by the time you get to the investors that you really want in your startup.

The one risk is that word really gets around in the investor world. Thus, a top-tier investor like Index, Kleiner Perkins or Draper Fisher would not want to hear that you've been going to the lower-quality investors at the same time when you've been talking to them. Going to too many investors also sounds like desperation, which it often is—but you don't want word to spread!

Although you may have top-tier investors that you target first after you've practiced your pitch, it is also wise to target other investors without too much delay. Clinging on to investors' "interest" may come back to haunt you if this results in too much delay.

8.7   Exclusivity

Investors normally request for exclusivity after they issue the term sheet in the period when they finalise the investment. This is to ensure that when the investor is investing its resources into finalising the investment, the startup does not use the term sheet to shop for other investors and try to find better terms for investment.

Sometimes, investors try to block startup companies from talking to other investors once they are interested in investing. This is to mitigate competition since no investor wants to get into a bidding war with another investor. The investor will then try to get the startup to sign exclusivity at the initial due diligence stage itself much before the term sheet has been provided.

We once had an investor who wanted us to sign the exclusivity when they began their due diligence. At this point, the investor had not provided us with any confirmation that if the due diligence was okay, they would invest. When we pressed the investor to confirm, they said they could do so but would not be able to provide the terms of the investment. The confirmation was effectively irrelevant, while limiting our ability to look for other investors.

Once the investor gives the term sheet, you need a few days to evaluate whether you broadly agree with the terms of the term sheet before you can finalise. Signing exclusivity before you can see the term sheet conditions including valuation will only limit your options. The right time to sign the exclusivity is when the investor also commits to invest subject to clear and quantifiable steps like the technology due diligence not springing red flags or legal red flags. At a minimum, like in a marriage, if you give a commitment, you need one in return.

For precisely this reason, it makes sense for the startup to hold out from the exclusivity for as long as possible. Other investors will immediately recognise if you have already received a term sheet, even though you are legally not allowed to provide any details. If you're finishing your MBA and have just received your first job offer, it takes about 10 seconds for another prospective interviewer to know if you have another job, simply from your confidence and how you negotiate possible conditions. Although investors would have you believe that the term sheet given to you is the standard one and the one they always sign, keep in mind that there's always room to negotiate.

Back to your startup experience, it is therefore no bad thing to have as many days as possible after you receive your term sheet before you get into exclusivity. And keep that time for only two things: to discuss with other investors who are not yet there and to ensure that the main cornerstones of the investment are palatable for you before you get into exclusivity. These cornerstones include valuation, founder exit, milestones and agreement on achievement and of course clarity on follow-on investment with conditions. Keep in mind that once you've signed, you've just lost your negotiating power.

Takeaway *When you're asked for exclusivity, get your ducks in a row—the clock is ticking.*

8.8 Expectation of Entitlement

All the problems are not always out there. I found this the hard way. We were pretty close to the term sheet when one of our technology leads came up with this idea that he was entitled to a bonus—a sign-on bonus, as it were. Now

I've heard of this being given by banks to the MBAs being hired. But, from an investor investing in your own company which was not only pre-profit, but pre-revenue to boot... That was a first! His view was that he was "giving" the investors the "opportunity" to invest in his technology that he had developed to the level where it was interesting for them. He thus deserved a reward.

This happens to be a common problem, since technology co-founders feel that the investors owe them something when they invest in their technology. As per their thinking, part of the investment made by the investors should come to the tech co-founders as an award.

It takes time to explain to the tech co-founders that investors are investing in the company that still continues to be largely owned by the founders. It is only when the technology delivers on the commercial objectives that investors will benefit. It is only at this time that investors will allow the founders to benefit by way of selling their shares or get some other entitlement.

The one thing to be careful about is to ensure that the tech co-founders understand the commercial reality and the investor's perspective. This could otherwise derail an investment by sending a message to the investor that the founders do not trust the technology to deliver and want to make an exit as soon as the investor invests.

8.9   Term Sheet

When the investors are convinced that this is a good investment opportunity, they will proceed to offer the startup a term sheet. This can be a document ranging from 1 page to 20. The term sheet summarises the terms within which the investment is envisaged. This includes the valuation, list of founders and shares held, shares given to investors and money to be invested.

In case of an angel or VC, the term sheet tends to be short and has clear terms of investment. Strategic investors frequently have very large term sheets of up to 20 pages and more, since they assume that they will not only invest more in future rounds but will also eventually want to integrate this into their other businesses. Their timeframe is thus 10–20 years or more, resulting in the more comprehensive term sheet.

An important element is the liquidation preference. This means that in case of dissolution of the company, the investors have the first right to their return. This is also reflected in their shares, which are normally preference shares with an average of 10 % interest/dividend annually. The conversion of shares from preference to equity shares should be 1:1. Some investors try to put this at 1:10. This would mean that for each preference share held, they get ten equity shares. Ensure you flag this out. Other important elements include board constitution, consent and veto rights of the investor, as well as right of first refusal, lock-up of founders' shares, tag along and drag along and non-compete.

When we first received our term sheet, we believed that the process had now been completed. On inquiring with our lawyers, we were told that at this point, <40% of the work had been done. We couldn't believe what else could remain after receiving the 20 plus page term sheet. Till we saw the transaction documents. Speaking of which. . .

8.10 Transaction Documents

If any founder suffers from the delusion that startup co-founders are at par with investors, this is a good time to get rid of it. Exceptions like Facebook and Groupon simply prove the rule—investors have the edge during the negotiation. Investors can live without investing in a particular startup—startups cannot survive without the appetite of risk that only investors have. The transaction documents are a reflection of when investors flex their muscles.

The purpose of the transaction documents is to have binding agreements between the founders and the company as well as to clearly define the rights and obligations of the investors, founders and the company. When the founders are desperate to commercialise their idea, they realise that the investors have the upper hand since they have the money. Due to this, the founders have to agree to the investors having certain rights and priorities over the founders. After all, the investors are investing into the vision of the founders and based on what the founders say they can achieve.

People always say that you need to have skin in the game when you do a startup. The reality is that you need to have your neck in it. That's how desperate you need to be to make it work. Anything less and you begin to treat the startup as a hobby. As investors know only too well, hobbies seldom become billion-dollar success stories.

We began our startup with a group of scientists who were comfortable with support from the government and grants from the European Union for multi-year projects. As any researcher will tell you, research projects are pretty flexible in their timelines and deliverables. It is assumed that some of what has been promised will not be delivered and more funding will be forthcoming to facilitate this in future projects.

At the time, one of my lead tech co-founders was fully employed by the university, with a stable salary. This became a significant disadvantage since he felt he could afford to delay the discussions with the investors in the hope of getting all his idiosyncrasies incorporated. His work with the university also gave him the illusion that the founders were on par with the investors and that the founders could afford to wait a little longer till the investors *came to their senses*.

In the meantime, the transaction documents grew larger and larger, as ever more clauses were incorporated, eventually reaching over 300 pages. The time that had passed since the signing of the term sheet was about 9 months. Finally, we had one disconnect remaining. The investors wanted the founders to provide a guarantee that between the time when the investors signed the transaction documents, thereby committing to investing, and when the shares were issued; the founders would not wilfully leak any company secret. Otherwise the founders would each be liable to millions in damages.

The technical co-founders got stuck on this point. They said that in the weeks between the time when the investor signed and when shares were issued, if the co-founders said anything in research forums, this could be used against them and they could be forced to pay the investor. It became so acrimonious that the technical co-founders said the investor was trying to make money by forcing them to sell their homes. The lawyers tried to convince them that the investor was a company with an annual turnover of over $100 billion, and it was unlikely that the investor was using the penalty paid by startup founders to reach its annual turnover.

The point took over 3 months to resolve. At the end, our auditors told us that since we were running out of funds, they would have to file for insolvency with the company registrar in 2.5 weeks. This was when we decided to take the plunge and sign the documents.

What actually happened was that the lawyers opened the board meeting, confirmed that the investor could become a shareholder by signing the necessary documents and closed the meeting. After about half a minute, with the investor having signed the documents, the lawyers opened the second board meeting and stated that the shares could now be issued to the investor. That was it. Within 2 days, the money was in the bank. After losing 3 months over it...

At the end, I was simply thankful that the investor did not walk away. One year between the term sheet and the money. And we lived to see yet another day.

8.11 Getting the Money

A deal is not done till the money's in the bank. No matter how many steps of the investment have been completed, no matter what level of commitment the investor has exhibited and no matter what exclusivities he has signed. It bears to keep in mind that anything can happen, and it does—whether it is to the company, conflict between founders, questions about milestones, changes in the competitors, government policies like subsidies or perception of future customers—all these and more can make investors nervous or make them wait till clarity emerges. In the meantime, the investment gets delayed. This in turn can put the startup's survival into jeopardy.

In case the money is coming from more than one investor, there are even more things that can go wrong. In one of our small rounds of intermediate funding, two investors who had already invested in the company decided to invest further to strengthen the cash position. We requested the bank to create a blocked account, and the escrow agent provided a letter confirmed by the company registrar (since the company was a limited company) stating that a certain number of shares were to be issued when the cash was in the blocked account.

After we received the formal approval, one of the investors decided to provide slightly different funds due to a reduced cash requirement. However, the bank refused to release the money from the blocked account since the letter confirmed by the company registrar stated higher amount of funds against issue of shares by the company to the investors.

Even though the company and the two investors were in agreement about the updated fund requirement and the now updated number of shares to be issued, the money remained blocked. Finally, the money was remitted back to the investors; the escrow agent prepared a new letter, confirmed with the company registrar and sent it to the bank. This time, the bank was asked to open not one but two blocked accounts, so that in case of any further discrepancy in one blocked account, at least the company now had the option to access funds from the second blocked account. At this point, it was fortunate that we had more than 3 months worth of funds in the bank. Otherwise, since our employees had a 3-month notice period, we would have had to formally fire them on account of the little merry-go-round with the funds.

It is wise to ensure that the agreements are structured in a way that shares are issued to investors immediately, and the investors no longer have the option to take their money back once it is transferred into the blocked account. This seemingly minor point, similar to Hotel California, where you can check out anytime you want, but you can never leave—is best illustrated by the number of times you wish you had written something different in an e-mail just after you press "send". Since investors get a constant flow of information when they are investing in a company, it is in your best interest to keep these safeguards in place in case the bride develops itchy feet at the altar.

Takeaway *Trust is fine so long as you have a big stick provided by your lawyers to back you up.*

8.12 Deal Breakers

It's possible to get the investors to agree to many different things during the negotiation. This really depends on the strength of the technology and the competitive scenario surrounding the deal.

Of course, if there are other investors also interested in the investment, and they are all vying to be part of your startup and share in the spoils, you can ask for a lot more and they will likely accept it. In order for this to happen, you'd have to have a lot of customers, a solution that either customers or advertisers are already paying for and no competitors on the horizon that may reduce your capability to generate profits. It also helps if your name is Skype or Facebook. But chances are, you're not there yet. The deal breakers are when you're trying to get there.

8.12.1 Exit

If you're in the process of getting your early funding rounds, this is being put by the investors into the company. Well, you may ask, what else is the money for?

When we began our company, one technology co-founder decided to ask for money because he believed he had "allowed" the investors to buy shares into the company. This money was for him—as a bonus. The investors took pains to explain that since he and the other founders still owned the majority of the company, the value of the company was increasing. The money was for the company to commercialise the technology. Only after some milestones were achieved could the investors consider a small exit for the founders.

Perhaps it is greed, ignorance or a misplaced sense of entitlement due to which technology co-founders feel that they have a right to get the money as a bonus when investors first come in. This needs to be clarified to the technology co-founders to avoid turning off investors. At the same time, if the company already has some revenue and is in the black, there is a possibility of negotiating with investors where some of the money is taken by the founders as recognition of what has been achieved so far. This is often the case when the technology startup has grown organically and has stable revenue and is looking for growth capital to scale up.

8.12.2 Competitive Interests

Technology founders or scientists work on multiple technologies through their research. However, during the time of technology commercialisation, investors prefer that co-founders avoid working on other technologies. This is to keep the team's focus clear and limit distractions.

One of my technology co-founders had an interest in multiple technologies. When told that investors would like him to focus on one technology's successful commercialisation, his response was that if investors could invest in multiple companies, what stopped him from creating multitechnology companies? After all, he had attained research excellence in multiple technologies. Good question in a fair world. However, since investors primarily invest in the team, they don't want to end up backing the losing horse.

Investors do not want the founders to begin treating the startup they have invested in to become a hobby where the founders begin focussing on another company. This has to be made clear to the team. I've mentioned this earlier—but it is really an essential "make-or-break" component that is critical, given multiple competitive interests of technology co-founders.

8.13 Limited IQ Intellectuals

Like I said earlier, a scientist is a person who is highly focussed on any one area of knowledge, which he goes to the extent of not only focussing the highest level of education possible in that area but also spends substantially all his working life in that area. This also implies that he has little if any experience in areas relating to business and finance.

When you start a company with other co-founders who are likely to be technical or from the scientific community, it is likely that they have not only never started a company before—and also have no idea what conditions constitute "reasonable". So don't throw caution to the wind when the time comes to close the deal and you notice many conditions that seem tilted towards investors. This is particularly so when the investors are VCs, but is equally likely to a lesser degree in case of other investors like angel investors or family funds.

There's a good reason for this imbalance. The investors are really investing in the team and the idea driven by the team. They are not investing in the idea without the team being on board.

Since the scientists in the team are used to "fairness" during their research, they expect the same during discussions with investors. Since they don't see this in the term sheet and even more so in the transaction documents, they ignore the fact that the money from investors is the only thing that can help them achieve commercial reality for their technical excellence.

One of your greatest challenges is managing your own team and keeping their expectations aligned with reality. Another challenge is to convey to the team that however fantastic their research results may be, they are getting duly compensated with the pre-money valuation of their equity, when an investor agrees to invest in them. Any future compensation will only happen when the founders achieve key milestones.

The risk of not being able to manage the expectations of the team during the time of closing of the investment round is that the investors may yet decide to walk away.

Takeaway *Never consider money till it's in the bank; never assume a limit on idiosyncrasies of tech founders; be cautious when giving them face time with investors.*

8.14 You

In the rush to close the deal, you will likely become the conduit in the negotiations between the technology co-founders and the investors. The scale of the challenge becomes clear when the co-founders have conditions that seem unreasonable to you and absolutely unacceptable to the investors.

When you see the investors on the verge of walking away—and this will happen several times before you sign on the dotted line and get the money—your main focus will likely be to get the issues of the tech co-founders sorted out and make them see sense and agree to the conditions of the investors that appear sensible. Your focus will also include trying to push back on some of the demands of investors that you find unacceptable.

What may fall by the wayside is the stuff that may be important for you. For example, if investors come in and decide to change the management team, you may be one of the first persons that become dispensable. This is because all the technical co-founders will be required till the company is able to transfer the knowledge from their minds to a replicable manufacturing set-up.

The investors may want to have one of their own people in to lead the business or ongoing communication with investors, either because they trust their own people more or even because they are nationalistic and they want someone from their own country to be the business driver.

To ensure that the investors don't walk all over you and the technical co-founders don't forsake yourself, you have to document your ongoing interests to drive the company as the business driver. This can be done by way of stating that you will continue on a full-time role as the business driver for a stated period of time. This period could be till the achievement of key milestones that could be over a period of 2–3 years.

By not sticking to a title like CEO or COO, you provide the right level of flexibility to the investors to bring in their own people while ensuring that you remain for as long as you believe you can bring value to your firm, not when the investors begin to consider your presence irrelevant. In addition, you should also ensure that you have a notice period of at least 6 months, since this is standard for C-level executives.

Your presence is not something that your technical co-founders will fight for; they are too inward looking for this. Once your work focus and the minimum duration is clearly stated in the legal documents, you get this point off the table and can begin to focus on more relevant points relating to making the startup successful.

8.15 Twist in the Tail

During the course of our investor search, we once came across an investor group that comprised two wealthy individuals. This group had made a success of wind energy in Europe, and we had confidence in their ability to help us do with flexible solar cells what they had done with wind energy.

Through the discussions we noticed that they sometimes spoke to one set of co-founders and sometimes to others. Due to this, seeds of doubt began to get sown between the founders, and founders began to questions the capabilities that each founder brought to the table. This should have cautioned us about the lack of transparency of this particular investor group. However, when you are looking for funding, you take every investor seriously; you simply cannot afford not to.

In the beginning of our discussions, we had indicated key cornerstones to the investor like the funding required and the baseline valuation that we believed was justified. The investor seemed to agree with all the critical elements giving us confidence to proceed into the due diligence.

After the customary due diligence, we received a term sheet from the investor. The terms of the valuation seemed very complex. On a deeper reading, we realised that this was a creeping valuation for the founders. Thus, the pre-money valuation began at 25% of the baseline valuation that we had considered, and for each milestone achieved, the founders ended up owning more and more of our own company. But if we failed to achieve milestones, we ended up with a minority stake on the first round itself.

As any entrepreneur will know, the milestones for a startup are moving targets. The startup overachieves on some milestones and is never able to reach others. Further, confirming achievement of specific milestones is far more difficult than it appears on paper.

We realised that this investor was not fully transparent and in alignment with what was earlier agreed. Since the investor had exhibited signs that his sense of ethics was not in alignment with ours, we took the then painful decision of terminating discussions. Ultimately, since we were able to get an investor who was fully aligned with our objectives and our sense of ethics, it was just as well.

Knowing whether you can be comfortable with the investor's sense of ethics is particularly important, since once you sign the term sheet, you effectively have to stop negotiations with other investors. If your chosen investor is less than ethical, you may be helpless to negotiate after you go into exclusivity with the signing of the term sheet. If you break negotiations with the investor, other investors realise that you may be difficult to deal with. This further hurts your chances of finding an investor.

8.16 When Techies Lead

As the business driver, you may be blessed with having a group of co-founders who truly understand the value of investors and are reasonable in what they ask for. You may have co-founders who know what value investors bring and what they want in return, i.e. they bring money and want a return on their investment. This happens when you achieve all your milestones agreed to commercialise your technology and continue to have an edge on the evolving competitor universe. Alternatively, your co-founders may be, well... techies.

We were closing our rather large fourth round of funding in late 2012. By this time, one might think our technology co-founders would have figured out what investors look for. But then, if they could understand what business people and investors look for, they wouldn't have been techies in the first place.

Two days before the investors were to come together across the table for the final signing for our fourth round of funding, the investors and the lawyers were sitting in discussions with us. The technical lead, who was responsible for the discussion on behalf of the company, wanted to discuss three important issues.

First, he declared that the milestones provided by the company to investors and mutually agreed upon months in advance were too ambitious. Second, he wanted the founders to have a guaranteed exit a couple of years down the line. Third, he did not want the founders or the company to be responsible for the next fundraising in the future and wanted investors to take responsibility for that.

If that sounds incredulous to you, that's exactly how it sounded to be investors and to their lawyers sitting around the conference room. Saying this, he said he had another meeting and walked out, leaving us to figure it out. There was palpable tension around the conference table since the lawyers saw this as a deal on the verge of collapse.

Fortunately, one of the individuals representing the investor had also participated in the earlier financing round. With him, we distilled the import of the three points. Regarding the first point relating to the milestones, we recognised that technology people only confirm something as being possible once it has been done, and they seldom if ever recognise stretch objectives. The second point, according to the investors, lawyers and anyone who understands business, was simply the technology lead behaving like an idiot since no investor will guarantee a return if the competitiveness of the startup a few years down the line is uncertain. Regarding the third point, investors cannot comment in future funding rounds unless the company is competitive. And if it is, not only the current investors but also new ones would find it an interesting opportunity, further boosting company valuation.

Again, senseless but extremely distracting ideas to bring to the table 48 hours before signing. It was only because we could read between the lines that the deal finally did get signed on the agreed time.

Takeaway *Never underestimate the risk when techies lead. There's a good reason you're there.*

8.17 Funding in an Evolving Market

As you speak to investors, it is imperative to know what makes your startup special and capable of delivering outstanding value on the investment of the investors. It is just as important to be able to tell a story of how the startup fits into the evolving landscape of competitors and customers.

There is a chance that yours is one of the startups pitching an idea in an evolving market segment. In such case, investors may have made not too many investments. In this case, the only customers may be the early adopters. There is however a much higher probability that the market where your startup wants to provide a solution already exists—and your vision is to provide greater value or similar value at lower cost.

Depending on the evolution of the market sector where your startup plays, there will be a failure rate which investors and the market will be acutely aware of. Your success in raising funds will depend on your ability to make the market scenario work for you. The various steps in the market evolution are discussed below.

8.17.1 Early Stage: Tech Shake-Out

In the early stage of evolution of a sector, investors take the portfolio approach. This implies that they invest in multiple startups that may have slightly different technology advantages or competitive advantages when addressing the market. Many of these technologies will fail to deliver or simply take too long since some fundamental science needs to be done before the technology becomes ready for commercialisation.

Investors may challenge you on why in your view your technology has a greater chance to succeed when so many other entities are failing. Defining the technical shake-out and recognising that this will result to consolidation, enabling the stronger firms to capture more of the market, enables you to benefit from the evolving technology landscape.

The flexible PV space was evolving rapidly in the mid-2000s. There were multiple technologies getting investment. Some of these were very simple to commercialise, but had efficiencies in the range of <5%, implying that they could convert 5% of light into electricity. The timeline for getting to market was thus very short, making them attractive.

Our efficiency was in excess of 15%, but the machines to manufacture this did not exist and the process to do so was only in the minds of our cofounders. During our pitch, we thus focussed on our medium- to long-term competitiveness. This drove away the financial investors who were looking at a short turnaround and quick exit. At the same time, this was attractive to industrial investors who conventionally took a long-term view, since they expected to be in this business 10–20 years down the line.

This was an effective strategy because when the time came to get additional funding and the investor market had dried up, our investors came in with additional funding. This in turn gave confidence to other entities that then came in as coinvestors, creating a virtuous circle.

8.17.2 Maturing Markets: Investor Return

If the market is a bit more advanced, a significant amount of money may have gone into the sector and the inferior technologies may already have been weeded out. The competitors who are still in the market are probably well funded compared to your startup. This is a strong talking point for investors, since their view is that it may be difficult for you to catch up if the competitors are ahead.

We once faced this situation in my startup. Our competitors had, in certain cases, raised 50–100 *times* more funds than we had. Clearly, they had advanced more towards reaching the market. Given this scenario, our pitch to investors was that if they were to invest in one of our competitors, they would get a tiny fraction of equity compared to if they were to invest in our company. Additionally, our advantage in being the second mover was that some of the machine designs were now available. Thus, we did not have to create the machines from scratch entailing a risk of a suboptimal design resulting in inferior output.

Fortunately, the investors realised that in the near future, we would also become a large entity like our competitors, since the market for cost-competitive alternative energy solutions was large enough and likely to continue growing for the foreseeable future.

Our investors also realised that since so much money had been invested in our competitors, the requirement for a return on that investment made them less competitive. We, on the other hand, had achieved far more, giving the investors a much bigger bang for their buck.

8.18 Exit Planning

It's said that the best time to negotiate a loan is when you don't need it. In the same way, the right time to plan for an eventual exit is when investors are funding the current round. This is not to say that some of their money can help the founders in making a partial exit. However, having an option for the founders to get a partial exit at the *next* fundraising or on achieving key (not all) milestones can result in a nice cash-out option for founders and early employees.

Having an option implies that you don't have to take it. Even though at the time of fundraising, you may feel that this is irrelevant and you would never consider selling part of your equity, things can change—not only with your mindset but also with investors and their perspective. Since the investors will put all manner of things to protect themselves, it behoves you to protect your own interest.

Takeaway Summary

1. *Don't assume you're smarter than investors. In particular, don't assume that you can get away by having a bigger ego than them.*
2. *Delay consortium building unless any one investor cannot commit to the full fund requirement. Remember there's no going back.*
3. *Don't assume financial return is key for all investors.*
4. *Investor alignment is key to consortium building. Let one take the lead so you deal only with one entity representing all investors.*
5. *Never underestimate that power of conviction. As long as you have conviction and excitement about your vision, there's no wrong way to present to investors.*
6. *When investors ask for all the info that you can provide, they may only be building market intelligence to invest in your competition.*
7. *Interest doesn't mean anything unless you have a clear committed timeline for the term sheet and beyond.*
8. *Never let someone else's advice supersede your conviction, particularly if he's not been there.*
9. *When you're asked for exclusivity, get your ducks in a row—the clock is ticking.*
10. *Trust is fine so long as you have a big stick provided by your lawyers to back you up.*
11. *Never consider money till it's in the bank; never assume a limit on idiosyncrasies of tech founders; be cautious when giving them face time with investors.*
12. *Never underestimate the risk when techies lead. There's a good reason you're there.*

9

Exit: Opportunity to Convert Equity to Wealth

Depending on the competition that develops as your startup commercialises, your exit strategy will continue to evolve. There are multiple factors that will determine the appropriate exit strategy. Having clarity about the options will enable you to control your destiny since the optimal outcome of your investors may not necessarily be the optimal outcome for you or indeed for your company.

9.1 Institutionalise Vision

You cannot easily replicate vision, and most often, absence of articulation of vision is substituted by short-term cost saving. This is why so many companies lose their edge and superprofits once the entrepreneurs exit.

The prime example of our time may be Apple. Since the demise of Steve Jobs, the company has yet to invent a new product category, other than the Apple watch. These are very high expectations indeed, but then, Apple has delivered precisely this over the past decade, creating a number of product categories. It is only new product categories that become the next big thing that enables a company to generate superprofits. You don't become the most valuable company in the world with a market capitalisation greater than the GDP of several smaller countries by being cost-plus.

If vision is not fully institutionalised when the founder leaves, it can leave the company precariously perched, since in the early stages of its being, the company is very fragile. After all the effort of creating the company, it is the onus of the founders to ensure that the company is positioned for growth and

© Springer International Publishing Switzerland 2016
A. Sethi, *From Science to Startup*, DOI 10.1007/978-3-319-30424-3_9

that the cornerstones due to which the company exists are well understood and articulated rather than being only in the mind of the founder, who subsequently leaves.

With Apple yet again, this is what happened when Jobs was asked to leave the company in 1985. The company went from having a laser-sharp focus on products of exceptional beauty and quality to trying to be everything for everyone after Jobs left, eventually doing nothing for anyone. That is when it almost went bust. All because Jobs' vision was not institutionalised at the time. Hopefully, this time it is.

Thus, when the vision is articulated and fully institutionalised, the leaving of the founder does not result in the company crumbling but continuing to grow and thrive. In such case, the founder can exit a wealthy man, but more importantly, do so with the recognition that he's created something of truly sustainable value.

9.2   Different Exits for Different Co-founders

It's important to keep in mind that your exit strategy as the business driver will be different from the exit strategy of the technology co-founders. This is because they are locked into the technology and will likely have a non-compete clause. Due to the limited areas where the technology co-founders can work outside the startup, this effectively results in a lock-in for them.

This non-compete clause is irrelevant for you, since as the business driver, your main skills would include transitioning technology into a successful company, building a team around the idea and leading the funding rounds while managing the expectations of the team and the investors. All these are not only easily transferrable, but are the most relevant skills for any young company and should hold you in good stead should you decide to do another startup.

Investors tend to have flexibility with regard to the business driver exiting at least part of his equity, once the initial milestones have been met. This is most common during future rounds of funding, and it helps if there are new investors investing at an ever-increasing valuation.

So when is it time for the business driver to move on and create the next buzz?

You'll be the first to know. Your zest might seem to decline. Your work will turn administrative. You'll look at your "first baby" objectively for the very first time. And the itch will reappear!

9.3   Fund Cycle of Investors

The reason that the optimal exit options for investors can be different from your exit options is that investors, particularly financial investors, have fund cycles. At the end of the fund cycle, the funds have to be returned to *their* investors. Thus, even if the company is not fully mature at the time when the fund cycle of your investors is nearing its end, the investors will evaluate an exit. This may be by way of a liquidity event, which could include getting new investors or find an entity to buy the company.

All minority shareholders normally have a tag-along right, so if the investors exit, this could be an excellent opportunity to exit at least some of your holdings. After all, your rights and obligations will be renegotiated with new investors in any case, notwithstanding your percentage of holding in the company.

9.4   Back and Forward Integration

Investor-related exit options aside, there are several options to exit from the company. The obvious option is to scale up and continue running the company. Here's what our startup faced towards commercialisation. Through the pilot, the market changed dramatically. Our American competitors in the clean energy sector imploded due to their inability to deliver on their inflated promises. Global investors got cold feet since in their view if our competitors could not deliver with a lot more investor money as compared to what we had, our vision of success was questionable at best.

At the same time, China began to consider this a moonshot, something that was so strategically important that they couldn't afford not to be *the* global leader in clean energy technology. China had already decimated the German PV industry by undercutting their prices so aggressively that Chinese products were lower than the cost of production of German PV modules. This was done by two ways: by providing large amounts of soft loans to local companies to build super-massive factories, to extract huge economies of scale. The second was by keeping their currency artificially low.

At this time, we were in the midst of our pilot production set-up, which would enable us to demonstrate replicability of our highly efficient and flexible PV modules. Our scale-up beyond the pilot plant to the first commercial facility of 100 MW would take substantially over $100 million. But compared to the scale of the Chinese competitors, who were building a capacity of over 2–5 GW, we would become hopelessly outsized. This would have a direct impact on the costs due to economy of scale. Agreed that the Chinese companies were building PV modules that were rigid, compared to our flexible modules. But contrary to what our scientists considered important such as world records in efficiency or flexibility, the only criteria of relevance to the end user was the low cost of electricity. And small size of production just wasn't going to get us there.

This was when we broadened our options. The initial plan of selling modules by scaling up was conventional, but ran the risk of being a non-starter if we took too long to get the funding to get the 100 MW facility.

Backward integration from selling modules implied selling machines incorporated with the necessary process that would enable our customers to produce modules. The benefit of focussing on machines was in the cash flow. You got up-front payment of up to 30 % on the customer placing the order and an additional amount in the range of 40 % even before you delivered the machine. The remaining amount was paid by the customer on installation. A company doing turnkey plants for an innovating technology was an attractive acquisition option for many larger companies. This could then become a sweet option for the founders to get an exit.

Compared to this, if we were to sell solar modules to end customers, they would pay on receiving the modules. But in order to make the modules, we would have to invest time and money to set up a commercial scale manufacturing facility, entailing huge capex costs. Thus, if we began investing in year 0, it would take 2 years to set up the manufacturing plant and another year before we could practically manufacture and deliver modules to customers. We thus had to ensure that we had enough money to survive for 3 years. Suboptimal, at the very least, given China's ambitions and the money being pumped in by the Chinese government.

Another option was to license the technology. This is the first thing that tech founders think of, given their experience with large companies licensing technology based on their research work. However, the revenue from technology licensing tends to be linked to subsequent sale of products by the acquirer and is normally much smaller than anticipated. It can therefore not be considered a sustainable value proposition.

The final option was to forward-integrate. This implied that instead of selling solar modules, we convert them into solutions like flexible chargers for mobile devices or panels that could be directly integrated into BIPV or building integrated photovoltaic solutions. By doing this, we again improved our chances of being attractive as an acquisition target for larger companies that were in the electric utility business and looking for complete solutions rather than components.

Not surprisingly, most technology startups have this opportunity to consider exits for the founder team by way of forward or backward integration. As the business driver, if your current investors do not have the patience and you do not know if the technology will deliver on the commercialisation promise and have an uncertain timeline, these are sound options to consider. You walk away with a wealth of experience, and as the business driver, your experience is the only one in the company that is possible to transplant to another entity or another industry.

Without considering all the options as well as the risks like lock-in and upsides like monetising your holding, it is never too soon to begin considering this. In fact, investors will expect you to have a clearly thought-out plan for how you expect to exit, because although you may have your emotions in the company, the only focus of the investors, specially financial investors like angels and venture capital entities in the mix, is to exit and multiply their money.

9.5   Partial Exit

Addition funding is an excellent opportunity to make a partial exit. Assume. Don't ask. If you ask investors if you can, their response will always be no. This is because they normally prefer to keep the founders locked in for as long as possible and deploy all their money into the company.

However, if this is not the first round of funding and if the round is at a higher valuation, it would clearly reflect on the progress made by the startup. This should justify a partial exit by the founders. Even though the transaction documents drawn up in the initial round of funding may not provide for an exit, it's good to keep in mind that new transaction documents are drawn up if new investors join in. In such case, the original transaction documents cease to be in effect and you, again, have the option of negotiating for your exit.

Several factors can justify a partial exit. Since it is commonly recognised that founders take lower salary than their market value, this can be a reasonable option. Investors may argue that the subsequent success of the company will enable the founders to cash out. However, most startups take a number of years to achieve the level of success that enables the founders to exit, via a route like IPO or trade sale. A partial exit, in such case, simply enables the founders to get some financial upside, particularly if the next round is at a higher valuation.

Another factor for a partial exit is the fickle understanding of the rules of finance by the technology co-founders. Take my own case.

Remember, I had started our company with five other co-founders, all of whom were PhDs? The first casualty happened a few months later when one of the younger members and his partner decided to have a baby. He had to travel by train for about 1 h to get to the office. His view was that after the baby was born (this was still some months away), he would not want to spend so much time travelling from his home to the office. He sold his share at cost to the other co-founders and went off to join a regular company. It's interesting to note that he did not lose faith in the technology or the future potential. He simply looked at his priorities and his office commute didn't fit.

The other casualty happened when we were quite close to getting our third round of funding. This young co-founder decided that he wanted to leave the company because he didn't like to give orders to a number of employees who were reporting to him as he didn't always have answers to their questions. His view was to try accounting as a profession as he enjoyed doing the accounts of the startup! I was able to get him back to stay at the company with the risk of taking a decision on his behalf that I believe was good for him, but was definitely good for the startup and something that kept the confidence of investors. A case in point demonstrating yet again that just because you've got a PhD doesn't mean you necessarily know what's good for you.

Much of the reasoning of the technical co-founders would be completely alien to any business founder or even a wannabe entrepreneur. However, all the technology founders I have spoken to in Switzerland identify with the reasoning provided. Interestingly, none of the technology co-founders of US companies can relate to this.

Technical co-founders can seldom identify with promises of money that are contingent on some uncertain events. They work on yes/no principles. It is for this reason that a partial cash-out is effective since technical co-founders understand this.

9.6   Exit After Strategic Investment

With investment from strategic investors, you have to consider a potential exit of the co-founders. Since the strategic investor may not have plans to sell the startup or get it listed in a stock exchange, particularly in a foreseeable timeframe, the founders may not have a clearly defined exit strategy via an IPO. Hence, you need to ensure that the timeline for the sale of the shares of the founders is clearly defined. The best option to ensure this is to have a VC or other financial co-investor since the financial co-investor will look after his (and by implication, your) exit.

As mentioned previously, an exit based on milestones can be contentious, since in a startup, some milestones will be overachieved and others will not be achieved. Getting agreement of whether milestones have been achieved may also turn out to be a grey area. Unless the milestones can be very clearly defined and the founders have confidence in achieving them even with a conservative scale-up target, the simplest method could be the option to the founders to exit at specific periods of time.

With a strategic investment, it is unlikely that you will be able to get a significant jump, if any, in your future valuation after your first option to exit. However, it is reasonable to consider upsides particularly if the investor is able to drive more value from incorporating your startup's solution in their value proposition. The easiest way to do this was demonstrated by Facebook.

Facebook brought Instagram for a billion dollars. When the founder of Instagram argued that his company was worth more and Facebook would in turn increase its perceived value with the acquisition, Facebook agreed to give a large part of the acquisition price in its own equity. Instagram thus got a lower price in equity, but was able to share in the future upside in case of increase in value if the shares of Facebook increased, partly driven by synergies between Instagram and Facebook.

9.7   Exit Prior to IPO

Andrew Mason founded The Point in 2007 with the backing of Eric Lefkofsky, a successful Internet entrepreneur. The focus of The Point was to get people accessing the website aligned together to solving problems.

One of the ideas that emerged from a campaign run on the website revolved around obtaining a group discount if 20 or more people wanted the same product. This was in 2008 when the USA was entering the recession caused by the sub-prime lending crisis. Groupon was born (Wikipediaorg 2015). The company pitched this as an opportunity for small businesses to generate cash by increasing customer traffic by giving discounts when big lenders were not lending. Groupon became the fastest growing company in history,

In 2011, Groupon decided to file for an IPO. Just prior to the IPO, the company decided to raise an additional round of funding. Of the $130 million raised, $120 million was paid to the founders of the company, instead of going into the company itself. More interestingly, of the total funding that Groupon raised prior to IPO totalling $1.12 billion, $940 million was used to pay back the three co-founders and early backers of the company.

When an investor invests into a company, he gets shares proportional to the amount paid based on the pre-money valuation of the company. If the company issues new shares, the money goes into the company. However, the other option is for the current shareholders to sell some of these shares to the new shareholder. In such case, the money goes to the current shareholders instead of going to the company.

In case of Groupon, the sheer amount of money taken by the founders makes it appear that they did not have complete faith in the long-term sustainability of the concept. There could have been few other reasons for founders to take out this quantum of money. Millions of dollars, yes, but hundreds of millions of dollars, doubtful.

Whatever the reasoning, Groupon illustrates an effective mechanism for founders to take an exit prior to an IPO or trade sale. If the company has the buzz, funding can be raised from current or new investors solely for the purpose of providing the founders with an exit by enabling them to sell their shares to the incoming investors. The impact of this action needs to be kept in mind since there is a thin line between a startup appearing to have the buzz and one that seems like a Ponzi scheme, since even in a Ponzi scheme, new investors' money is used to pay the existing shareholders.

Reference

Wikipediaorg. (2015). *Wikipediaorg*. Retrieved December 1, 2015, from https:// en.wikipedia.org/wiki/Groupon

10

Technologies That Made It: And How

In a series of interviews, stories of some of the technologies coming from ETH Zurich have been provided. The interviews show the challenges faced by the founders and the team towards commercialisation and how, in spite of everything, they're on the way to commercial success.

Stefan Tuchschmid started his PhD at ETH Zurich in 2005 as part of a large research team with 16 PhD students from all across Switzerland. The goal was to develop the most realistic surgical simulator for hysteroscopy, the examination of the uterus with scope. In summary, the project was about doctors practising their surgeries on virtual patients. In 2007, Stefan recognised the potential of commercialisation and value in the market. He recognised that one of the main challenges in medical operations was practising the actual surgery prior to doing it.

Through his PhD, Stefan recognised something simple—this was an opportunity to get funds to build a prototype without the requirement of any external funding. The initial funding and the knowledge of senior researchers and

© Springer International Publishing Switzerland 2016

A. Sethi, *From Science to Startup*, DOI 10.1007/978-3-319-30424-3_10

the professor responsible were simply available. This would otherwise have been either impossible or very expensive to get. Towards the end of the research project, the team had finished building the prototype.

The next challenge was commercialisation. He decided to enter business plan competitions and was the first-ever winner of Venture Kick, an annual competition in Switzerland with an award of CHF 130 K (about $140 K). Shortly after winning the competition, he raised an equity round of another $1.5 million from angel investors towards commercialisation.

Stefan started VirtaMed with five other co-founders. The focus of VirtaMed was to get knowledge from simulation to simulated surgery.

In the beginning, Stefan was not even supposed to be the CEO, but at the last minute, the more senior co-founder left to join McKinsey thrusting Stefan into the role.

Takeaway *Entrepreneurship is about grabbing opportunities that come your way and realising that either you will succeed or you will learn - or experience a bit of both.*

Stefan cultivated his relationships with the original co-founders who continue to have a strong link with the company. As a result, several years later, the senior co-founder left McKinsey and joined the company as COO. Another of the six co-founders was an ETH professor. The professor has continued to bring value by way of research relationships as well as thought leadership.

Takeaway *Cultivate your academics. They can open doors to C level executives of fortune 500 companies that startups cannot even aspire to reach.*

When Stefan began to look at the market, he saw a competitor doing hardware in the area of training for medical doctors. At the same time, he recognised that VirtaMed's strength was the simulation software. So instead of working on making a software and hardware solution, Stefan decided to focus only on the software. Further, to leverage the work that the hardware competitor had done, Stefan decided to focus on doing the software and got the other company to do the hardware of human body parts for VirtaMed. This enabled the company to get rid of all the supply chain, quality assurance and logistic-related challenges of manufacturing hardware.

Some benefits of doing software included seamless replicability and ensuring that if the prototype worked, the scale-up would work. Another key element of software was the capability to fix things that were already in the field via the cloud.

Stefan also learnt the lesson on appearances. The solution could in principle be provided on a laptop computer, but users were hesitant to pay a high price for the simulators. On the other hand, as soon as the software was integrated in a nice-looking system including the appropriate human body part that the specialist doctors could practise on, it was possible to sell the simulators at over $100,000 per simulator.

Takeaway *Integrate software and hardware. If the package looks sophisticated and leaves room for imagination, customers will pay more for it. It's about perceived value.*

As the company grew, multiple layers were added. As CEO, Stefan saw himself doing micromanagement. To transition out of this, he decided to take a 3-month sabbatical, where he completely went off the grid and went to Australia for surfing. On his return, he realised his absence had helped differentiate between processes already running properly and processes that needed additional work in order to run independently. This was his way of stepping back from operational details in order to focus on company strategy.

Eventually, he decided to hire a person to be responsible for production. Even during the interview with candidates, Stefan realised how much more the candidates knew compared to the knowledge within VirtaMed. In retrospect, he realised that they had waited too long to get a production head.

Takeaway *Production capability is a mindset and very different from technology excellence. The former is critical to commercialise successfully.*

Hiring good people was one of the most challenging aspects of starting the company. Stefan found that hiring technical people was much easier than finding good sales people. Few senior people were willing to leave a corporate job and join a startup. The investors told him, "find a sales person, you're a techie". He found someone in a rush, but had to let him go after a year. It was then that Stefan realised that he was actually the best-suited person for closing the initial large deals.

Takeaway *CEOs cannot delegate responsibility for sales in the first years of a company. Their passion, knowledge and authority are key to close deals.*

The company began by having a clear IP strategy. It decided not to file for patents, due to the challenge of doing software patents. Instead, it decided to have trade secrets. The practical implication of this is that trade secrets can be held by the company indefinitely, unlike patents. But the question for the company was always how to ensure that its solution was not being copied. To mitigate this risk, VirtaMed converted its technology blocks into silos. Thus, even if someone was able to crack one component of the technology, he would not have access to everything.

Subsequently, the company decided to file IP but only as a defensive measure or to ensure freedom-to-operate. Ultimately, summarises Stefan, "the best protection is to be faster than the competitors."

Investors

Stefan presented to a number of investors and a group got interested in the company. This group hired an external firm to do due diligence and the firm simply called a group of prospective customers to check interest. Naturally, without knowing more about the product or technology, the prospective customers said no, and the initial market due diligence was not favourable at all. Fortunately, only a few days later, VirtaMed was able to close first sales of the products in exactly the same market. The investors took the leap of faith, and 7 years hence, these investors are still there and see good annual growth and strong future prospects.

Stefan's initial plan was to do 2–3 financing rounds. However, within 2 years, VirtaMed was able to secure large medical device companies as customers and were thus able to scale the company on the back of this. If you have customers, you don't need investors.

Motivation

Stefan's view of working in a startup is simple; you should continue working on it if you're excited about going to work at least 3 days in every week. Otherwise, it's time for a change, either within the company or to try something new. This is a common thread among entrepreneurs: they believe they can. They define what they want to do based on what drives them and what enables them to make a difference. The money is incidental because it's a by-product of the value they create.

Upsides

As the CEO, Stefan's responsibility is to define the culture of the organisation. It is therefore interesting that Stefan regularly takes Wednesdays off to look after his young baby.

Stefan also recognised that being an entrepreneur also provides a phenomenal level of freedom, not only in how long you want to take a summer break but also in how you want to define the evolution of the company. He also sees it as an opportunity to create his own legacy.

Going Forward

VirtaMed now has a turnover in eight digits and a growth forecast of high double digits (details confidential). Suffice to state that the investors are very happy with the company and the team recognises that VirtaMed will be a game changer in the future where telemedicine and virtual medicine aspire to reach those in need, wherever they are in the world, and at the same time, continue to mitigate risk of surgery by practising virtual surgery.

Expect to hear about VirtaMed's impact in the future.

Wulf Glatz began his PhD at ETH Zurich with a view to design micro-thermoelectric generators. Wulf could have taken one of the two approaches. The first approach would have focussed on nanostructures that would advance efficiency on the nanoscale. The second approach was to design generators with the capability to be scalable by reducing cost and ensuring replicability. Said Wulf, "If you look at why thermoelectric generators haven't been widely used but only for niche like space applications, it's all about the cost. There are two ways of bringing down cost. One is to improve efficiency. The second is to have a better manufacturing approach and have a technology that is truly scalable. I focussed my PhD on something that is truly scalable. I thought it would lead to success in the real world." greenTEG was the result of research driven towards real-world deliverables, rather than research for the sake of scientific progress.

The idea

Wulf continued, "I didn't start my PhD with a view towards starting a company. But through my research, I came across other people who had started companies, or persons who were working in startups. That's when I started considering my own startup."

In the beginning, he found it tough to get some functional devices. He had almost given up on having a real device when he saw another chance when Lucas joined the group with electrochemistry background. Wulf had shown the concept with some simple metals. The background of Lucas enabled the team to work with more efficient semiconducting materials. The results made the team realise that the idea could have real-world potential. "We decided that if our solutions could reach a certain level of performance, we could consider starting a company."

Towards the end of his PhD, Wulf had submitted the first draft of his thesis to his professor, who asked him for some more information for which more experiments were needed. At the same time, he asked himself a simple but profound question, "do I want to write a PhD thesis that sits in someone's drawer, or do I want to do research on something that carries on and creates real-world value?"

Deciding on the latter included changing the material composition, which was a bit like going back to the drawing board. That meant that for 5 months, Wulf worked towards completing his PhD without a salary, "because I'm then at the point where I can start a company."

After his PhD, Wulf started working with IBM research, since there was no funding to start the company. The team won an award, which gave valuable publicity and some credibility and helped win the first R&D grant, which provided salary for one person for 3 years. The team took this as the starting point and founded the company with this as the basis. Wulf left IBM and decided to take the leap.

Team Challenges

The company wanted to hire someone for tests and measurements. "We received applications with mediocre people who asked for $150 K annual salary. We finally got someone who had okay references, but I let my team overrule my gut feeling and decided to accept him. We had to lay him off within the 3-month trial period, since he simply wasn't delivering. It was tough since he had personal problems. It wasn't a good feeling. But it taught me that you have to trust your gut. It also taught me that sometimes you have to be the bad guy for the good of the company," says Wulf, pointing out one of his learnings.

When the company began the transition to manufacturing, they needed a person with manufacturing experience. They hired an experienced person with electrochemical manufacturing experience. He brought know-how of industrial manufacturing, critical during the design of their first production line. Since the new production expert did not have a research background but was from industry, he followed each step given in the production manuals. This meant that by having him working with the manuals enabled the team to identify gaps in the manuals, making them really bulletproof. These steps were important for ensuring consistent end products, critical for moving from R&D to commercial manufacturing.

Investors

"We started too late, and underestimated the importance of keeping investors in the loop. It's such a painful experience to go look for funding, that when it's done, you want to forget about it and you don't even want to touch the topic till however long your money is going to last. This was probably our biggest mistake," observed Wulf. The team didn't keep up the relationships with investors who had not participated in the seed round. Neither did they invest time in broadening their investor base since they had a financially comfortable situation for such a long time.

Don't neglect investor relations. "I remember in the first round, where I recall thinking that if I didn't have to have ongoing discussions with the investor, I'd be able to do so much meaningful stuff to advance the company. But this was short-sighted," said Wulf. Keeping on going contact with investors is a little bit of effort, but this will save a lot of effort later on, which is like starting from zero all over again.

Takeaway *Keep a network, keep them informed.*

Investors invest in the team. How they perceive the team is based on their gut feeling and their trust. You can't generate trust instantaneously, however, it is something you have to build up.

Market

greenTEG in the fortunate situation that they are in a niche market where they can be profitable with their current production. The next step for the company is to take the product to the mass market. The current production has demonstrated the viability of providing a solution that has relevance to customers and at the same time is capable of scalability. Today, it is high priced, but when greenTEG scales up production, the cost will come down dramatically. The company strategy is to scale-up on a stepwise basis, by demonstrating value for larger customers, and roll it out to the larger market as demand grows. Most importantly, the strategy is driven by revenues covering costs, since strategies for the future are irrelevant if there is uncertainty of survival on account of cash flow challenges.

Scale-up depends on how quickly the market evolves. The market has so far grown slower than expected, and many competitors scaled up too aggressively. This resulted in financial difficulties for these companies since the customer market didn't develop as fast. Observed Wulf, "Once investors lose faith, it's very difficult for young companies to recover investor trust, where trust is all you have going for you." And as every startup knows, investor trust is critical till you're in the black.

With regard to approaching customers, Wulf had a practical approach that captured the conservative business philosophy of greenTEG. "We had R&D departments as early customers, since our focus was to get early revenues. Then we started cold-calling and approaching commercial customers with our product. You get a different level of feedback when you actually show customers a physical product, compared to showing a presentation, since customers can actually touch it and tell you whether this is a product or a prototype, and can begin to tell you what's missing. But customers don't take a PowerPoint slide promising something too seriously, since they probably have been approached several times with people promising something and they don't believe you till you put something on the table. You need to put the prototype with the data sheet and they will tell you if the interface is bad and the packaging needs work. This is when you can really get into an interaction and if you're fast and if they see that you're doing big improvements, you've got your first paying customer."

Continued Wulf, "We had to educate our team that simply because your sensor has a 10× higher resolution doesn't mean it's a value proposition if the customer doesn't need that higher resolution. So it's not about faster, higher or better, it just needs to fulfil the specs of the prospective customer. There's no sense in overachieving in specs if you underachieve in others. You shouldn't be wasting time on those you're excellent at, if this excellence is of no relevance for the customer."

Takeaway *Go out and start talking to customers. Show them your product. Get their feedback. Adapt and do whatever it takes to fulfil their requirements. Revenue is magic.*

Exit

Wulf has valuable nuggets regarding investors. "For most investors, it's always important to have an exit option. When we began, our vision was the challenge of building the company based on our technical expertise and bringing what we've developed to the market. But our conversations with investors also made us recognise their view. We now recognise that our investors have a different cycle, which begins with investing. For some investors, their cycle is completed when they are able to exit their investment and return the money to their investors. For others, their cycle is complete when they buy the rest of the equity. It is critical to have alignment with investors regarding their exit."

Rushing to close rounds with disparate groups of investors is indeed the greatest risk for founders, since an investor in a rush to exit may compromise the valuation of the company or force the company to sell at less than optimal market conditions. This is also what makes investor matching tricky, because one set of investors may be looking for an exit and others may have another view. It was likely a burnt entrepreneur who said of his rush to get investors: *marry in haste, repent at leisure.*

Going Forward

With tomorrow's technology of converting temperature variation into energy, a pragmatic mindset rooted in reality and customer revenue as their driver, expect to hear a lot more about greenTEG.

Born and brought up in Switzerland, Manuel Aschwanden went to the USA for his Masters. He was considering doing his PhD while starting his company. He spoke to professors at ETH Zurich about the option of the PhD with a specific focus on developing his own idea towards commercialisation. One professor gave the nod and Optotune came into being.

Manuel teamed up with two other students to commercialise his idea regarding provision of tuneable optical devices based on elastic polymer-based materials. He used his time during his PhD to develop a prototype. In his words, "How else do you get chance of having the best technical resources combined with the brightest technology and research people and work on developing a prototype for a breakthrough idea. It was a great opportunity to have 3 years of development time". By the end of his PhD, he had the proof-of-concept. He knew that in principle, it would work.

Company: Focus and Evolution

Optotune's focus is to provide tuneable optical devices based on elastic polymer-based materials. In other words, the lens changes its shape for faster focus. These electrically controlled lenses had billions of cycles, compared to traditional lenses where the focus mechanism was driven by mechanical motors. The lenses also had higher speed of focus and reduced servicing due to fewer moving parts.

The company looked at the evolving market for machine vision. They were very well positioned to address the market for cameras on machine vision systems. This turned out to be one of the first markets and Optotune began to supply hardware for this industrial market. In the area of medicine, eye cameras and dental cameras also realised the benefit of using this technology, since it provided a combination of speed and reliability. Since the lenses are often put into equipment that costs over $10 K, reliability enables greater uptime and less loss of indirect revenue.

Technology

Optotune began with electroactive polymers. However, this was a complex technology that was simply not mature enough at the time. The company then looked at what this technology enabled and discovered that it was excellent for tuneable lenses. They then switched to electromagnetic actuators, which also had the same effect of controlling tuneable lenses. However, the latter technology was highly reliable, since it had been used in loud speakers for several decades. It was therefore easily available, highly reliable and used simple and proven processes. Consequently, it was cost-competitive.

Optotune made the decision to use old-fashioned technology to address a new market, since they recognised the real argument, which was cost and reliability based, for addressing a new customer segment, rather than using a new technology for the sake of the technology.

On coming up with new products, Manuel has a simple but elegant approach. "Talk to customers. Figure out their problems. Design the solution. It's shocking how seldom this is done."

Investors

Manuel held discussions with many investors. However, the conditions seemed one-sided and entailed significant dilution of the equity. Often, investors would start by saying that they would provide a $10 million pre-money valuation for investment. But on reading the fine print, the team would realise that if some milestones were not met, the valuation would be $2 million.

Ultimately, the team decided to focus on organic growth. Their view was that it would be better to work with strategic partners rather than get investors with strings on board. The fact that the company already had revenue streams to ensure survival had a strong bearing on this decision.

In order to get initial revenue, the company decided to lease its key product for the consumer market to a large strategic partner company. This forced the team to get back to the drawing board and focus on other revenue opportunities for future growth."

Takeaway Tech entrepreneurs often cling to technology, rather than the value to customers. Recognising that customers simply don't care is the first step to commercialisation.

Team Challenges

Originally, Optotune began with four founders. Three were technical and the fourth was legal and financial. However, the fourth founder was not fully committed since he continued to keep his day job. While the three technology founders were working 80-h weeks, the fourth person spent his time either trying to understand what was going on or questioning small spending decisions.

The team took the difficult decision to get him out of the company. It was an important learning; hire based on commitment, capability and fit into the team and the vision.

The second decision was whether to get the professor into the company as a shareholder. The view of the team was that to be a shareholder; it was imperative for the professor to quit his job and demonstrate his commitment or, at the very least, reduce his work at the university by a certain percentage and get similar compensation from the company. Ultimately, the company did not get the professor in.

IP Strategy

Optotune's IP strategy has been to file patents on features and geometrical design only. Thus, the company considers materials and process as trade secrets.

The team decided to have an aggressive IP strategy to ensure that competitors were unable to copy their products. This was also a safety measure since often small two-man customers ordered their lenses and subsequently tried to file patents on products that used these lenses.

In order to mitigate the risk of patents filed by existing customers on products with the Optotune lenses that would block new customers from using these lenses, the company filed on the website www.ip.com. This website put the information on the public domain on an anonymous basis. But this then became prior art by becoming public information with the date of publication. Thus, if a small customer subsequently tried to file patents on the same information, he was unable to do so since the information already existed.

The benefit of making product ideas prior art ensured that Optotune was able to sell to multiple customers that wanted to use their components to produce equipment for addressing the same market.

Going Forward

Manuel's conviction is that the best is yet to come for his company. Solutions that were earlier only the domain of Star Trek like 3D holograms are now becoming a reality. Manuel notes with some satisfaction that Optotune components have enabled these solutions.

On a personal level, Manuel's learning curve has been so much steeper than that of his peers from his education days. "As an engineer, you may make an average of $3 million through your career. But as an entrepreneur, even if you fail and lose $100 K, you'll make much more due to the phenomenal exposure of seeing the full picture. Add to that the opportunity to have dinner with some of the most successful people in the business, who see you as a peer, since they've been where you are and know your struggles, I wouldn't change a thing."

Doing a startup has provided Manuel with a greater sense of perspective. Regarding innovation in big companies, he says matter-of-factly, "They are rigid and simply don't innovate. Don't underestimate the power of innovation."

But it's coming up with new product areas where Manuel is most optimistic. "Seeing the world through the eyes of technology has made it entirely too complex. The real opportunity is to make things simple."

With a turnover in eight figures and a growth rate that Manuel would rather not say, albeit with a smile, the future looks bright, through the Optotune lens.

Patrick hails from a family of successful entrepreneurs—his grandmother ran the family company in her time which had been started by her father. His uncle ran a large European transportation logistics company.

Patrick says, "Very early on, I wanted to be an entrepreneur. Even through university, I dabbled with trying new things, like importing products via eBay and selling them on Ricardo, Switzerland's (more high-end) answer to eBay".

Patrick always had the talent to see the big picture and maximise on what was available. When he had finished his Masters degree, he realised that he could do research as part of his civil service, in lieu of mandatory military service in Switzerland. He used this opportunity to do research in his area of interest, which ultimately culminated in his PhD.

Patrick was clear that his learning was to prepare him for entrepreneurship and looked for opportunities to learn more. "ETH had a Master of Advanced Studies in Management, Technology and Economics, or MAS MTEC program, a 2-year program for working people. This was free for ETH students pursuing their PhD, but cost about $19,000 for external candidates. So I enrolled myself for the course and did this in parallel with my PhD. Considering the fact that you could do the MAS MTEC program for free if you were at ETH, it shocked me to find out that I was the only ETH student in the program. Perhaps most ETH students were either not aware of this or felt that it would be too much effort. I, however, felt that this would provide me with additional tools towards starting my company. I don't recall taking too many holidays through the duration of the program, but the knowledge was phenomenal".

Foray into Entrepreneurship

He started his PhD at ETH in the hope of finding a technology that he could commercialise, rather than for the sake of pure research. Patrick's work during his civil service resulted in an idea about nano-printing using electromagnetic fields. He chose this area for his PhD and focussed on making his process stable and replicable. The technology that achieved nano-printing was based on an innovation that ionised nanoparticles of gold or other materials suspended in a liquid and pulled the tiny quantities with extreme precision to the surface by using electric fields. This was different from conventional printing where the printing ink was pushed through the nozzles. The printing technology was indeed so precise that Scrona was able to create the smallest printed colour image in the world, highlighting a group of clown fish. The entire image could fit in the diameter of a human hair.

Funding

In order to address investors, the company needed to have not only a technology but also a customer group that recognised the value of the technology in providing superior products to the end users. Touch screens were seen as a major market where current technologies didn't provide a good solution for larger screen sizes, especially for notebooks. Scrona saw this as a huge billion-dollar market since touch screens and curved display screens were the future. However, the anticipated growth into large screen sizes was strongly hampered. In a market where many players had lost huge amounts of money on the unfulfilled promise of a growing touch notebook market, nobody would invest in an unproven technology. In addition, as is often the case, while the next-generation technology tries to address emerging markets, the currently available solutions are already adequate for the current market.

In Patrick's words, "My biggest mistake was to assume that just because I had invented something that was revolutionary, investors would give me money for commercialising it. Little did I realise that people don't invest in you if you're far away from the market".

Tech to Startup

In 2013, Patrick was selected for specialised coaching at the Innovation and Entrepreneurship Lab (ieLab) of ETH Zurich as his nano-printing technology was considered a high-potential technology with significant future potential. The ieLab was an incubator where teams driving high-potential technologies were invited and supported for 18 months as well as paid $150,000 as financial support to take the first steps in commercialising their innovations.

Team Challenges

Patrick began to experience something that most startups go through, viz., team conflict. One of the four co-founders found the focus on pragmatic solutions was taking him away from his zone of comfort of pure research. His lack of excitement about the startup also translated to low motivation and resistance to working all hours to make it happen. This gave rise to friction between the team members, something that could have resulted in a swift implosion of the startup.

After much deliberation, the team decided that everyone would be better off with this fourth co-founder exiting the company. The delay in setting up the formal structure of the company paid off at this time. This was because the split was acrimonious and could have resulted in ongoing conflict if this co-founder had continued to be part of the decision-making in key decisions like investors and valuation on account of his holding equity.

What Market?

The team soon established their company Scrona. The challenge of what customers to address remained. The long-term customer value was great, but immediate survival by way of customer revenue or investor funds was critical.

Patrick's main challenge was to identify a market for the technology. It was clear that in the medium to long term, highly precise and replicable nano-printing would revolutionise multiple industries, including display technology, printed electronics and life sciences. The question was to establish a beachhead by identifying a market that was ready for this futuristic technology. In retrospect, he says, "Thinking rationally, we should not have tried to commercialise such an early stage technology. We were simply too far away from any application. But we were in love with the technology."

He learnt a valuable lesson from his initial struggles: don't focus on the fancy technology, focus on the business case.

The company then contacted watch companies for providing high-quality microstructures on watch-faces as a security feature and as a customised component whereby the microscopic gold image or a personal symbol could be imprinted on the inside of the crystal watch-face. Several discussions with watch companies later, Patrick realised that the sale cycle was going to take much longer than expected.

In the meantime, the team noted that it was really difficult to see images using regular magnifiers. They began working on creating a small and thin microscope that could be controlled by a smartphone app.

During meetings with senior executives of large Swiss watch companies, executives recognised the strategic value of nano-printing, but personally exhibited more fascination in the immediate value of the microscope than in the nano-printing solution. The team sensed that this microscope might have a larger immediate potential market, particularly since current solutions available in the market were simplistic and with very limited functionality.

With the strong technical background and driven by excellence, the team began perfecting the microscope. They called it μPeek. It was the size of a credit card and thinner than a phone.

With very low and dwindling funds, the team decided to bite the bullet and test the market. They put this on the crowdfunding website, Kickstarter. The amount requested was relatively high at $125 K, simply because this was required to cover the fixed and variable costs associated with making the device and staying afloat in the meantime.

This was a last-ditch effort of a spirited and extremely talented team. The technology lead had the astute business sense to soak up market needs, adapt and commercialise.

On Kickstarter, μPeek broke through the $125 K ceiling within 10 days. By the end of the 30-day campaign, Scrona's μPeek had backers worth about $250 K or 200% of their goal. The team had survived to see another day.

The future looks bright for Scrona. Patrick's new challenge is to see how the company may be able to handle both the microscope and nano-printing business verticals. But when customers want one of your products, and you happen to hold the world record for the technology of the second product, it's a good problem to have.

For Scrona and μPeek, the path ahead, each tiny nanometre of it, is paved with gold.

SENSIRION
THE SENSOR COMPANY

Since a very young age, Felix Mayer knew that he wanted to be an entrepreneur. Perhaps it was driven by the fact that his father and his grandfather were entrepreneurs, albeit on a much smaller scale, with a local business and fewer than ten employees.

Felix chose a different path to getting there. Instead of choosing to go to a university after finishing school, Felix decided to go into "berufslehre", or apprenticeship in high school. What this meant was that when Felix was 16, he began to do apprenticeship for a few days each week and went to school for the remaining days. He did this apprenticeship for the next 4 years, while continuing his education in parallel. This gave him a flavour of working with his hands to develop an understanding of electronics. Since his motivation was to understand how things worked, this apprenticeship provided Felix with an opportunity to practically figure out how things worked. It also provided him with a keen sense of business early on in life.

Perhaps most importantly, the apprenticeship provided Felix with an overview of how inefficient work could be in big organisations and how difficult large organisations were to manage. "For the standard employee, it was absolutely not clear who was taking decisions and why are they taking decisions. There were so many things that were just a waste of time and not efficient." Due to this, he realised that the focus in large enterprises was more on following the process than on deliverables. This was a valuable lesson, learnt early enough to influence his choices later on.

Since his teens, Felix had a fascination with flying. When he was 16, Felix took flying lessons and qualified as a hobby pilot. At 24, he began to give lessons to others who wanted to take up this hobby. Most of the people who come to learn flying were much older than him and managers in large companies. The experience of teaching people who were more used to giving rather than taking instruction provided Felix with an insight into the challenges in leading people. "Leading people comes down to knowledge and conviction. And between you and your instructor, there's only one person who really knows what all switches in the plane do when you're 500 m in the air."

With three children of his own, Felix recognises how entrepreneurship can develop early in life. In his words, "kids should learn how to sell fruits. That'll give them a flavour of entrepreneurship early on. During my summer holidays, I used to collect marroni (sweet chestnut) and sell it for pocket money. It taught me a simple but valuable lesson about how business works". His own passion was for science, not for its own sake but for the ability to take a scientific breakthrough and make a business out of something new.

On whether entrepreneurs are born or made, Felix's response is a vexing question for today's children and future entrepreneurs. "Our school system is such that children don't come in touch with business. How can we expect them to get excited about something if they don't know the first thing about it? Through their growing years, if all that the children know is education, and nothing about how business actually works, how can they get excited about starting out? How can they be motivated to study hard if the role of studies appears to have no link with the real world?"

Sensirion co-founder Moritz Lechner complemented his experience by having learnt teamwork and team leadership, not in a classroom but in Pfadi, the Swiss equivalent of Scouts, where he led large teams. The leadership experience that Felix and Moritz gained in their formative years was to become the foundation of a company that's already a global player in the world of sensors.

Technology Challenges

Felix draws a clear line of distinction between university research and R&D towards commercialisation. "There are things that behave differently in practice than what simulations suggest. For example, the stability of a sensor cannot be predicted. You have to physically do it, you have to test it and then you have to optimise it. You can't simulate it. This is something you don't learn in university. In university, if you're doing work on a sensing effect, you write a paper and it's done. In your startup, your sensor has to be stable for 15 years. This is a commercialisation challenge that is completely underestimated when technology people start a company."

"Stability is also where our competition is failing. It's relatively easy to make a humidity sensor, but far more challenging to make a humidity sensor that is stable for 20 years."

Financing the Startup

Felix and Moritz were clear that they wanted to start something new. But the sensor technology was not the first technology they looked at. "I wrote a patent on the technology that enables showing moving images in tunnels of public transport, like underground railways", said Felix. Finally, they decided to commercialise the sensor technology they had researched through their PhD and founded Sensirion. "We wrote our thesis and our business plan in parallel."

Funding to finance the company was a significant challenge. At about the same time, Venture competition was introduced. This was backed by McKinsey in Switzerland and ETH Zurich. Their company Sensirion was recognised as the most promising technology for the year and won the Venture award in 1998 that provided the team with very good visibility and helped to get into contact with many potential investors.

"In the late 1990s, the tech bubble had not yet burst and it was relatively easy to raise funding. But many tech companies focussed on raising money to bring them to the stock market. VC investors like to exit at the earliest opportunity and sometimes force the company to go to the stock market. We didn't want to do that because we wanted to build a company. We decided to go with private investors who have a long-term perspective."

Like any technology-based manufacturing company, forcing an exit too early would have risked bad decisions that would have haunted the company for a long time.

"The role of my wife, who's also a physicist, was key. If you want to start a company, you first have to discuss with the people closest to you. You definitely need the understanding and support of your spouse. This is because all the evenings and weekends you spend trying to make the startup work will break the relationship if your spouse doesn't support you."

Felix continued, "The first 5 years were very tough. An example of the sacrifice that we made was the delay in having children so that my wife could continue working and provide financial support while I worked on starting Sensirion." In spite of having an option to continue getting paid by the university as a researcher or work in a large company while trying to get funding for his company, Felix decided against it. "How can you convince an investor if you're not all in?"—words to live by.

Today, the total funding raised by the company is in the small double digit millions, raised over a few rounds, but more important, the original investors are still on board. It's been over 15 years for the original investors. But when the exit does occur, the patience of the investors will have been more than worth it.

Steps to Commercialisation

The most important components towards commercialisation were summarised by Felix in three words: reliability, stability and replicability. Most research done by researchers and scientists is done with a view to finding out new output by tweaking the input or the process.

With turnover significantly in excess of $100 million, the focus on innovation became apparent by the money that goes into research and development. Sensirion invests over 30 % of its turnover into it. In the words of Felix, "Switzerland has the highest salaries in the world. We are not good because we have cheap products, but because we have better products driven by innovation and technology. But finally technology can help for both, making products better and also cheaper in production. With a base in Switzerland, we can't compete on our salaries. So our only opportunities for growth are either to provide new products that help our customers to create new solution categories, to make things better, or to get the production cost down by smart use of technology and automation. We do all three of them."

IP Strategy

Felix has a clear idea of what should be captured in patents. "If you develop something new, you need to have a strategy for how to protect your IP. For everything you can reverse engineer, we try to protect with patents. But if you do some of the production processes in-house, you can also protect knowledge by keeping it secret. The focus of Sensirion is to be fast and innovate constantly. And we do want payback for our investment in innovations."

With the amount that the company invests in IP generation via R&D, it is no surprise that Felix takes patent infringement very seriously. On risks of IP infringement, Felix's response is telling. "Asian companies copy the outer feel of the product. But if you look inside, the technology is completely different, because they are not yet on our technological level. Those who copy us are European and American companies."

Looking into the Future

"We are in the lucky situation that we have had good growth. We have also consciously diversified into multiple markets. One segment is the mobile market and the second is everything else." Today, Sensirion products are ubiquitous in products that we are surrounded by and ones that surround us. Examples include mobile phones and medical devices as well as automobiles or lately also smart homes.

"It's an interesting time to be an entrepreneur as there are so many opportunities in technology. It's easier to build up something when everything is growing. In the long run, there are always opportunities. Entrepreneurs always find possibilities. That's why they're entrepreneurs."

With regard to his own exit plan, "Sensirion will always be a part of me and I will also be a part of Sensirion. But to really build something, it takes time."

Looking Back

One of the important things Felix feels he had known when he was starting out was how to find out which investors were the right ones and how to negotiate with them. "There's no learning curve. They have a lot of experience and you're a complete novice. Once you sign on the dotted line, you're stuck in the relationship for a very long time."

Felix's advice to young technology graduates is two thought bullets:

1. *Half day off-site*: "Plan based on scenarios. Not everything you plan will happen. Keep room for flexibility and take half a day every month without computers, where you take the team offsite and discuss questions like *Where are we? Where do we want to go? Do we still want to go to the same place as when we started?* and *How do we get there, given the current scenario?* As an entrepreneur, this is the most important role. But it's easy to forget because there's always something more urgent. But it pays off."
2. *Meet customers early*: Regarding customers, Felix's advice is simple and to the point. "Go to customers early. It's never too early to know what customers are willing to pay for." Technology entrepreneurs want to finish the product first before they go to customers. It doesn't work. It's very difficult to make the right product, without interface with customers.

With the world becoming ever more connected as we head into the Internet of things, expect a Sensirion sensor to help you make sense of it all.

11

The Golden Era of Entrepreneurship: Putting It into Perspective

For most of history, entrepreneurs and original thinkers have been vilified and discriminated against rather than celebrated. And this was what happened to them during the good times. During most of the other times, they just got their heads handed to them on a platter.

11.1 Women in Europe

In the Middle Ages, women in Europe came up with a novel idea. Equality!

They then began looking for emancipation. This meant simply asking for their rights to be treated as more than objects and have some rights, rather than asking to be treated on par with men in all respects. In return, it is estimated that between the fourteenth and eighteenth century, hundreds of thousands of women were systematically massacred in the name of witch-hunts to mitigate their power or relevance (Wikipediaorg 2015a).

So much for that idea.

11.2 The USA in the Last Century

As recently as the nineteenth century, the first wave of industrialisation in the USA, most industries were established by well-regarded families since the investment required for setting up this manufacturing was so large that it was beyond the means of the common man. Individuals like Thomas Edison, who rose to prominence from a very ordinary childhood and defined an entire industry, were the exception rather than the rule.

© Springer International Publishing Switzerland 2016
A. Sethi, *From Science to Startup*, DOI 10.1007/978-3-319-30424-3_11

This has changed over the last century in general and with more rapidity over the past decades with the advancement of technology. Individuals armed with a new idea could now commercialise their idea without huge investment. There was very little downside to failing with a new idea since this was the time before all the manufacturing jobs were outsourced to China. This was the time when the USA came on its own with the mantra of being the land of capitalism.

11.3 Arab Spring (Wikipediaorg 2015b)

This is the story of many countries with one underlying theme: the limitation of opportunity for entrepreneurship for the majority combined with state assets held by those in power.

The discontent of being denied a better quality of life had long simmered in the populations of these Northern African and Persian Gulf countries. Many of these countries had concentration of wealth for those in power and autocratic rule, limiting opportunities for wealth creation for the large majority.

The countries where this occurred include Tunisia, Algeria, Jordan, Oman, Egypt, Yemen, Djibouti, Somalia, Sudan, Iraq, Bahrain, Libya, Kuwait, Morocco, Mauritania, Lebanon, Saudi Arabia, Syria, Iran and Palestine. The sheer number of countries with discontent is a good indicator of how widespread this concentration of power and limitation of opportunity was.

Taking Libya as an example, Gaddafi held on to power for decades by virtue of a combination of factors. These included keeping the level of education within the country low but by doling out money for free healthcare while keeping state institutions weak and devoid of clear leadership and clearly defined authority. Opportunities for free-market entrepreneurship were denied to a large swath of the population.

The revenue of the country was driven, not by innovation or free-market-driven excellence in any market sector but by way of natural resource exploitation from sale of oil. This gave the population the proverbial fish instead of enabling them to develop the tools to catch their own.

The countless lives that have been lost to the cause without any clear end of the conflict in sight for many of these countries are a clear indicator of the challenges that have to be faced for the privilege of being an entrepreneur.

If you are reading this, it's more than likely that you have the fortune of belonging to the part of the world where free markets exist and entrepreneurship is a given. In such case, it's good to keep in mind that equal opportunity is not a right but a privilege earned due to the strife of those who have come before you.

11.4 Russia: Coming of Age

Russia has struggled with decades of socialist outlook. From communism, the country moved dramatically towards an open economy after the break-up of the erstwhile USSR. The public institutions that normally support the functioning of a free-market economy, however, were not adequately mature to facilitate this. This resulted in the most politically well-connected individuals benefitting most from the privatisations, by capturing the value of the natural resources of the country. This was to the detriment of the population at large.

This spate of privatisations resulted in creation of pockets of extreme wealth in the hands of the oligarchies. The pockets of wealth were only possible because this wealth was on account of natural assets like oil and minerals. Even today, Russia is largely dependent on the revenue from its natural resources rather than from its industry, which is still at its nascent stage.

Russia recognises this anomaly as well as the fact that economic development is largely driven not by natural resources but by equitable distribution of wealth from knowledge-driven industries. To address this, Russia is trying to leapfrog technology development by trying to import research and manufacturing in tomorrow's industries like nanotechnology.

Russia's asset is a large number of highly skilled engineering and manufacturing talent. What it lacks are entrepreneurial visionaries since they had been suppressed for so many decades. The human mindset is indeed the most difficult to change.

11.5 China Versus USA: An Entrepreneurial View

China has captured the essence of entrepreneurship even as the USA seems to be missing the point. The main focus in China is not just being the manufacturing hub but the innovation hub for the world. The internal focus is shifting from "made in China" to "designed in China". This is a dramatic shift and one that is likely to have long-term repercussions in global wealth creation and distribution. Innovation is the main driver for wealth creation as well as job creation, particularly for high-quality and high-paying jobs. Needless to say, the main beneficiaries of entrepreneurship are the entrepreneurs. In addition to getting kudos across the board for employment generation, they also end up capturing the major portion of the wealth that is created.

The USA, in the meantime, seems to be focussing on employment generation. But when a 50-year-old steel worker in China is earning $12 per *day* for the creation of a bridge in Silicon Valley, it is not easy to see how the US workers can compete (Nytimescom 2015). This is particularly because in order to get employment and remain competitive, the US worker has to be more than "x"-times better to deserve a pay of "x"-times more. In a global economy, higher salaries in mature industries can only be possible on account of state protectionism, rather than free-market forces. If this is done widely enough, it also contributes to the weakening of the country's competitive position.

In the short term, the leadership position of a particular country can enable the country to influence other countries to its advantage, even as its financial position weakens. Today, we are seeing this with the USA, where there is a lingering suspicion that the USA not only encourages conflict but also gets revenue by selling weapons to both sides of the conflict. At the same time, its financial situation is increasingly in dire straits, as reflected by Hillary Clinton's remark to Australia's prime minister on the latter inquiring why the USA was not more tough with China, "How do you deal toughly with your banker"? (Ewen MacAskill 2010)

The advantage that the USA has over China is not financial but mindset related. The USA is very comfortable with trying new things. China, on the other hand, is largely a traditional society where people do what their bosses tell them. In other words, Chinese people are not as freethinking but are more hierarchical. So the only thing that may stymie China to more effectively compete with the USA is China itself, and of course the one-child policy, due to which supporting the pensioners may take a bite out of China's development aspirations.

At the same time, an important question needs to be asked: Can lack of progress in a competing nation for the foreseeable future be a sustainable source of competitive advantage? The answer will determine future leadership of nations.

11.6 Indian Class System

Over the last two millennia, Indian society had been so strongly divided that those from the lowest caste—the "untouchables" or "Harijans" as they were later called—were not even allowed to cross the paths of those from the higher castes. Their lot was writ in stone right from birth. Then came the class system—this was essentially based on the socio-economic structure and not strictly by birth (unlike the caste system). Till the late twentieth century, the ruling classes, made primarily of the higher castes in villages or small communities, came to be known as the feudal class. This class of people had absolute power to decide the fate of the rest.

Recent findings by American Journal of Human Genetics show that although distinctions began to appear almost 3500 years ago, these caste divisions became more strict about 2000 years ago (Livesciencecom 2015). Individuals within each group began to practise endogamy or marriage within their group. Different groups were also discriminated against and prohibited from specific activities like participating in religious rituals or access to education.

If you were one of the countless individuals from the "lower castes" in India over the past 2000 years, you would not have had the opportunity to be heard, let alone to take your idea towards reality. Education itself was restricted to a select few.

There has, thus, never been a time in India like what exists today, to come up with an idea and drive it towards achieving its full commercial potential. India has transitioned more in the past half century than since the past 2000 years. The pace of change has continued to accelerate with the advent of the Internet, more so in India than in most other countries. Today, investors only look at the capability of your idea to be the next Flipkart, the Amazon of India. The website, not the forest.

The land of the billion shopkeepers is also the land where a billion people are comfortable being entrepreneurs. Treat them with respect.

11.7 Jews over the Millennia

Jews have always brought out strong feelings in people.

It's safe to assume that the Jews have always been entrepreneurial by recognising opportunities amidst strife. Their ability to monetise on these opportunities for wealth creation made them very wealthy. This was not simply over any one period in history. On the contrary, their entrepreneurial bent was very well recognised consistently over the past 2000 years.

I highlight here the view shared by many historians regarding the history and evolution of Jews over the millennia. The wealth creation over the centuries is the result of the activities of Jews relating to commerce. These are in turn the result of their religious tenets. In the centuries prior to 70 AD, Judaism was focussed on two tenets: the Temple of Jerusalem and the reading of the religious text Torah. During that period, both of these activities were confined to the elite class, the Rabbis and scholars.

Prior to 70 AD, this reading was limited to the priest class (the Rabbis and scholars). However, the Jewish-Roman war in 70 AD destroyed the Temple of Jerusalem (Wikipediaorg 2015c). Since this temple was one of the main pillars of Judaism, its destruction resulted in the dispersion of the religious leadership from the high priests of Jerusalem to a much wider Jewish audience. This in turn eventually transformed Judaism to a religion that required every Jewish man to read the Torah in Hebrew, as well as send his young sons to school or the synagogue so that they could learn to read as well.

In those ages where going to school was expensive and took time away from doing manual work at the farm, this was a huge investment of time and money, particularly since illiteracy was the norm. The consequence was twofold. The first was after investing to study in schools, going back to work at farms did not provide the right return on investment from schooling. The second was more profound—Jews realised that this education enabled them to better understand the laws of commerce due to which they were able to get into other professions like banking, shopkeeping and trade.

Since Jewish community was always a minority wherever it went, they found it more effective to work as a cohort. This enabled them to focus on accumulation of power in any particular segment of industry more effectively.

Over the past 1800 years, their entrepreneurial capabilities have been so well recognised that Jews have been expelled from over 100 regions including 31 countries due to their business acumen, sometimes more than once (Wikipediaorg 2015d; Biblebelieversorgau 2015). Being minorities wherever they went, Jews were restricted from many activities considered a privilege of the majority or ruling classes. One of the activities that they were not restricted by was trade, since this was often looked down upon. But they converted this same trade into a highly profitable enterprise, flipping a liability into an opportunity. The refrain has always been that they have been smarter than the Gentile or indigenous population and have thereby been able to accumulate wealth to the detriment of those less capable. Somehow, that almost sounds like capitalism.

Seemed a pretty tough time to be an entrepreneur.

11.8 The 1 %

Behind the prosperity of a country is the opportunity given to anyone with an idea and his right to risk his all in pursuit of that idea.

In the thirteenth century, Venice had become one of Europe's wealthiest regions. The main reason for this was the Colligenza (Acemoglu and Robinson 2012) or the *commenda*, where a company was formed for the purpose of a single shipping expedition. Anyone was allowed to invest in this. This Colligenza was therefore egalitarian and attracted all manner of risk-taking entrepreneurs as investors for the merchant voyages.

This risk taking resulted in a lot of social mobility, where new people joined the ranks of the wealthy. With wealth came political power, which partly migrated from the existing elite to the newly created wealthy. The existing wealthy and political elite saw their political power eroding and shifting as a consequence. To mitigate the risk of ever-more people joining their ranks, the wealthy elite decided to create *Libro d'Oro*, or the "Gold Book", an official register of the Venetian nobility. This meant that only those whose names were in this book were now allowed to invest in new ventures.

Over a period of time, this also resulted in economic benefits and rights being limited to the nobility. Society moved from being inclusive, where every entrepreneur had equal opportunities, to one that was more extractive and where only the elite had the rights to new ventures. This was like saying that simply because Bill Gates created Microsoft, only his children should be given the right to create new startups. However, when these people became sufficiently wealthy, their focus changed from wealth creation to wealth preservation. They began to become more risk averse.

By the end of the fifteenth century, the wealth and influence of Venice in shipping had begun to wane. By the seventeenth century, Venice was no longer a power in shipping and could only rest on the laurels of its past.

From being a global powerhouse in the thirteenth century on account of being the first fully inclusive society in the world to getting reduced to selling coloured glass trinkets and pizza to tourists, it's been a steep downward spiral and a direct consequence of becoming an extractive society. By the end of the seventeenth century, a man armed with an idea would have ended up with just that: the idea.

Thus, what began as a capitalistic society eventually moved to a society where only the wealthy were given the right to look at new ventures and opportunities. This eventually led to Venice's irrelevance in international shipping and as a haven for entrepreneurship.

11.9 Poverty Within Plenty

It is often seen that nations with the most natural resources see the maximum disparity within wealth. This usually occurs because the most powerful groups within the country grab these natural resources to further consolidate their political position.

Since the revenue generated by these natural resources serves the purposes of the leading group, there is little motivation to cater to the requirements of the other groups. This is most stark within oil-producing countries. Nations with the highest amount of natural resources like oil see the maximum disparity in the wealth of their population.

It appears that the ease of monetising natural resources into money brings the poverty of money itself into sharp relief, resulting in huge disparity of wealth and social inequality. In case of public unrest, hand-outs are given rather than opportunities that could lead to a better quality of life.

The impact of wealth accruing from natural resources thus goes to minimise new wealth creation from innovation, since new wealth creation in the hands of innovators and entrepreneurs would usurp power from the existing elite, thereby upending the wealth-hierarchy and closely connected political status quo.

11.10 True Wealth of Nations

Much of the technology of travel did not change over the past 2000 years - till 200 years ago.

In the context of history, it is only the twentieth century that saw the glorification of entrepreneurs. As people moved away from off-grid communities to cities in search of a better life, the need to find jobs to fuel this mass immigration arose. The wealth of nations, which till the twentieth century was primarily based on natural resources, transitioned to having the capability to add value to raw materials.

As stated previously, till only a few decades back, countries with the highest amount of natural resources were considered to be the wealthiest. However, the pendulum has swung so dramatically in recent decades that today the truly wealthy nations are those that are able to add most value by way of their skills and human resources. To do this, these nations focus on inclusive development, where all members of society are encouraged to focus on learning a skill. Since society develops because of the efforts of all its members, the benefits also percolate equitably. These nations boast the maximum per capita income and the highest average living standards. It is due to this reason that Switzerland, which has arguably some of the lowest natural resources in the world, was nominated in 2014 as the best country to be born in, by The Economist magazine (Economistcom 2015).

Fewer natural resources force people to hone skills or get technology-based education. Lack of natural resources also encourages the nation's leadership to encourage its population to learn these skills and keep the benefits that accrue by using these skills. It is a combination of these two factors that subsequently becomes a source of sustainable competitive advantage. This is the true wealth of nations.

11.11 . . . And It's Free

Perhaps, the greatest resource available today with the power to reach out to the world, or to change it, lies within our reach. Before 1990, had someone told us that it might be possible to communicate with someone in another country instantaneously, we would have been willing to pay quite a premium for the privilege of doing so. That was the time when it could take several weeks for a letter to reach another country. International phone calls were expensive to exorbitant at this time.

Come 1995, we began to get access to the Internet and e-mail, for free. Human beings are adoptive creatures and can adjust quite rapidly to the good life. And so, we began to take for granted that although letters by post or snail-mail require stamps that cost money and entail delays and risk getting lost, e-mail is and should be free. This platform in fact is a privilege, of a scale that humanity has never seen in history and should not be considered a given. With security issues, the days of unfettered access may well be numbered.

11.12 Putting It into Perspective

It is only when you understand the challenges that anyone with a new idea had through history that you can begin to recognise the incredible time that we live in (Fig. 11.1).

The Internet is an amazing leveller. From a person sitting in Nigeria, masquerading as a rich widow, whose only request is to have your bank account number so that a large sum of money may be transferred to you, to a person who comes up with an idea to track the most attractive girls at Harvard, which he later calls Facebook—all you need is a laptop, an internet connection and a little imagination. There has never been a time in history where the barrier-to-entry was so low.

It is important to keep in mind that this right cannot be assumed for perpetuity. However, today, it exists, and it is yours with which to mould the future in your vision.

11.13 Yours to Lose

Look beyond the over seven billion people in the world with a feeling of simply being one among the multitude. Visualise all of creation including the stars, galaxies and the entire universe. It is when you recognise that perhaps humanity is alone in all this, that you begin to gain a greater appreciation of who you truly represent, and that your purpose is indeed to build a better tomorrow for all mankind, rather than simply getting food on the table (Fig. 11.2).

Fig. 11.1   Entrepreneurship: a historical perspective

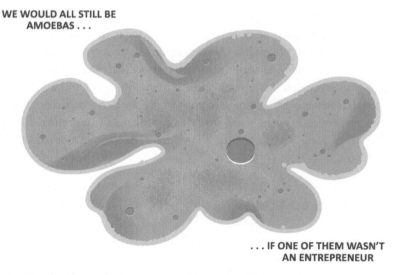

Fig. 11.2   With your **next** idea, the world will be a better place

By not recognising your calling to be an entrepreneur, the future may be yours to lose.

11.14 The Art of the Possible

Understanding how difficult it was for those who came before us and the knowledge of their struggles to be the original entrepreneurs makes us better appreciate the unique opportunity that lies ahead of us. In this way, opportunities are like good health—often taken for granted.

The ability of anyone armed with an idea, and perhaps a computer, to not only dream a future that he could influence, but also make a reality is what is remarkable for this generation. This luxury of being able to visualise something from being a mere idea and taking the opportunity to make it happen is beyond science; science is but the enabler. This - is an art.

This is the art of the possible.

References

Acemoglu, D., & Robinson, J. A. (2012). *Why nations fail: The origins of power, prosperity, and poverty.* New York, NY: Crown Publishing Group.

Biblebelieversorgau. (2015). *Biblebelieversorgau.* Retrieved December 1, 2015, from http://www.biblebelievers.org.au/expelled.htm

Economistcom. (2015). *The economist.* Retrieved December 1, 2015, from http://www.economist.com/news/21566430-where-be-born-2013-lottery-life

Ewen macaskill, E. M. (2010). *The guardian.* Retrieved December 1, 2015, from http://www.theguardian.com/world/2010/dec/04/wikileaks-cables-hillary-clinton-beijing

Livesciencecom. (2015). *LiveSciencecom.* Retrieved December 1, 2015, from http://www.livescience.com/38751-genetic-study-reveals-caste-system-origins.html

Nytimescom. (2015). *Nytimescom.* Retrieved December 1, 2015, from http://www.nytimes.com/2011/06/26/business/global/26bridge.html

Wikipediaorg. (2015a). *Wikipediaorg.* Retrieved December 1, 2015, from https://en.wikipedia.org/wiki/Witch-hunt

Wikipediaorg. (2015b). *Wikipediaorg.* Retrieved December 1, 2015, from https://en.wikipedia.org/wiki/Arab_Spring

Wikipediaorg. (2015c). *Wikipediaorg.* Retrieved December 1, 2015, from https://en.wikipedia.org/wiki/Siege_of_Jerusalem_(70_CE)

Wikipediaorg. (2015d). *Wikipediaorg.* Retrieved December 1, 2015, from https://en.wikipedia.org/wiki/Edict_of_Expulsion

12

The Inside Track: What Drives Entrepreneurs and What They Won't Admit

There are some things that entrepreneurs won't easily admit. These are the same things that make them tick.

12.1 The Most Difficult Step

It's not ensuring the success of the startup that is most difficult. It's not even the journey, however arduous and difficult. Indeed, the most difficult thing is taking the first step. If you're in a job, it's not easy to put in your papers and step into a world of uncertainty.

But here's the curious thing—if you ask an entrepreneur what he would be doing if he were not involved in his current endeavour, his response is not likely to be "I'd be doing a 9–5 job in a big company". The more common-place response is "I would be engaged in an activity that gives me fulfilment or that enables me to make a difference" or "I'd be trying to start something else". Monetary stability, the key driver for the majority holding jobs, is hardly ever the motivation for entrepreneurs.

12.2 It's Some Ride

Since you're following your dream, it does not ever seem like work. This is why entrepreneurs seem to work longer and harder than everyone else.

A lifetime ago, when I was still with the large company and responsible for establishing relationships with young startups in Europe, I used to wonder what made the founders tick. I noticed that they were always available, week,

© Springer International Publishing Switzerland 2016
A. Sethi, *From Science to Startup*, DOI 10.1007/978-3-319-30424-3_12

weekend, day or night. I asked one founder if in retrospect, he felt that given all the hard work involved, what he would do differently. He said, "If I had known how much hard work it was going to be, I would never have started. Now that I know how amazing it is, I wouldn't change a thing".

The founder's response was intriguing and I only fully understood it when I started my own company. If you have to ask this question, you will not be able to understand the answer. Once you start your own company, the question becomes irrelevant.

It's work only if you're a cog in the wheel along the journey without having the option of reaching the goal or if you're stuck in a box doing the same stuff every day. One of the challenges with a job is that you very seldom have the opportunity to see the big picture, let alone have the responsibility to make a meaningful difference. This is the privilege of being an entrepreneur. There's a good reason why so few entrepreneurs go back to a salaried job.

12.3 Cost-Benefit of Entrepreneurship

Entrepreneurs won't tell you that it's not really rocket science. Incidentally, rocket scientists can be hired. With the experience of my own first company, I now know that several of the technology co-founders would have been much more comfortable with a stable salary and bonus (plus, of course, the pension fund and fixed annual holidays) instead of equity. If more people doing jobs were to compare the risk and returns associated to a job with those of being entrepreneurs, there would be a lot more of the latter.

12.4 When the Smarter Guys Work for You

The daily 9–5 grind provides security to most people. Most people like stability, however ethereal it may be. Entrepreneurs take advantage of the perception of security by hiring people who are frequently smarter than them, but haven't taken the leap.

12.5 Managing Risk

The average company in the Fortune 500 has a half-life of 15 years (Wiredcom 2015). This has reduced over the past decades, which means that the average time for which you can expect to do the same work is 2–3 years. This implies that every 3 years, you will have a new job that will last only for 3 years. Incidentally, have you known or heard of people who got fired despite having done wonderful work, simply because the companies were closing that particular department? This doesn't happen often if it's your own company.

12.6 Resume Makeover

If for some reason, despite being bitten by the entrepreneurial bug, you still are keen on returning to the job market—for any position of real responsibility—the one thing that companies look for is the capability to lead in uncertain times and be able to see the big picture. In other words, they all seek an entrepreneurial outlook. Since nothing substitutes for having being an entrepreneur, your resume will absolutely stand out if you ever consider joining the ranks of the employed again after having been an entrepreneur.

The opportunities that subsequently came my way covered a broad spectrum and included the option to run a fund, manage the European branch of an investment bank focussing on clean energy, be the CEO of startups and be part of the venture arms of large conglomerates. None of these would have even considered me as a viable candidate before my startup experience.

But, having stepped down from the management team and from active management of my first startup, I decided to take a sabbatical. I decided to spend time evaluating new ideas.

When I met old contacts over a cup of coffee and was asked what I was doing, my answer invariably was that I was enjoying my coffee. Contrary to my expectation that they would feel I was wasting my time by not doing anything actively, they all appeared to think that I was doing something that took a lot of courage. This was interesting since I thought taking a step back to figure out what to do next was the easiest thing possible.

12.7 A World of Driven People

One of the first things I noticed when I became an entrepreneur was the varied backgrounds of the people I began meeting. These people were all driven by their convictions and followed their own true north. That made them fascinating individuals.

Dario Schwoerer is one such individual. Dario's story began several years ago when he was a natural scientist and avalanche expert in Davos in Switzerland and a professional mountain guide in his spare time. In his words, "the key to change the course is to inspire and fascinate your crew for your new vision followed with action. Vision without action is just a dream…and action without a vision a nightmare".

It was his work with nature that inspired Dario to embark on a world record expedition connecting sport and the environment and recognise incredible potential to bring people together, break down borders and build a global community via his organisation www.toptotop.org (Toptotoporg 2015). The unique concept of the first expedition over the seven seas to the highest top of each of the seven continents by human power (sailing, cycling, climbing) and nature's force (wind, solar) is what drives Dario. This has already got almost 70,000 students worldwide involved.

Being on the road or the sea or climbing and cleaning a mountain with volunteers, Dario has been an inspiration to thousands since he began his journey in 2002. He is living the story of safeguarding our earth for the next generation. He and his elk are truly an inspiration. Knowing Dario has also been a humbling experience and epitomises what's possible if only one has the will to lead change.

12.8 And the Surprises

I've already mentioned about the call I had received from the World Economic Forum (WEF) regarding the Technology Pioneers (Weforumorg 2015) award, where the only criteria was pioneering a solution with potential to have the greatest impact on humanity. About thirty people were honoured by the WEF every year and invited to attend the meeting in Davos.

One of the many interesting meetings included the time when I was having a drink at a social event organised by WEF in Davos. This elderly gentleman approached me and began talking about my work. Clearly, I was forceful in my conviction about my work. After I shared my story and convictions for about 10 minutes, I asked him what kind of work he did at Credit Suisse, since the badge that he was wearing on his coat lapel simply stated his name and the name of the bank. Very apologetically, he stated that although he was the chairman of the bank, he was not really a banker. In fact, continued Flavio Cotti, he had been the president of Switzerland in 1991 and 1998.

Unforgettable was also the time I bumped into someone who introduced himself as Haakon, during a coffee break at the WEF. In the course of the conversation, I inquired whether he was representing a company. His brief but polite response was only that he was from Norway. As an entrepreneur, my first instinct was curiosity. When I inquired again (rather persistently, to my subsequent embarrassment) how he happened to be at WEF, Prince Haakon sheepishly mentioned he was representing Norway since his father was the king.

As Hugh Grant remarks to Julia Roberts in Notting Hill, it was all "surreal but nice".

12.9 Being Boss

A major perk of doing your own thing is that there's no boss anymore. This is so rare in the conventional business world that one does not even know how to relate to this. As soon as you move to your own startup, you feel a great sense of fear of the unknown as well as a sense of liberation. There is now no one between your product and the market—and your main edge is your vision. And, of course, there is no boss to report to anymore. Even if you hire a person to become a CEO, he will always treat you with deference even though you may not have any formal role. You are the one who has enabled them to have their roles. It's empowering to be on the other side.

12.10 You're More Equal

Some people are more equal than others. Take family-owned conglomerates. These include individuals who may have worked on your level—but who happen to be family members of the entity. Their treatment and their progression within the said entity will always be different since, although everyone is considered equal, they are just more equal than others.

By starting your own thing, you suddenly leave the conventional rat race and can no longer be measured by conventional criteria. Suddenly a salary discussion becomes irrelevant since some of the coolest individuals in the business world like Steve Jobs and the Google founders did not seem financially constrained by getting a salary of $1 per year. On the contrary, having a lower salary is now considered a badge of honour, where you are now sacrificing for your vision.

Even heads of relatively large enterprises treat you as an individual rather than as a number since your enterprise could be the next Google.

12.11 Better Work-Life Balance

As you are not required to be in the office from 9 to 5, you are able to balance your work requirements with spending more quality time with friends and family. You make time for things that matter most. When I started

Flisom, I often used to work from home, which enabled me to spend an amazing amount of quality time with my young children. This was indeed a privilege. At the same time, I was able to get work done when it needed to be done, thereby optimising my time and working when required rather than sitting in the office and getting frustrated while waiting for action to happen.

12.12 You Generate Time

When you do your own thing, you only look after strategic (read interesting) things and delegate the operational or administrative (read boring) work to others. This leaves time to consider the important things like future ideas on go-to-market or innovation. This is where maximum value is generated. This is also why companies try to lock in the entrepreneurs who started them in the first place.

12.13 New Opportunities

One thing you realise when you've started something once is that you need to know very little indeed to commence on something new. And when you realise that new ideas are not something to be scared of, it becomes much easier to come up with or commercialise new ideas. Once you have the glimmer of the second idea, you know that technology can come from labs and universities, manufacturing people and admin staff can be hired. Even potential business drivers can be identified who would be very glad to come on board when the funding happens and who, in the meantime, would be quite happy to work gratis on the promise of equity or stock options, if only to get out of their humdrum day jobs.

All you need to know is how to pinpoint the red flags, whether they relate to the team, technology, IP, timeframe or market.

It also becomes apparent that the one thing that most technology teams are missing is someone who's done it before to come in and tell them that it's possible to commercialise their technology. And finally, once you realise that the most important element in a startup is the vision to start it (and that it's always possible to hire experts for any operational area), it becomes easier to commercialise new opportunities.

12.14 New Comfort Zone

Jobs provide us with a comfort zone. We enjoy the perceived stability because the edifices where we work give a feeling of permanence and solidity. Doing your own startup really enables a much greater appreciation of what you are truly capable of. Most entrepreneurs I've encountered said they never imagined that they would be able to achieve as much as they did.

12.15 Building Your Own Brand

Over a period of time, the brand name of your company can attain significant value. This never translates to employees but always to the entrepreneurs. This value is released on the partial or full sale of the business or can be reflected as goodwill on the share price of the enterprise, whether on the price that new investors are willing to pay to invest in the company or on listing on a stock exchange. By the same token, companies become extensions of entrepreneurs rather than entrepreneurs being extensions of companies, unlike an employee of a large company, whose work identity is always as an extension of the company. Due to this, the next company you start is likely to benefit on account of your credibility with investors and future team members, on account of your having done it before.

12.16 Rent Versus Mortgage

A job generates salary so long as you're at it, unless you're lucky enough to get stock options that translate into serious wealth. Microsoft has created thousands of millionaires, as has Google due to stock options. But in case the job is all you have, once you quit, you can't take any of the wealth you may have enabled the company to create, which is reflected in the capitalisation of the company. But when you own the company, you own part of the wealth in addition to getting a regular salary. This is exactly like the difference between rent and mortgage, where at the end of a given period, you own the house if you've taken a mortgage. If it's rent, you only pay so long as you stay. When you walk away, you're on your own again.

12.17 The Next One

Although it may be too early to start thinking about this just yet, doing a startup is often a one-way street. The buzz makes it very difficult if not impossible to consider going back to a conventional job and being segmented to a constrained area, particularly once you begin seeing the big picture. This is also the reason entrepreneurs most often come back to entrepreneurship.

12.18 Going Back

The route from working in a large company to being an entrepreneur is much simpler than the route going back. Entrepreneurs are able to see the big picture of how companies operate and how different departments like marketing, finance, HR, strategy and production are parts of one whole entity. Even though managers within companies treat these departments as their fiefdoms, it is the entrepreneurs who recognise that without all these parts focussed on one direction, the entire enterprise would fall apart.

For these entrepreneurs, going back to a job would be akin to fitting back in a box and doing exactly what you're told to do, rather than trying to capture opportunities whenever they become available.

Having broadened your horizons also makes it difficult at time to fit back into the environment you left—the geographic boundaries and views contained therein. This was what Mikiko[1] of Japan experienced. She was a classmate during my MBA and, for a long time after the MBA, she resisted returning to Japan. Considering she was from a family that was in the business of supplying parts to car companies, I found this reluctance difficult to understand. Years later, when I ran into her in Japan, she told me the real reason. Japanese women who leave Japan to go for advanced education are not accepted back into Japanese society, which is very traditional and male-centric.

Since the traditional role of women is clearly defined as being homemakers and being subservient in this male-dominated society, they are no longer considered viable marriage prospects because they no longer fit the mould. On her return, she also found the traditional system unfair to women. She wanted to be treated at par with men, as was common in the Western world. For Mikoko, leaving Japan to pursue her MBA may have been difficult, but returning was impossible as her expectations had evolved and the gap was too large. The place that she had left all those years ago no longer existed.

---

[1] Name changed to protect identity of individual(s)/entity

12.19 Full Circle

There is a certain thrill in the chase. We've all experienced this, whether it was the feeling of fulfilment on learning something new and doing it the first time or finally landing your dream job. The feeling of starting your own company, which changes from being a figment of your imagination to something tangible and real with a life of its own and with the capability to exist beyond your own lifetime, is the closest we can get to immortality.

Beyond the reasoning of countries and management writers of the positive impact of entrepreneurs to the economy in particular and to society at large, it is the very personal sense of accomplishment and having made a tangible difference that makes entrepreneurs go to the next one.

Beyond all the frustrations and challenges, the sense of fulfilment comes from knowing that you have self-worth that is not dependent on belonging to a large corporate but in the knowledge that the next large game-changing company or, indeed, an entire industry may spring from your guts, wisdom and conviction.

References

Toptotoporg. (2015). *Toptotoporg*. Retrieved December 1, 2015, from http://topto-top.org/

Weforumorg. (2015). *Weforumorg*. Retrieved December 1, 2015, from http://www.weforum.org/community/technology-pioneers

Wiredcom. (2015). *WIRED*. Retrieved December 1, 2015, from http://www.wired.com/2012/06/fortune-500-turnover-and-its-meaning/

About the Author

Born in Nagpur (Maharashtra, India), Anil Sethi made his way through education, arming himself with CA and ICWA degrees (where he ranked among India's top candidates) and equipping himself with an MBA from London Business School that further honed his business skills as a visionary and entrepreneur.

Since childhood, he was disinterested in the "normal school stuff"—but what set him apart from the others "bored at school" was his intense need to know "why" certain phenomena happened the way they did. His curiosity was unquenchable and his energy high. This continued into adulthood. He knew he is here to make a difference.

The Indonesian tsunami provided him the first opportunity to break into his role as an entrepreneur. His debut experience of starting Flisom AG led to an enormous plethora of learning and unlearning. And, as he evolved into

© Springer International Publishing Switzerland 2016
A. Sethi, *From Science to Startup*, DOI 10.1007/978-3-319-30424-3

a serial entrepreneur, his experiences and learnings refined his skills further. Apart from Flisom AG, Anil has founded Swiss Extension GmbH and is a cofounder in a number of other technology startups.

Among his many recognitions, Anil was honoured as a Technology Pioneer by the World Economic Forum in 2007. In 2010, he was invited to be part of the Swiss delegation to the USA led by the Swiss President. Among his other activities, he is often a speaker at international conferences. He advises technology startups and aids them in fund-raising; and helps investors in evaluating investment opportunities.

Anil lives in Zurich with his wife and two children.

His debut book is a guide to what to do—and more importantly what not to do as an entrepreneur. It is an essential read for first-time entrepreneurs as well as established ones—for it brings out facts and throws a certain element of freshness into history, while heading towards an exciting future of constant change. Putting entrepreneurship into perspective, the book is a guide to being the change you want to see.

Executive Summary: Format

The format below may help in formulating the executive summary.

COMPANY OVERVIEW

Put a couple of paragraphs on background, where you're coming from, the idea and where you plan to make a difference. Capture key highlights including vision that are not addressed in points below.

KEY INVESTMENT HIGHLIGHTS

(Put 3 to 4 bullets, ideally one line each, *never* more than 3 lines per bullet.)
Competitive advantage (tell the investors why they should invest in you).
Where do you expect the business value to come (now/later)?
Do you have IP? Mention it. Also mention IP strategy including freedom to operate.
Barriers to entry (if any) (can depend on exclusive research partnership and customer relationships (and lock-in), in the future, becoming a platform).
Mention demonstrated capabilities, particularly those relevant for the startup.
Poised to benefit from market growth (and government regulations?).
Experienced team augmented by key advisors who have done it before.
Recognition or "what have you done so far". If customer relationships locked in, take it higher up.
Why are you compelling for investors?

TRANSACTION OVERVIEW

Provide details regarding how much are you seeking to raise, what for, and then raise how much, and subsequently for what, additional commercialisation activities. And of course, what milestones you expect to reach with the funding (more competitiveness, scale product, etc.)?

Important Considerations

Keep in mind that the investors are interested in milestones you achieve with the money you raise. Focus on deliverables and time, therefore, with the money raised.
Finally, break text with visuals, graphs and pie charts and graphs to illustrate market, size, growth, etc.
Don't be conservative with your numbers. The investors will do it anyway.
Keep the text brief. Fewer words ensure focus on the important ones.
Keep the executive summary to a maximum of two pages.

Most importantly

Believe and let your passion show. It's not just about the numbers.

© Springer International Publishing Switzerland 2016
A. Sethi, *From Science to Startup*, DOI 10.1007/978-3-319-30424-3